LOVE IN CONDITION YELLOW

Love in
Condition Yellow

A Memoir of an Unlikely Marriage

Sophia Raday

Beacon Press
BOSTON

BEACON PRESS
25 Beacon Street
Boston, Massachusetts 02108-2892
www.beacon.org

Beacon Press books
are published under the auspices of
the Unitarian Universalist Association of Congregations.

12   11   10   09   8   7   6   5   4   3   2   1

This book is printed on acid-free paper that meets the uncoated paper
ANSI/NISO specifications for permanence as revised in 1992.

Text design and composition by Yvonne Tsang
at Wilsted & Taylor Publishing Services

Library of Congress Cataloging-in-Publication Data
Raday, Sophia
    Love in condition yellow : a memoir of an unlikely marriage / Sophia Raday
        p. cm.
    ISBN-13: 978-0-8070-7283-7 (hardcover : alk. paper)
    ISBN-10: 0-8070-7283-4 (hardcover : alk. paper)
        1. Raday, Sophia, 1964–   2. Wives—United States—Biography.
3. Married Women—United States—Biography.   4. Military spouses—
United States—Biography.   I. Title.

    HQ759.R236 2009
    306.85092—dc22
    [B]   2008046953

Most of the names and some details and characters in this work have been altered
for the sake of clarity and to ensure the privacy of individuals.

For B., who has a hero's heart

For one human being to love another human being: that is perhaps the most difficult task that has been entrusted to us, the ultimate task, the final test and proof, the work for which all other work is merely preparation.

—Rainer Maria Rilke, *Letters to a Young Poet*

In White you are unprepared and unready to take lethal action. If you are attacked in White you will probably die unless your adversary is totally inept.

In Yellow you bring yourself to the understanding that your life may be in danger and that you may have to do something about it.

In Orange you have determined upon a specific adversary and are prepared to take action which may result in his death, but you are not in a lethal mode.

In Red you are in a lethal mode and will shoot if circumstances warrant.

—Jeff Cooper, *Jeff Cooper's Commentaries*

CONTENTS

ONE   Spark 1

TWO   Reconnaissance 13

THREE   Cultural Exchange 27

FOUR   Behind Enemy Lines 34

FIVE   Individual Liberties 52

SIX   Constructive Engagement 69

SEVEN   Allegiance 82

EIGHT   State of Alert 98

NINE   Preemption 106

TEN   Casualties 121

ELEVEN   Culture Wars 136

TWELVE   Drive On, Soldier, Drive On 159

THIRTEEN   Quagmire 178

FOURTEEN   Hearts and Minds 184

ONE

Spark

The unexpected is disconcerting.
—Jeff Cooper, *Principles of Personal Defense*

M Y COUSIN GEORGE FROWNS AT ME. "Did you ever call my friend Barrett? Remember I told you he went into the Reserves and then became a cop in Oakland?"

I am instantly wary. Lowering my wineglass from my lips, I put one hand against the textured plaster wall to steady myself. I have prepared myself to talk about politics, about the Dayton Accords, Rabin's assassination, or the budget impasse. But George's question is going in an even more unpleasant direction, a direction that could lead into my love life in general. I want to avoid that at all costs. In fact, my mom had to cajole me into attending this party, assuring me no one would notice the redness around my nose and the way my eyelids are slightly swollen.

I stall, mumbling, "What? Barrett? Oh yeah..." and glance around my cousin Molly's house. Is there some way I can derail this conversation from its inevitable terminus? The house is eclectically decorated with my aunt's modern paintings and my nieces' artwork; the Christmas tree, strung with cranberry garlands and popcorn, gives off its heady smell of pine. I want to chitchat and drink my glass of wine in peace, avoiding the tangle in my chest. So what if I am over thirty and not married? So what if I got dumped yet again?

I point out a woodblock near me, gray clouds against gold and auburn mounds. "George, is this Taos? When did your mom do this?"

George waves away the art, saying, "I gave you Barrett's number, right? Did you ever call him?"

I shake my head. Yes, George gave me Barrett's number a while ago, probably at another family holiday party. I've heard about Barrett for over a decade now, ever since he was a cadet at West Point with George. When Barrett was in the Ranger battalion, his apartment was furnished with only a bed, a box as a nightstand, and a nine-millimeter pistol. He once dragged a manhole cover home with him after a night of drinking. Perhaps the favorite family story involves Barrett yelling at a superior officer at Walter Reed when George was in the hospital there with a brain tumor. As a plebe at West Point, George had headaches and dizzy spells for weeks, but none of the authorities took it seriously. Instead they accused him of trying to weasel out of boxing. An inebriated Barrett expressed the whole family's frustration, yelling at a superior officer: "That's *my* buddy in there! The one with the brain tumor! Don't tell *me* I can't see him! You all who thought he was faking, why should I listen to you? You all didn't even believe he was sick!"

I hear George saying I should just give Barrett a call. Really. Not for a date or anything, just for fun. But I know that's just subterfuge. I know my cousin is doing a mental calculation of my age and wondering what's wrong with Sopapilla, as he affectionately calls me. Where's the boyfriend? Where's the husband-to-be? My stomach muscles catch as George pulls a pen out of his shirt pocket and grabs a notepad from Molly's bookshelf.

George and I spent a lot of time together about ten years ago when he was assigned to Fort Ord as a first lieutenant. On the weekends, George and another lieutenant would meet me and my best friend Missey in Tahoe. We'd ski together during the day and argue politics late into the evening. George and Jake were soldiers; Missey and I were peace activists; Reagan was president. We argued about the arms race and the U.S. opposition to the Sandinistas in Nicaragua and revolutionary groups in El Salvador. But somehow we always seemed to end up at Vietnam. I think the maddest George ever got at me was when I bemoaned the loss of our soldiers there. "We sent those kids over there to die, and for what? What do we say to those mothers and wives and children? Sorry, we thought this was a domino but it wasn't? Oops?"

That was the first time George jabbed his finger menacingly at me, his words flying out accompanied by small units of spit. "Don't you *ever* (jab) *ever* (spit) say that a soldier's death is a waste (jab, jab). *No soldier's* (spit) *service is ever* (jab) *wasted* (jab, spit)."

Our most recent major argument, a few years ago now, involved the Gulf War. I had posted a handmade "No Blood for Oil" sign on my car. At a dinner with George and my mom, I tried to voice my objections to our invasion of Kuwait, my belief that we should have tried economic sanctions first. A cigarette bouncing dangerously from two accusatory fingers, George hissed at me, "George Bush drew a line in the sand, you hear me? He drew a line in the sand and backed it up! Now that's leadership! That's what this nation needs!"

Taking my hand off the wall, I push it out palm forward toward George in a gentle protest, in the universal sign for "Back off, I can handle this." Has he forgotten who I am? What does he think—that I'm going to discuss Gandhi's experiments with truth with his gun-toting Republican friend?

I may no longer get arrested at the Nevada Test Site or at divestment protests. And it's been years since I scaled Moffett Field's barbed-wire fence with a friend to spray-paint "Work for Peace" across the "Be all you can be" recruitment billboard. But that doesn't mean I have given up on social justice. Okay, I'm not married. But that doesn't mean I'll date just *anybody*. It doesn't mean I've suddenly given up all my core beliefs!

Besides, I am still hoping that Nathan—the guy I've been seeing up till recently—will come around. Nathan is the kind of guy I can picture myself marrying: men's group attending, Robert Bly reading, naked in the woods drumming. Nathan and I look so good on paper. We like the outdoors, traveling, reading. We are both seekers, do a lot of yoga, read about Tibetan Buddhism. We *should* work. So why don't we?

Just before our recent disastrous trip to Nepal, Nathan invited me to go see Thich Nhat Hanh at the Berkeley Community Theatre. We were both enchanted by the Vietnamese monk's soft-spoken simple admonitions to find peace within and let it radiate out. Present moment, wonderful moment. When you are mindful, you see into the true nature of things, how a flower comes from soil, from decay. This is the sort of spirituality I expect to share with a partner. Maybe our getting back together will be the flower that blossoms from the garbage of our recent journey together.

Keenly aware of approaching family members, I whisper to George that I appreciate the thought. Any normal person would get that subtle signal that I am not interested. *Look, I appreciate the thought.* But not George.

"Tell you what," he bellows, "here's his number. I'll tell him to call you, too." Brandishing the slip of paper.

It's time to change the subject. Pronto. I cast about desperately, finally hearing myself say, "Hey, what do you think of the Dayton Accords?"

George says, "C'mon, it's not a date. I just want you two to meet, that's all."

Maybe if I just take the damn paper, George will stop broadcasting to the whole party that Sophia can't find a man.

"Barrett? Are you talking about Barrett? He's cute!" Molly's daughter Mallory exclaims.

"I always liked the B-man too. He's definitely got a special something," Cousin Matthew adds.

Despite my embarrassment, I realize this is an odd triangulation. Thirteen-year-old Mallory thinks Barrett's cute and my thirty-one-year-old gay cousin thinks he has *je ne sais quoi.* Hmm.

The workday's finally over and I'm home on my bed. I've pulled out Nathan's most recent love letter. Like a scientist mapping the human genome, I am mapping my relationship with Nathan. How did we get from Point A, where Nathan wrote me—*My dear Sophia, I want you to know that I see you. I see you are a rare and exceptional woman who walks in the world with power and grace. I see your passion in work and play and I see your soft, intense beauty both in and out. I love you.*—to Point B, where he announced, during our recent month-long trip to Nepal, that he could no longer kiss me?

Nathan and I had rare moments of deep connection. When we shared our self-doubts, I felt some kind of magic at work. It was like Nathan was a mirror: he reflected back someone I recognized, the confident exterior masking the deep self-doubt. My body hummed with warmth when he shined the light of his attention on me. I felt filled up. I felt high.

My therapist and my friends like to remind me how atypical those moments were, how unhappy I was in the long stretches between them. And I have to admit that's true. I've been wading through a dark ocean of rejection since our parting at the Bangkok International Airport, but every now and then a little silver flicker of insight has flitted past. Then I see I am not so much in love with Nathan as in love with *Nathan-prime*, the Nathan I believe he could become. But these insight-fish are too slippery to hold onto. Soon I am back to my familiar slog. I showed Nathan a part of myself I really hadn't shown anyone before. And then he closed down, distanced himself from me, and couldn't even tell me why. I try to shut out the obvious: that he saw something in me that repelled him. It's so much easier to psychoanalyze him. And as it happens, I think I have his issues pretty well worked out.

He just got scared. We just need to reconnect; I can be stronger. I can suppress my need for his attention. I can be undemanding. God, if he'd only just *listen!* If he'd only just let me *help!* Doesn't he see that *I am only trying to help?* Because if we could sort things out, then we could have those moments, that shimmering soul-union, *all the time.* And that's true love, right?

Across my down comforter, data from our year-long relationship are strewn: love notes, my journal, unsent letters, my calendar.

I glance at my Day-Timer. George's note with Barrett's number is stuck to the open page. If I do meet him, should I wear my "Bad Cop, No Donut" button? Maybe I'll casually mention how I hovered around the edges of the Lockdown Lockheed protest in 1986. The police van pulled up next to me and other surprised stragglers, disgorging five or six officers who hurtled toward us in riot gear. I spun away and ran madly, almost blindly. I would downplay, I think, the sheer animal terror I felt, the feeling of being prey. Instead I'd emphasize how I found myself in front of a hotel, where I slowed to a pretend-calm walk, slipped into the lobby and out the back entrance, eluding capture. Ha! Of course I wouldn't tell Barrett all of my stories regarding the police, particularly why I still start to shake when I get pulled over, but it might be fun to tell him that one.

I look back at Nathan's most recent love letter, a card showing the faces of a man and a woman leaning together, their profiles blurring into one another. The couple's skin is golden like the sun, the lips red, and instead of hair there is a Garden-of-Eden-like jumble of ripe roses, grape vines entwining, peas and tendrils mingling, daisies blossoming. I sigh. Tonight is a Thursday and my housemate and I are hosting friends for *Seinfeld* as usual. I hear Jaime banging in the kitchen as she gets out the chips and salsa, and searches for the bottle opener. I have to put the letter aside and head out to the living room.

As our guests arrive, I slump into the wicker couch and start down a rutted mental path. Things were going fairly well before Nathan and I went on the trip to Nepal. Okay, he didn't like to have sex as much as I did, and we were working on that. But on the trip something changed. "I don't want things to be so heavy," he'd said.

Am I heavy? Am I dark? Isn't it more likely that *he* is just afraid of commitment?

A shout interrupts my thoughts. "Sophia, how's it hangin'?" my friend Sal bellows upon arrival, and leans down to give me a peck on the cheek.

"It no longer feels right to kiss, because kissing might mean forever, and I'm just not sure," Nathan had said in Pokhara, a week into our trip, just before we trekked the Annapurna Circuit, a favorite loop through the Himalaya among adventure travelers.

The doorbell rings, my dog Dave barks, another friend arrives. Jaime flutters to the door, immediately inquiring about Sasha's hot date last weekend. Sasha's arm waves the question away; it was a bust but at least she got to eat at a great restaurant.

In Kathmandu, Nathan had wanted to sample the food at what was reputedly its best restaurant. Hours later I'd come down with a violent stomach flu. During a lull between my episodes in the bathroom, for reasons that weren't clear to me, we needed to change hotels. Nathan had carried me up four flights of steps to get to our new room. Surely that was a gallant and loving gesture? I dwell on this data point in particular, rotate it around in my mind, train a microscope on it. But I was so weak and dizzy that everything is hazy—the dinner, the pukefest, the hotels. Just one clear image—the stairwell of the new hotel, whitewashed and cool, where Nathan stopped to rest, gently dropping my legs from the fireman's carry position. I stood draped against his lean, muscular body, his heart thumping under my cheek. I felt happy despite the nausea. He was taking care of me. He loved me.

The only trouble is that blur of a conversation before we'd moved hotels. Is it real? Did I dream that he said the new hotel was "a better value?"

"Who wants an Anchor Steam?" Sal yells.

"Not me, I'm having green tea. Anyone with me?" says Jaime.

It feels kind of good to have people around, as long as I don't have to talk.

The Annapurna Circuit is dotted with teahouses. We stopped at different ones for breakfast, lunch, and dinner, and then stayed at the last one for the night. Each evening, I ordered a "hot bucket" and bathed myself in a dark hut. Then I collapsed in my twin bed across from Nathan. For weeks, up and down gold and brown hillsides, through massive gorges, over rickety Indiana Jones–style bridges, I asked nothing of him. I sat daily and chanted, *Om mani padme hung*, a traditional Buddhist mantra that Tibetans use to regain calm in times of tribulation. I read Rilke's *Letters to a Young Poet* and Peter Matthiessen's *The Snow Leopard*. I drew spiritual strength from Nakendragiri, our ninety-five-pound porter who carried Nathan's and my pack the whole way, taking his sure-footed steps through the snow in flip-flops. If Nathan didn't want things to be heavy, I would hide the clutch of fear in my gut, squelch the requests for reassurance that rose to my lips with nearly each step.

Hiding my feelings in intimate relationships comes naturally to me. I grew up with an older brother who got my parents' attention by acting out, so I took the opposite approach. I got straight As, walked the dog, made the beds, helped with dinner. This made my parents happy while at the same time allowing them to focus less and less on me. Somewhere along the line I got the idea there was something about me that did not inspire care. And later, watching the popular girls, I decided it was the desperate fact of my need that was the problem. So as an eight-year-old, I put my stuffed animals away and stopped crying when I got hurt. I cultivated a James Dean look with a purple jean jacket and boondockers, resolved to start smoking as soon as it was feasible.

Although I loved the outdoors, animals, and climbing trees

much more than dolls or dresses or makeup, I slowly became more and more trapped in my own tough girl act. The only way I knew to get approval from my parents was by suppressing my hunger for their attention. Certain older boys could somehow see what my parents could not: that I was so desperately lonely I would submit to secret embraces that I didn't understand and that left me empty and ashamed. To my busy parents—my mom a pioneering career woman, my father an eccentric early computer engineer—I was a blessing, a child who seemed to take care of herself. Yet even when I floated next to Nathan along the mountain path, independent, undemanding, he didn't want to kiss me. It felt oddly familiar, just like the boys of my youth who would pretend they didn't know me in the halls of elementary school.

Jaime and my other good friends all tell me, "It's not *you*, Soph, it's *Nathan*." Even Nathan said he wished I weren't so hurt by *his* limitations. I nod when they say this. I nod as if I comprehend. And I delineate Nathan's faults. But secretly I don't understand what the hell they are talking about. He doesn't love me. If I were different, maybe he would. Doesn't that always redound to me?

I slip out of the living room to grab a beer and dip into my bedroom to glance at the answering machine. There's a message! With each flash, my body tingles. Is it? Could it be?

I reach for the play button but hesitate. I want to savor the possibilities. Staring at the blinking light, I imagine a reunion, a fullness of connection that will erase all my self-doubt. I probably stand there a full minute before shaking myself and pressing the button: "Hello, Sophia, this is Barrett McAllister. Your cousin George Csonka said I might call. You can reach me at 555-8686."

The spot where I fold my hands in yoga—my heart center—sags. It's not Nathan. Of course not. I am a fool. I play the message over and over, staring but not really seeing the silver buttons on the phone, listening to the brusque formal voice over and over. "Your cousin George Csonka said I might call." "George Csonka said I might call." "...said I might call."

He uses the subjunctive, I muse. And correctly.

"Hey, Jaime—" I yell, "come listen to this."

Jaime and I met just after college, and she has shared my Berkeley cottage for nearly three years. When I find the right guy, and she finds the right gal, we plan to all live together. She wants to build a solar cabin somewhere off the grid. I want a rambling house with a view in the Berkeley hills. When we get to the part where Barrett says the last part of his phone number, "eighty-six, eighty-six," Jaime starts giggling. I start laughing, too. It's the no-frills message, the clipped prose, said without any humor or irony. It's so coplike.

Jaime calls our friends in from the living room to listen to the message. When it's done, she lowers her voice and imitates Barrett, "Eighty six, eighty-six, over!" Everyone hoots except my friend Mark, our lone male guest, who looks at us all quizzically. "What's so funny? It sounds just like a message I might leave."

My friends all think I must call Barrett back. The women think it sounds like a great lark—Sophia, the pot-smoking feminist, will go on a date with a cop. I have to go, they insist. It's an adventure. "You're a secret agent!" Sal cries.

Everyone else chimes in, Sasha telling me it would be good for me to get out, Jaime chortling about the fact that I'll be going out with a cop one week, and off on a motorcycle ride with my lesbian friend Alexandra the next. They're laughing, high-fiving; they can't wait for me to report back.

"Plus," Mark says, "he might be a nice guy." But he is pretty well drowned out by the squeals of *Tell us all about it!*

On the morning of my lunch date with Barrett, I begin the day with my regular routine. I sit in the gray stillness of my living room, a cup of warm tea in the crisscross of my legs. I focus on my breath until the rush hour traffic of my thoughts has calmed. Then I summon the first of several images I am hoping will help me move forward with my life. I stand by an open door, Nathan outside in the vestibule. Without malice, but firmly, I shut the door and turn my back to it. Good-bye, Nathan.

Then I move to the next image. I am standing by a rushing river. I picture Nathan again, in the water, clutching the end of a rope, his lean legs wiggling with the current. *Snip! Snip!* I cut the rope cleanly with giant scissors. Away Nathan drifts, over a large waterfall, and out of sight.

• • •

Barrett and I are meeting for lunch at a café near my office in San Francisco. As I walk by the storefronts, I glance at my reflection in the glass. I see a statuesque blonde in a pleated miniskirt that shows off her long legs. She looks confident, not nervous or even timid. That's me?

The minute I open the door of the café, a man steps toward me, hand outstretched. "Sophia? Hi, I'm Barrett McAllister."

His handshake is firm, formal. I can see the whiteness of his scalp on the sides of his head where it is almost shaved. On top is an oval of half-inch black hair. I am surprised to find he is much shorter than Nathan, shorter than me, even—an inch or so less than my five foot ten. Mallory thinks he's cute? I suppose he isn't bad looking, although his buzz cut emphasizes his slightly oversized ears. In his mock turtleneck, tweed jacket, and glasses, he seems rather...well...*ordinary.*

Barrett looks from the floor to my forehead and back again, and I am startled to realize that the Man, in this case, is shy. His eyes find an open table nearby. With obvious relief, he pulls out a chair for me. Once we sit down, he stutters, "Uh-h-h, I'm sorry I had to reschedule. I'm glad you were able to change it to today."

"No problem. Has your leg healed?"

"Yes, thank you, it's much better."

"How did you injure it?"

"Well, I was chasing some dope dealers and I jumped over a fence and landed wrong."

I look up from my plate with anticipation. Taking a deep breath, I slowly exhale the words as if I am very tired. "Man," I drawl, "don't you think drugs should be legalized?"

He ponders this briefly and for the first time holds my gaze. "Yeah, you're right," he says, and then flashes a grin that is pure fourteen-year-old boy. I suddenly understand why Mallory likes him. "Sure, let's legalize drugs," he says. "But tell you what—there should be *no* drug treatment." Then he chortles, a loud "Heh heh heh."

I am momentarily confused. I expect him to be outraged by my suggestion, thrown off-guard, maybe even angry. Instead he seems to be having fun.

"Are you joking?" I ask sternly.

"Sort of," he replies. "Look, I know tons of people smoke pot, and I don't really care. But nothing destroys a neighborhood quicker than a bunch of young bucks hanging out on corners slingin' dope. You want your kids walking by?"

My face warms. This is not how I've planned the conversation to go. I have this horrible feeling he might have a good point. I sputter something about legalization allowing regulation.

Barrett just gives me that boyish grin again and says, "How 'bout an iced tea?"

He orders our tea, then asks what I'd like to eat. When I tell him, he turns to the waiter. "I'll have a Reuben please," he says, "and the lady will have the veggie panini."

We look tentatively at each other. "So…," I venture. "You live all the way in Livermore? Thanks for driving up to the city."

He tells me he likes driving. Plus, there's a great gun store around the corner. I decide not to touch that one. I ask if he lives by himself. He says he does, with his dogs, then corrects himself: just one dog. He recently had to give one away. He's gotten too many tickets for the barking while he was working overtime. ("Barking tickets, get it?" Fourteen-year-old grin again.) He has gone to visit Beauty over the weekend at her new home and wonders if he's made the right decision. He murmurs, as much to himself as to me, "It'll be better for Beauty. The lady's home all day and she has lots of room to run." Then he says it's his remaining dog, Oscar, that he worries about. Oscar misses Beauty.

I tell him about my dog Dave, how I like to take him out after work for long runs at the Berkeley Marina. "You go alone?" he asks, squinting at me. "In the dark?"

I wouldn't like to admit that I get a little spooked on my nighttime outings to the marina. That as I get farther and farther from my car, I have to remind myself that my dog will protect me, that the dark hides me as well as any bad guys, that I am strong and trained in self-defense. I go bungee-jumping and extreme skiing and on solo runs in the dark because I love the aftermath, the momentary feeling of having won the battle against fear. It is the closest thing I know to peace. I might get a little prickly if some other friend intimated it was not safe to run alone in the dark. But Barrett is a police officer and a soldier. It's his job to be protective. I can pretend his question stems from a sort of de rigueur professional concern. I don't have to protest. Prompted by his simple concern for my safety, I can allow an unfamiliar wave of comfort to wash through me.

At the end of the date, he insists on paying the bill. Then he says his days off are Wednesday and Thursday and would I like to get together again? For one whole hour I've hardly thought about Nathan. I say, "Sure."

TWO

Reconnaissance

Time spent in reconnaissance is seldom wasted.
—Unknown, alternately attributed to Sun Tzu,
Napoleon, Custer, and Sir MacPherson Robertson

A T DUSK, THE MAN-MADE HILLS of César Chávez Park in Berkeley look vaguely lunar. The park is built on top of the old Berkeley municipal landfill at the edge of the San Francisco Bay. Every ten years or so, they have to repave the entry road because as the garbage underneath degrades at irregular rates, the road becomes a bumpy series of whoop-de-whoops. I've parked in my regular spot, on the dirt shoulder at the southern edge of the park, just before the road takes an abrupt turn left and heads toward the bay and the Berkeley Marina. From my parking spot, I look out on an inlet where an old giant boat is moldering. Like something out of *Mad Max*, the boat is draped with tires and multicolored oil drums. Basquiat-like graffiti adorns its sides. A tiny dinghy tied to it signals that someone still inhabits it. I look at it and smile. The best part of Berkeley is the way it can transform the ugly and banal into something quirky and interesting.

When I open the door of my Subaru hatchback, my dog Dave bounds out. As usual, I admire his masculine grace. Dave was a gift from my late father, and I have often thought of him as some sort of guardian angel assigned by my dad to look after me. And look after me he does. One friend commented, "You are Dave's sun; he isn't just faithful to you, he *orbits* you." Sometimes when I look at him, his physical beauty hits me so hard that I start to cry. He has a golden retriever's build, a shiny red, brown, and black coat that emphasizes his broad chest and lean muscles. If I throw a stone into the water, he will jump nimbly along the large rocks bordering the inlet, then leap in a masterful arc into the water. Or, if we are at the beach and I go swimming, it doesn't matter how rough the sea is, Dave will swim in after me, disappearing for long scary moments as the waves hit him, then emerging and continuing steadily toward me.

Now he looks at me for a signal of which way we will go tonight—the wide potholed path toward the field with the pampas grass waving at its edge, or the loop around the rolling hills of the park proper, past the methane vent, toward the boats, where we can see the lights of San Francisco when it's not so foggy. "Hang on, buddy, we're not going anywhere yet," I tell him.

When Barrett didn't call me, I was hurt. So *he* didn't like me either? I mentioned it to George and he chuckled, saying Barrett's just not that kind of guy. If I wanted to see him again, I might have to make the next move. So I left Barrett a rehearsed-to-sound-casual message: "Hi—just wondering how the life of crime-fighting is treating you? Would you like to get the dogs together for a walk on one of your nights off?" He called back the same night and we made a plan for a walk and dinner. As I wait, I wonder what kind of car Barrett has and whether he'll be able to find our meeting place. "Just give me the address," he'd said impatiently. "I can find it."

"No," I'd insisted, "it's not that kind of place. I have to give you directions."

I just have enough time to wonder how deep the garbage is buried under my feet when Barrett pulls up in a blue Blazer with a white stripe. I don't know Barrett well but the vehicle jives with my first impression: masculine, sporty, unpretentious. I'm excited to see him. I spent the weekend skiing and that always brings me back into the grace and power of my own body. I tell myself I feel free because I could never be serious about this redneck soldier turned cop. But there is something more, something I noticed on our first date: he has a quiet confidence that makes me feel I can show my tomboy side without threatening him. At Barrett's suggestion, we plan to have a steak dinner after the walk, and I already know I'm going to have a vodka tonic. I feel unbound, light. In my black leather flight jacket and jeans, I am Beryl Markham on an adventure with Denys Finch Hatton.

As Barrett passes me, he raises his hand in a minimalist hello. To the point, not flashy, I think, as I watch him steer the Blazer expertly into the remaining dirt shoulder just in front of my car. Clad in jeans, a plaid shirt, and a brown leather jacket, he quickly gets down from the driver's seat, opens the tailgate, and starts futzing with a tan crate in the cargo area.

In no time a black-and-white dog—lab-size, but with a spaniel's enormous floppy ears—emerges from the car, then jumps up and down in place at Barrett's side while Barrett closes up the back of the truck. I notice the dog is wearing a strange bulky collar. Barrett commands him sternly, "Sit, Oscar, sit!" Oscar looks at his master warily, sits for a second, then quickly resumes bouncing. "Sit!" Barrett cries again.

My dog Dave barks once and walks toward Oscar slowly, legs stiff, holding his tail erect in the flag of the alpha dog. I want to move closer to Barrett, shake hands, say hello, but I know that once Dave reaches Oscar, Barrett will have no hope whatsoever of controlling his dog.

"Dave, stay. It's all right," I say, and Dave walks back to sit by my side.

Barrett is holding Oscar's snout in his hand and speaking to him sternly. I wonder how often he gets the dog out to run. Oscar seems full of nervous energy and I doubt Barrett will be able to control him while there's another dog just a few yards away.

"He seems really excited," I say. "Can he come over and meet us?"

Barrett hesitates and Oscar bounds over and jumps up on me. He has soulful brown eyes, like his master. Dave growls and resumes his stiff-legged hauteur.

"Damn it!" Barrett yells. "Oscar, sit! Oscar, stay!" As Barrett strides over to the dog, I recognize the soldier's march, the same purposeful walk George has. Oscar has lain down on his back near Dave and is wiggling his legs gaily as Dave gives him a thorough sniff. "Just a sec," Barrett grunts, leaning over his dog, "I've just gotta switch on the training collar. I haven't been working him enough lately."

"What is that thing? I ask, kneeling down and putting my fist out for Oscar to smell.

"It's a training tool," Barrett says in a low voice. "Damn dog doesn't listen. He's so undisciplined; I never know when he'll run into the street."

"Training collar? But it doesn't shock him, does it?"

"Look," he says, straightening and picking up some sort of remote. "These collars are great tools. I use one to keep him from barking. And this one for obedience training. He has trouble paying attention when he needs to. This gets his attention."

Oscar has righted himself and is running in crazy patterns. In one abrupt about-face, he starts running toward the street. "Oscar!" Barrett bellows. "Oscar, come now!"

The dog continues his mad running dance, when suddenly I hear him yelp. He stops running and shakes his head. My stomach compresses, folding into a tight lump.

"Oh, my God." I turn to Barrett. "You shocked him."

"It doesn't hurt him, it just gets his attention. Really."

I walk toward Oscar automatically, not sure what to do. "But didn't you hear him cry?" I am enunciating each syllable, as if I am talking to a child or a crazy person. "Just don't. No more. Please."

Barrett strides past me, "Look, don't freak out, it really doesn't hurt that much. I've tested both collars out on me."

"What?"

"Yeah. Watch, I'll show you." He presses the collar in his hand to his Adam's apple, "It really doesn't hurt, I swear. Watch. *Woof!*" he yells. "*Woof woof!*"

I stare at Barrett barking into the collar and looking at me imploringly. I don't know what to think. Here is a person who can't see that his crazy nervous dog needs reassurance, who thinks the answer is to administer pain, and yet I can tell by the concerned look on his face that he's upset that I think badly of him. He's feverishly trying to shock himself so that I will feel better. He says, "Okay, I can't get this to work on me right now, but really, really, it doesn't hurt. Do you want to try it?"

"Oscar just needs to run," I say. "He's totally hyper. Let's get into the park a bit; he'll be fine. Please, I'm sure you don't need to use that collar."

"I'm afraid he won't come when I call him. He's so spastic."

"Look," I say, and use a happy voice. "Oscar! Here, boy!"

Oscar, who has been wriggling on his back by Barrett's feet, stands up and looks at me. "Here, boy! C'mon!" I say, my voice lilting in happy excitement. He starts to trot toward me. I kneel down, waving my hands in front of my chest like I am fanning myself, "Good boy! Here, boy!" The dog breaks into a run toward me, and I amp up my joyful encouragement. When he arrives into the circle of my arms, I shower him with affection, stroking his head and chest vigorously and praising him, "Good boy! Good dog, Oscar!"

I look up to see Barrett walking toward me. I worry that he will be angry, that I appear to be one-upping him. "Beginner's luck, I guess," I say and am relieved to see he is smiling and the taut lines of his face have loosened.

"I'll be darned, he likes you."

When I stand up, Oscar places his snout between my thighs like he is trying to hide. I pat his soft head and gently tug his ears, and he seems to relax. "It's okay," I say soothingly, not sure whether I'm talking to the man or the dog. "It's okay. He just needs a little love."

We choose the path toward the methane vent, a concrete tube surrounded by chain link that sits incongruously amid the rolling green of the park. It is dark now, and foggy, and we cannot make out the stars. Since the park and the surrounding areas are all landfill, I wonder how it is that one vent can work for those acres and acres of garbage. I remark to Barrett that there is something poetic about this reclaimed ugliness—that on the weekends, the place is filled with kite flyers. Everything from stunt kites to massive dragons to the simple diamonds favored by little kids will dance together above the old dump.

He says, "Huh."

I try a different tack and tell him of my ski weekend. There was new snow, and my friend Mark and I spied members of the ski patrol making their way to the top of a closed area. We took a chance that they were about to turn the signs from "Closed" to "Open," and we began hiking up the knoll to where they were. Already behind a few other powder hounds, Mark and I were racing them and each other. I felt lithe and strong, and because I was lighter than Mark and the other skiers—all male—I was able to stay on top of the new snow and promptly pass them up. When the patrol turned the sign, I was there first, queen of the pristine blanket of snow stretching below me. Whooping, with the snow billowing up around my legs and even kissing my back under my parka, I swooped and glided through the snow, claiming it for myself.

When I finish relating this story, I am grinning, full of the freedom and triumph of that run.

Barrett says, "I think you're the cockiest girl I've ever met."

For some reason, this makes me very happy. Perhaps he understands bravado. I laugh and turn to him. "So, do you ski?"

"I haven't been up much in the last few years. I don't get that much time off, with the SWAT team and pulling a lot of overtime."

"But what do you do for fun? Do you bike? Hike? Rollerblade?"

"Rollerblade!" he guffaws. "Uh. No. Don't rollerblade. Don't wear spandex, either. That's for guys with beards. But yeah, I've got a mountain bike. I don't really hike much unless it's to keep up with my land nav skills."

"Your what?"

"Land nav. You know—land navigation. Orienteering."

"Oh. Like map and compass?"

"Yeah, exactly."

"Huh. So that's fun?"

We can see the lights of the Albany Racetrack vaguely in the gray distance, and as we turn the corner and face west, the wind rolling in under the Golden Gate hits us hard, and we have to lean into it and raise our voices. Barrett pulls a wool watch cap out of his pocket and tugs it on his head.

"I guess mostly I work. I was a salesman for a couple of years after getting out of the army and, man, I just hated it. I worked real hard but the sucking up to people, the shmoozing, the lack of real mission, real camaraderie—it just felt like I was slowly drinking pure acid. Every day, drip drip drip. Acid."

"So being a cop suits you better?"

"Aw, yeah, definitely. I like being outside. I love to drive. I love the rush of chasing turds. I can't believe they pay me. Shit, I'd do it for free."

I am examining Barrett's words and phrases like they are puzzle pieces. I hope that if I arrange them the right way, they might form a picture I can understand. But "turds"? I feel a weight in my gut. This is what I was afraid of finding in Barrett—afraid that because he is a cop, he has become hardened to people's humanity. He sees the worst in people, day after day; and out of self-preservation has had to turn off his ability to be compassionate. Perhaps cops should be highly trained in self-care and should have a mentor like therapists do, someone to help them carry all the pain and anger they see. Otherwise it inevitably damages them, and they become a part of the perpetuation of trauma and anger.

Calling people turds disturbs me, and to go along with something like that without registering my opposition in some way is giving tacit approval. *Silence equals complicity,* as we used to say in my college activist days.

Remember, this is anthropological research, I remind myself. We're just hanging out. We don't have to agree.

To Barrett I say, "Yeah, I always wished I could work outside, too. Some days I get to the office in the dark and leave in the dark. I just can't stand not seeing the sun. It's not living. I mean, besides reading, pretty much everything I like to do is outside."

"Me too," he says, "although I work swing, so I'm outside, but it's mostly at night."

In a quiet voice I ask, "So you call them 'turds'?"

"What?"

"Turds. You called the people you arrest 'turds,' didn't you?"

"Oh. Well. No, not exactly. Did I say turds? I should have said suspects, that's usually what we call them…mostly we say suspects."

I don't believe him, and I guess it shows in my face, because he flashes me a guilty grin.

"Except the really bad ones. Okay, yes, some of the really bad ones we call turds."

"How do you know they are really bad?"

"Oh, you know. You just get a feeling. Or you see them all the time, over and over again."

"I just don't like the idea of calling human beings turds."

"But come on, some people are just evil, aren't they? They're just bad, they really are. Like the guy who kidnapped Polly Klaas, he's a turd, no doubt about it, Jesus, a little girl...That guy needs to go," and he makes a quick wringing motion with his hands.

Something in my chest tightens and I wrap my arms around myself.

Barrett says, "Do you know a cop stopped that guy when he had her in the car? He stopped the guy, and he didn't save her. Jesus, I don't want to ever make a mistake like that. I could never live with myself."

He really is noble in a way, I think. He wants to help people, especially those who are vulnerable; he wants to protect them from harm. From harm I can barely even contemplate. I am fascinated to look at him, stand next to him, and know that he travels in and out of the world of my nightmares. Barrett is part of a monolithic bloc of impassive guys with bristly mustaches and mirrored sunglasses whom I generally try to avoid. I can imagine him in his uniform looking tough and scary, but now I see him in his plaid Royal Robbins shirt, his Wrangler jeans—barking into the dog collar, looking at me with that worried expression—with those eyes that crinkle at the corners when he smiles. This juxtaposition is somehow exhilarating, like I have slipped between the cracks of a concrete wall and found some lush, secret world.

Barrett is saying something about having read a book recently about Polly Klaas. The author thinks there is a white slave trade ring in the Bay Area. He thinks the Hells Angels are involved, having branched out from producing and distributing speed. I hear an eerie piercing cry and see the black shadows of bats flit by. I imagine that in the landscape of Barrett's mind, the marina is dark and sinister, the fog hiding obscure threats. Suddenly Barrett stops walking. "Oscar! Where is he? Oh, shit. Oscar! Oscar!"

"He's probably with Dave. Don't worry, he'll come," I say, putting a hand on his forearm. He turns and strides back the way we came, bellowing the dog's name. I take up the cry with Barrett. "Oscar! Oscar! Dave! Come!"

Barrett's fear is contagious. As I yell, I start to feel cold seeping into my chest and shoulders. I said it would be okay, I told him to let Oscar run. Maybe I was wrong. Maybe the dog won't come back. Maybe he'll run out on the Marina Road on the other side of the hills. I imagine headlights and a dark shape, screeching brakes.

Barrett is twenty paces ahead of me now. I round a corner and see the methane vent spewing its orange flame toward the gray clouds, when the dogs come into view. Careening down the hills toward us, the dogs are a light shape and a dark shape, side by side, nipping at each other's necks.

Barrett calls me over the weekend and invites me to go see the movie *Heat* with Robert De Niro and Al Pacino. Even though we parted after our steak dinner with only a hug in the parking lot, something has changed. There is a physical vibration between us and I am eager to see him again. I tell myself this physical ease, this ability to be myself, must come from dating without marriage in mind. It's great not to worry if we fit together perfectly. In so many of my relationships, I've tried to reshape myself, to force a fit like a little kid trying to smash the wrong piece into a wooden puzzle. But since I am not serious about Barrett I can be free. I have finally become a truly modern woman. I will take a lover for fun and not because I am searching for a husband.

He arrives at my doorstep on the appointed night with a brightly wrapped package. "A little something for later," he says. As we go out to the curb, I sense him starting toward the passenger seat of his car and I unconsciously react by moving toward the driver's side. Then I stop, confused.

"Do you want me to drive?" I ask.

"No," he laughs. "I'm just opening your door for you."

"Oh, right."

Once we are in the car, he says, "So you said you liked Thai, right?" pulling a fat Yellow Pages from the backseat. "I made reservations at three different places, I wasn't sure which you would like." He thumbs through the book to some pages he's dog-eared.

"Hey, it's nice of you to go to all that trouble."

"Well, an old commander of mine once said, 'Time spent in reconnaissance is seldom wasted.'"

I laugh. "Well, I hope one of them is Cha Am, because that's my favorite."

He looks uncertainly through the book. "Umm..."

"Don't worry, let's just go there. It's close, it's good, and we're early enough to get in without a reservation."

We find a tight parking spot on Shattuck near Chez Panisse; Barrett parallel parks swiftly, with a mastery I find, absurdly, rather sexy.

"One correction with the wheel," he comments. "That's all you're allowed if you want to pass the driving part of the police test."

We enter the restaurant, passing a table where an African American woman is wearing a kente cloth headscarf. As we sit down at our table, he mutters, "I don't know why people do that."

"Do what?"

"Emphasize their differences so much," he says, gesturing toward the headscarf with his menu.

I stare at him, a giant alarm going off in my brain. "The kente cloth? You're kidding. I think it's great. It's about celebrating her heritage. Don't you believe in diversity?"

"I think diversity is the problem," he slowly replies. "I think we should all be…" He pauses, searching for a word, "…*pureed.*"

I feel my breath being pulled down, like my internal organs are free-falling in my body. I don't know exactly what he means, but my fears about white police officers are filling in the blanks. He wants a world of homogeneous people? Everyone looking exactly the same, presumably just like him? He doesn't want a mixed bouquet? He doesn't want many different kinds of whole grains; he wants bland white bread?

"I went to a funeral this weekend," he says softly. "One of our recently retired officers died—black guy, cancer—and I thought I should go, you know, pay my respects."

I am gripping my menu hard.

"Because to me, we're not black or white, we're all blue."

I realize I've been holding my breath and let it out in a whoosh. "Well, that's cool, I guess."

"Yeah? Well, so I walk in there, and all of a sudden I realize I'm the only white guy there."

"Oh. I see." I pause. "But it's still cool that you went."

"It wasn't *cool.* It was stupid. I just made everyone uncomfortable."

"Well, maybe you made them uncomfortable at first, but you probably made some of them think, too. If more people acted like you, things might change."

"Things aren't going to change in a city like Oakland."

"What are you talking about? Of course they could change. If you look at history, there is a slow but clear march toward human progress, toward greater freedom and understanding between people."

"I don't see that. I don't see it at all. I see a history of human conflict that will continue forever. I believe in what Plato said, that 'only the dead have seen the end of war.'"

"So...what? Everything leads to Armageddon? We aren't learning social beings? Geez, then what's the point? Why are we here?"

He looks at his plate and shakes his head. "I don't know. I don't have all the answers. I'm just a simple soldier."

I am deflated. I'd assumed that's why he was a cop, to try to help people. And "a simple soldier"? He is *not* just that. I have always believed that the privileges I have enjoyed—the opportunity and resources to get a first-rate education—should be repaid in some way by helping those who don't have the same possibilities. That's why I studied public policy. That's why I work in grassroots economic development. I try, although admittedly my impact has been frustratingly small, to alleviate poverty. I point out to Barrett that he is among the best-educated people in this country. He went to an elite college, has his master's in business. He has analytic skills.

"That may be true," he says, "but I'm not like you. I'm not trying to save the world. I'm just a simple soldier doing my duty the best I know how."

I push my chair away from the table. Oh boy, I think. We could not be more different.

Thank goodness I'm not serious about him.

Driving home from the movie, I ask Barrett, "So when you're off duty, do you ever carry a gun?"

He laughs, his crew cut bobbing, "Always, Miss Sophia. Got one on my hip right now."

My first reaction is a little rush of delight. I like having a secret knowledge of Barrett's other world.

When we get to my house, we sit on the edge of my bed and I open the little present he has brought me—two shot glasses and a flask-size bottle of vodka. We pour the vodka, clink glasses, and

sample. I kick off my shoes while Barrett tells me how his dad preferred vodka since it didn't make his breath smell of alcohol. I yawn
elaborately, stretch out sideways on the bed, and pat the area next to
me. He pushes the heel of each cowboy boot off with the ball of the
other foot and places his gun on my side table. Then he lies down
on his back with his hands behind his head.

I snuggle into the crook of his arm and he puts his arm around
me. He smells of leather and bayberry. I am heady with the vodka
shot. I take a breath. The room is dim and warm, and I like that I
am making the moves. Sliding my hand onto his chest, I begin to
nibble his neck. He turns toward me and we kiss. His lips are soft
and moist; his kisses gentle, tentative. I realize he is following my
lead. I try to lose myself in the feel of his rough cheek and soft lips
against mine. I try to stop thinking and just enjoy holding his upper
lip between my lips, gently biting. The heat of his chest under my
hand is inviting me in, but something is not letting me go.

I glance at the nightstand next to my bed. Looking at the gun
now—matte black metal with a textured grip—I am not excited
anymore. "What kind is it?" I ask.

Barrett is gently biting the back of my neck and exploring the
gap between my sweater and my pants with one finger. "Mmmm?"
he says, and glances over. "What? The gun? Oh. It's a Sig Sauer,
P-two twenty, forty-five caliber." He runs his hand up along my
ribcage.

"Have you ever had to shoot anybody?" I ask.

Barrett sighs and rolls onto his back, putting his hands back under his head. "Just once. Not counting dogs."

"What happened?"

"A guy tried to shoot my partner."

"Really? How?"

I can feel my body stiffening and I start to understand why the
gun disturbs me and why I am afraid to hear Barrett's story. The gun
reminds me of the fact that despite my own admiration of non-
violent principles, of peaceful conflict resolution, part of me worries that there are situations where nonviolence will not work. Like
when someone is pointing a gun at your partner. I honestly don't
know what one should do. Morally, that is. Gandhi would say to
resist without bringing harm to anyone—maybe throw yourself in

front of the bullet? In all my readings about Gandhi I felt so sure he was indeed a *mahatma*, a great soul. His convictions landed in my heart with the weight of Truth.

There was only one teeny thing that bothered me: the way Gandhi renounced his responsibility to his family, certain in his faith that God would take care of them without Gandhi's help. Somehow that didn't seem right to me. I have never told anyone this because it seems crazy for me to question Gandhi. He is so far superior to *me*. But it niggles at me. It niggles at me that he didn't want to protect them especially. If your loved one needs help, particularly if your loved one is being attacked, I just can't see not trying to stop it. Even with force if necessary. *Regrettably*, yes. With sorrow, yes. But still.

"We were stopping a car with three male blacks and a child in it." Barrett begins. A child! Good God, Barrett shot someone and a child was there, a child was involved.

He continues, "One guy ran and Thompson chased him and got him into a headlock. I was running to help when the first shot went off. The guy was trying to shoot Thompson by arcing the gun over his own head. I grabbed his wrist but he jerked it away. He shot again. The gun was waving around in front of me, but I couldn't grab it. I had to do something. So I shot him three times."

"Point-blank?"

"Yes. I kept shooting until I heard his gun fall."

My teeth are pressed hard together. Barrett is taut, his body remembering. Given my various minor run-ins with the police, I tend to imagine myself in the place of the suspect—desperate, afraid. I've never really imagined myself in the place of the police officer, never understood his fear. But I feel it now in the tense muscles of Barrett's body, and the way mine shivers with adrenaline, just imagining.

"Did you kill him?"

"No." He pauses. "Unfortunately. Put three holes in his side, though. That's why I changed to this gun, in fact. I used to use a Smith & Wesson forty-oh-six, forty caliber, but let's just say, I wasn't happy with the results." He laughs grimly, a half-chuckle, half-cough. "He was able to walk right into the courtroom. They gave him six years so he'll be out in three."

"And he never hit Thompson?"

"No. He missed."

We lie there a while in silence. I turn to him and snuggle my face into his neck. He strokes my hair. The air in the room has become heavier, the room darker. I roll away from him but pull his arm over me so my body is cupped into his. His arm feels solid and sure, slung over me, even now that I understand his strong exterior protects layers of fear, of foreboding, just like mine. Suddenly I wish I could show him a different world, of rich crumbly loam, beach fires, the happy shouts of children. I stroke the hand resting on my hip. "Don't worry," I whisper after a long while, "we're safe here."

THREE

Cultural Exchange

In country where high roads intersect, join hands with
your allies.
—Sun Tzu, *The Art of War*

ON OUR FOURTH DATE, I INVITE Barrett to the Harlem Boys'
Choir. I have seen the choir before and was moved by the
gawky boys in their bow ties singing so beautifully. In my mind, I
portray the whole evening as a sort of joke; I am the secret subver-
sive in Barrett's life, showing him black youth in a new context. I
am acutely aware of Barrett being a white cop in a predominantly
black city, the city where the Black Panther party was born, born
in large part to counter police brutality in African American neighborhoods. Oakland is still a place where American racial politics
seem particularly fierce, where everyone's actions tend to be viewed
through a racial lens. I don't think I'm being condescending. As
usual, I am just trying to *help.*

He arrives carrying a small bouquet of wildflowers and wearing
a brown herringbone sport jacket, yellow and blue striped tie, brown
pants, and loafers. Perhaps he is colorblind, I think. A lot of men are.
I feel a surge of excitement when he grins and hands me the flowers.
Pink warmth slips up my neck to my cheeks and I laugh. I put the
flowers into a vase and call out a good-bye to Jaime, who smirks at
me as I head out the door.

Once again, I find the music lovely and uplifting. I close my
eyes and let the clear notes ripple over me like soft raindrops, and
I answer their waves with tears. Barrett doesn't cry but sits alert in
his chair, leaning toward the music. I feel connected to him, and a

flicker of euphoria runs through me, that he and I can meet across the expanse of our different lives.

As we leave Davies Symphony Hall, the boys of the choir are waiting in a receiving line. Barrett has a favorite, the littlest boy with giant ears, and he wants to wait and shake his hand. I go to pick up our coats from the coat check, then lean against the wall in the entryway to wait for him. As the crowd flows by, I imagine Barrett with the choir. How would those boys feel if they knew he has chased young black men through backyards, hoping to tackle them before they can swallow their merchandise? I am afraid I know the answer. They would hate him, just knowing that much about him. I want them to know him more fully, see his complexity, as I am beginning to, but I worry, too. If there are those who don't see his humanity, who hate him for his uniform, his professional role, what will they think of me? And if I come to love someone who is clearly identified with one side of a bitter divide, the side that I have considered in the wrong historically, what will that mean for me? Can I still hold onto my own convictions?

Wouldn't it be something, I wonder, if we could all just be *individual people,* and if neither "young black man" nor "white police officer" had to carry so much historical freight in my mind, or in Barrett's, or in anyone's. It occurs to me that maybe that's what Barrett meant when he said he wished we could all be pureed. I didn't understand his comment that way, because we speak a different language and are communicating through a haze of historical mistrust and suspicion. But perhaps it's the same thing we all long for: to be seen with fresh eyes and an open heart. Still, remembering the lady in the kente cloth, I wish Barrett could imagine a world in which differences weren't a bad thing. A world in which differences were interesting and exciting and didn't preclude an open heart.

On the drive home Barrett is whistling and telling me how his ears were really big when he was a little boy, too. That's fairly easy for me to imagine since his ears are still somewhat prominent. Barrett says the little choirboy was shy and didn't want to look at him at first. Then he says the kindergarten kids in East Oakland still wave and smile when he drives by in his police car. But by they time they hit eight or nine, he says softly, they pretty much already hate you, already call you Peckerwood.

• • •

Barrett suggests we get a bite to eat. Neither of us had much dinner, but by the time we get back to the East Bay, it is after eleven. Not much is open except fast food places.

He asks me what kind of fast food I like. I tell him I really don't eat fast food much, and if I have to, I just go to whatever's closest.

"C'mon," he says, "but are you a Wendy's person, Burger King, In-N-Out?"

"Seriously, I don't really know. Which do you like?"

"Well, geez, I eat fast food all the time, usually it's all that's open when I'm working. I don't have a favorite. It's more that I pick based on what I'm doing."

"What do you mean?"

"There are places that have the best fries, or the best burgers, and then there are places that package better, like if I'm going to have to eat while driving, or if I'm picking up chow for the whole squad."

"Well, what's the best for hungry people after the Harlem Boys' Choir?"

"I'd say Nation's," he says, turning in. "It's clean and they serve breakfast all day and they have good pie."

Barrett orders two eggs over easy, a side of sausage, a slice of peach pie, and coffee. I ask for a chicken sandwich and a club soda. It turns out they don't have club soda so I get Sprite. He eats with gusto and I notice the greasy food is giving his lips a nice shine. They are really very attractive lips, expressive and sensual. And he has beautiful teeth, straight and white. I enjoy watching his lips and teeth work on the food he is eating. In fact, everything Barrett is eating looks really appetizing: the toast dipped in egg yolk, the sausages (even though I usually don't eat them), the pie.

"Can I have a bite of yours?" I ask.

"I bet it takes a lot of heart to get into that choir," Barrett says, sliding his plate over.

"Heart?"

"Yeah, heart. It's the most important thing in the world, I think, that and loyalty. Gotta be loyal to your team. Otherwise you're not worth your salt."

I wonder what he means by heart. I think I have heart, the way I can empathize with anyone. I think of the time my car overheated, the temperature gauge spiking into the red zone, steam billowing out of the hood. I pulled off the freeway at the first exit, which deposited me into a tough part of Oakland. I found a phone booth in the parking lot of a liquor store and was trying to call Nathan, to ask him to come help me. When I saw the kid with the hood pulled up around his face coming toward me on a bike four sizes too small for him, I knew he was bad news even as I told myself not to assume. I knew enough to jump back in my car, lock the door, and roll the window up.

When he stopped by my window and hissed, "Givemeyour moneybitchorI'llkillya," I'd already registered that my briefcase was behind my seat, and even though I didn't know if that was a gun in his pocket or his finger, I wasn't about to get out of the car. Yet even as time slowed and I watched myself turning on the ignition, there was another part of me. Even as I said a prayer that the car still ran and figured who cares if I fry the engine; even as I half heard tires screeching and got back on the freeway and pulled over to watch my chest heave and heard someone sobbing, another part of me was back with him. That part of me was asking, "What happened to you? What did you learn that made you so hard, so cold?"

But somehow I think this is not what Barrett means by heart.

"What I miss most about being a soldier," he says, "is the camaraderie. Sometimes I think I never should have left."

"Why did you?"

"My ex-wife really wanted me to. But I can't blame it on her. I guess I was frustrated with the command. Heck, I'm probably better off where I am now. I see more action in a week than I'd see in a year in the army."

"You know, they tried to recruit me into West Point," I say. "Sent me this fancy invitation to an open house."

"You would have hated West Point," he says. "Not that you don't have heart, but you're much too kind and sensitive for the military."

I smile.

"But you're still on my team."

It's just not fair to let him think that about me, when the person

I hate most in the world is a cop, Mark Cochinard. Cochinard, as in *cochino*, I've always thought. "Pig." There is a big knot in my gut. There is only one way to untie it.

"I don't know if I'm always kind," I begin. "Can I tell you something that you can't tell anyone else?" There is a vacuum in my solar plexus, sucking at my gut and lungs, and I am beginning to get the shakes, remembering.

Barrett says, "Sure, I'm good at keeping secrets."

"Really?"

"Really. People tell me stuff that's secret, and I don't tell anyone. I know a lot of other folks find it really hard to keep in, but I don't. So people tell me, and I don't tell anyone." He shrugs. "I just don't need to."

So I tell him how Mark Cochinard stopped me and my then-boyfriend Rafael, about two miles outside Austin, Nevada. Austin's town sign pronounces it "the loneliest town on the loneliest highway in America"—and we were two miles *outside* it. Cochinard said he was about to let us go, then added, "Just one last thing. Do you have any firearms, contraband, or controlled substances in the vehicle?"

Barrett chuckles. "That's absolutely textbook. Just like they taught us in the academy. Gets you to let your guard down."

After Cochinard found my little pipe with the weed in it, he handcuffed us, took us to jail, had us strip-searched and put in separate cells. As a parting comment, he told me Rafael would be deported and I would "never see him again." Dave the dog was put in the exercise yard, where there was a cold rain coming down. I could hear him barking through the three-inch metal door, even after it clanged shut behind me.

Barrett gives a low whistle. "All over a tiny bit of weed?" he says. "That'd be a ticket here."

"Yeah, well, it's a felony there. I didn't know, either."

"So what happened?"

I explain how Rafael was not deported. That there was a plea bargain down to a misdemeanor for me, and then the charges were dropped against Rafael once I agreed to testify that the weed was mine. I tell Barrett about going to my sentencing with my bag packed with seven bras, seven pairs of underwear, and seventeen books, as the probation department had recommended that I serve thirty days in county jail. But since my father was terminally ill with cancer, the judge relented and sentenced me to one hundred hours of community service and a two-thousand-dollar fine.

Barrett sits back in the red padded booth and shakes his head slowly. "I'm really sorry that happened to you."

"Yeah. Thanks." Now comes the clincher. I take a deep breath and say, "I really hate that cop."

"I bet!" Barrett says. Broad smile.

Absolution.

Later I will notice that almost everyone who gets to know Barrett has to go through this confession phase. They have to tell him their personal experience with a police officer, especially if it's bad. They have to hear what he thinks, his explanation of why the guy was a jerk or why he didn't help or why he wasn't more polite. It is our way of separating Barrett from his uniform.

Barrett is facing his empty pie plate but looking at me sidelong. "Now I have a story to tell you," he says. I make a question mark with my eyebrows. So he tells me about how as a rookie, he picked up some overtime doing security at a Grateful Dead show.

"I love the Dead," I say.

He nods. He'd figured. His job was to keep the traffic moving. He saw a guy walking alongside of the cars waiting to exit, stopping now and then to hand them something out of his backpack.

"You thought he was selling drugs?"

"I was sure of it. And I was right. I approached the guy and asked to see his backpack. It was full of weed. I couldn't believe how blatant he was. So I arrested him on the spot."

"And then?"

"And then all the other cops laughed at me and told me they never press charges for drugs at Dead shows."

In my room, Barrett slings his Harris tweed over the chair along with his regimental tie. Where I am lean and long, Barrett is powerful and compact. I know before he takes me in his arms that he will be solid. He can keep secrets. He can stand firm in the face of the ugly world I'd rather not think about. And he can stand here and kiss my neck, running his hands up and down my back. I explore his starched white shirtfront with my palm and open the top buttons. His kisses are warm and firm. I glide my hand around his neck to the back of his head. The hair is prickly around the sides, soft on top.

Since Christian times, the forbidden fruit has most often been depicted as an apple; but the truth is the Hebrew word in Genesis is generic, meaning simply "fruit." Given the climate of ancient Mesopotamia, the area most likely to have been the setting for Eden, some scholars assert the pomegranate is a more likely choice. My personal vote goes to the pomegranate. The apple is far too upfront—what mystery is there in its thin skin, its bland white flesh? Much easier to believe in the mysterious pomegranate, with its slightly bitter web of cells hiding sweet red juicy secrets. It takes time and work to consume a pomegranate, unpeeling the thick skin, navigating through the maze to the interior kernels, and savoring each surprising burst.

Maybe this is the secret. Loving without trying to make yourselves into a matched set. That's why there is this ease. This must be the freedom of loving without an agenda, not trying to force myself to fit where I don't. It doesn't matter. Nothing matters to me but the brush of his chin against my cheek, the feel of his fleshy earlobe between my lips.

FOUR

Behind Enemy Lines

We are not fit to lead an army on the march unless we are familiar with the face of the country—its mountains and forests, its pitfalls and precipices, its marshes and swamps.
—Sun Tzu, *The Art of War*

NEXT TO THE BEDSIDE, DIRTY PLATES are heaped among take-out boxes, a sock or two, a crumpled shirt. Most nights we order in Thai or Chinese, usually right around the time Jaime gets home from work. She notices Barrett's Blazer out front and walks in with her hands in the air, yelling, "Hold your fire!" Or she scrunches up her nose at the smell of Barrett's mu shu pork and mutters something about dead animals. Barrett and I laugh and take our dinner into my bedroom.

I am learning the beat, the pulse of him, delighted to find we can match rhythms despite our different backgrounds. He is full of surprises that make me stop for a moment, recalibrate. The first surprise is his soft skin, a pleasure to rub my cheek against, making tangible the yin and yang of him, the tough and the gentle. I ask him why he joined the military and he tells me of his alcoholic father. He tells me how he and his brothers would steal money from his father's wallet when he was drunk. Then they'd go buy food, burning the pork chops in the pan and each boy eating six of them at one sitting. Looping back to my question, he finally answers, "I guess... I guess I was looking for a family."

When I touch his smooth chest, I find the boy he once was. I think of him alone on a bus from New York City, soon to become a cadet at West Point, looking for a place to belong, a home. He tells me about marching with a hundred-pound pack when he was in Ranger school. How he was so hungry, he would say he had a sore throat so that he could eat the cough lozenges that were standard issue. When I stroke the wide muscles of his thighs, I am there with him in a Florida swamp, drenched in sweat, weak from hunger and fatigue. The muscles of his legs, back, shoulders come from hard work, not from the gym. I find the place on his left thigh where the quadriceps seem to suddenly part, leaving a divot where lean sinew should be, and learn it happened when he was four years old and ran into a post on the monkey bars. I admire each strand of his life individually and absorb them without question. I don't ask what they mean. I don't chafe at the contradictions inherent in my intimacy with him. I don't wonder what the future holds.

His stomach has a thin layer of softness, a pillow where I lay my head when we talk. Barrett tells me his father didn't like the word "cope"; he didn't like "issue." If the boys uttered such words, their father would throw his cocktail—vodka and ice—at them. If the boys avoided saying any words he didn't like, he'd make them wrestle during commercial breaks.

"And your mom?" I ask.

I feel his pectoral muscles stiffen slightly under my palm. "She died when I was twelve. Breast cancer."

I draw a breath. "So what was she like?"

"Dunno. I don't remember much. She was very strict. Strict and very frugal. Guess she had to be; I don't think my old man ever gave her much money after he left her. Made us peanut butter and butter sandwiches for lunch. I never could get anyone to trade with me. But I don't really remember being with her. I can't really remember what she looked like, just the images from photos."

But you were twelve, I wonder to myself, you should still have memories of her. Later I will find his boyhood diary from the time around her death, page after page filled with a simple entry: "I forgot." "I forgot." "I forgot."

He is quiet now and I run my hand up along the clavicle, cupping it around the back of his neck. Drawing my knee along the fur of his legs, I push up on my right elbow, lean over him and kiss each of his eyelids. Then I put my cheek to his chest where his heart thumps a soothing cadence.

"I wonder sometimes if we caused it," he says.

"What do you mean?"

"Three young boys, you know. My dad left her soon after my youngest brother was born. Then he took off for Vietnam. We were a handful. We exhausted her."

"You didn't cause it," I say, looking up at him. "You were just being boys. You couldn't have been any different."

He looks past me and shrugs slightly. For a second I have lost him to the past, and I can see him willing it all blank, pulling himself back to the present. When he looks at me, his eyes have their familiar glint of playfulness.

"We were a handful, but she kept us in line. Used to make us cut our own switches down at my grandmother's farm. She'd whip us and my Grandma Lily would yell from the front porch, 'Give 'em another lick, Charlotte! Give 'em another lick!'"

I want to comfort him, to heal all of his hurts. I want to go back and find the little boy standing at his mother's bedside. Yet I am not conscious that I am falling for him. The current we are floating in is too powerful, leaving no eddies for reflection. I am not fazed when he comes to me on a weekend afternoon, trembling, early home from work, saying, "I really wanted to see you. This has never happened to me before. I wanted to see you so much."

I am no stranger to the power of physical desire, the sorcery of shared secrets. I know all too well it doesn't mean love, it doesn't mean forever. I've made that mistake many times. I've held a lover like a child in my arms, rocking him, telling him over and over he was a good boy, that I loved him, until finally the tears flowed down his cheeks. I thought that connection would hold us forever. But it didn't. I've learned through countless disappointments—the many times when I mined my soul, unearthed my secrets and offered them to a lover like precious jewels, thinking that would bind him to me. And one after another they oohed and aahed over my treasures and went elsewhere.

This all feels too effortless to be love. I associate love with adrenaline. With that feeling deep in my belly that I get before the roller coaster heads down the biggest plunge. Nerves tingling, teeth clenched: to me love is something akin to fear. Beyond the ease, I assume that my true love will match my feelings, will cry when I cry, laugh when I laugh, become part of me, die without me. This can't be love because Barrett maintains a kind of equilibrium; even when he comes to me trembling, it doesn't scare me. He doesn't seem tortured or desperate, just hungry, eager. It's so easy to tell Barrett of the traumas that shaped my early sense of self: my loneliness as a seven-year-old, how I stayed home to walk the dog after school while the other kids my age took the bus to town to buy Bazooka gum and baseball cards, of my parents' talk of divorce, of the dog being sent away to a farm.

Before I know what I'm doing, I am telling him of my father's death from pancreatic cancer. In the last hours, at his house, when he started to hemorrhage, he asked my mom for me. I was in the bathroom, throwing up. When I went back to his bedside, he murmured to me, "The gun...is it locked up? The gun."

My mom had called an ambulance and I could hear the sirens getting louder. I told my father I'd take care of it. I explain to Barrett, and maybe to myself as well, that I thought he'd wanted me to be sure the gun was locked away. Then the paramedics rushed in. I held his hand as they carried him down the steps on the stretcher, and it hit me: he wanted me to give him his gun. He wanted to use it. He was agitated, trying to sit up, maybe trying to express the last wishes, the last thoughts, he would ever have, and I tried to soothe him, calling him by the pet name I had given him in my toddlerhood, the anglicized Hungarian word for father. "Api, can you try...can you remember your breathing exercises?"

He took a deep shuddering breath and lapsed into unconsciousness.

What I am trying to tell Barrett is this: my father had always believed my act. He really thought I was strong. And then, then, at the most important moment, he had asked me for help, had believed I would have the courage to let him do it. And I had misunderstood. And maybe, maybe failed him.

But while Barrett listens, he doesn't follow me down these dark tunnels. Instead, he only says softly, "Ya know it seems to me your rucksack's heavy enough. You don't have to *add* to it."

Because he is so calm, I even tell him that I still think about Nathan, that I can't reconcile how strong our connection was at times, those moments when he seemed to understand me thoroughly. How on the anniversary of my father's death, I stood with Nathan at the edge of an ice field near the Annapurna Base Camp and shouted my father's name to the mighty ring of mountains surrounding us. Nathan shouted his grandmother's name, and then took my hand. I tell Barrett that I believe those moments exist apart from time; they can't be erased. About my puzzlement: how can you share a moment like that and yet later your lover does not want to kiss you? Barrett just listens and nods, solid as the Himalaya.

I glide along, enchanted, filled with awe to discover this new landscape, this unfamiliar terrain, stark in some ways but also surprisingly beautiful. One morning, with our bagels on paper plates and a shared jug of orange juice, we wander out to his backyard to eat. Wiping cream cheese from his lips with his sleeve, he gets up, goes to a shed, and comes back with a BB gun. He lifts it to his shoulder and aims at a plastic bucket on the far side of the pool. The BBs rap against the fence behind. "Can I have a try?" I ask. Barrett hands me the gun. I shoulder it, pull the trigger, and the bucket dances. Barrett whistles.

Later, after he has left for work, I wander around his house. Barrett lives in Livermore, a rodeo town turned bedroom community on the outskirts of the San Francisco Bay Area. Across the street from his subdivision are wineries, stables, and a long windy road that leads to a mine. He has plenty of space for one person yet his possessions are fairly modest. A punching bag hangs in the garage, laundered clothes lie rumpled in a pile on the guestroom bed. In the rarely used pool out back, leaves are drifting. An aqua bucket outside the sliding glass door provides multiple days of water for Oscar. On the mirror of the master bath, I find a postcard of Nelson Mandela as a young man, wearing boxing gloves. All is unadorned and steadfastly masculine. The living room is sunken and boasts a large stone fireplace, mahogany furniture, burgundy and navy accents. The bookshelves are lined with books like Colonel Jeff Cooper's *Principles of Personal Defense*; S.L.A. Marshall's *Night Drop: The American Airborne Invasion of Normandy*; Sun Tzu's *The Art of War*; and *How to Tell if Someone Is Lying*.

None of it sets off alarm bells in my head. Such is the languor brought on by the ease of the current moment. I am like a cat stretching in the sun, indifferent to the needs of the future. I smile affectionately at the Mandela picture and think vaguely that it means we must feel the same way about race relations. Then a moment later I think he lives in a black-and-white world and I will bring him some color. I think given that his mom died when he was twelve, that he has two brothers, lived with his dad as a teen, went to all-male junior high and high school, then to West Point, then into an all-male Ranger battalion, he sure needs a strong woman in his life.

Then one day, in bed, as I am arched above him in ecstasy, he whispers something I can't make out. Clasping my waist with his arms, his cheek between my breasts, he turns and looks up at me, says it again, louder. "Sophia, I'm falling for you."

He is falling for me? I can't stop a rush of joy from stripping away my last layers of protection. *He* is falling for *me?* I begin to tell him I feel the same way, in the first flood of pure genuine affection. But even as I begin to speak, even as I start to whisper "Me too," I feel dread's sharp whip. This opens the door to the future; this will shine a light on the vast dark spaces between us. We are too different. This is not supposed to happen. He is a man, a tough man. Men like sex just for the pleasure of it; they can be physical without falling in love. I thought I only had to guard my own heart; his was a sure thing. His was safe, wrapped in layers of Kevlar, covered by blue and camouflage uniforms, protected by bandoliers strapped across his chest.

I sit up high in the passenger seat of Barrett's Chevy Blazer as we go through the Taco Bell drive-through in Tracy. Barrett finishes ordering, assuring me I will like their super tacos as long as I use the hot sauce generously. After receiving our order, he hands me the bag and the drinks and drives toward the exit while closing the window. Then suddenly he brakes, and reverses the window back down. "Hey, Rick!" he yells.

Rick appears at the window in a beat-up baseball cap, sunglasses, and flannel shirt.

"Hey, bro," Rick says. "What brings you out here?"

"We came out to do a little mountain biking, then we had to do a code thirty-three run for some chow. Rick, this is my girlfriend, Sophia," Barrett says, jerking a thumb toward me.

I smile at Rick, start to say nice to meet you, but can't quite catch his eye. He barely nods at me, instead saying to Barrett in a low voice, "So thought you should know Cunningham wants to talk to me about that four-fifteen family the other night. I'm supposed to go up to the eighth floor next Wednesday."

I take a sip of my diet Coke, wondering what they are talking about. I look down the street at a mirage of wavy liquid shimmering up ahead.

Barrett says, "Don't worry about it, I was code five in the house, and you had nothin' to do with it. It'll be okay."

"But I saw how worked up that cat was when he came out in the street. You had to handle your business. I'll sure tell 'em that," Rick says.

"Just tell 'em the truth, bro, code four."

Hello! I want to shout. Hello, I'm here! I exist! What the hell are you guys talking about? Handle *what* business? This creep Rick is giving me the feeling that he is ignoring me because I am (a) female and (b) not a cop. I don't like him. I don't like the way I can't see his eyes behind his glasses. I don't like the whole arrogant way he holds himself. I especially don't like the way he pulls Barrett away from me and into their little clubby cop world. A place I am no part of, where they even speak a different language. What's with the whole conspiratorial whispering? What's the eighth floor?

I look from Rick's impassive face to Barrett's. Then I pan back, taking in the whole picture of Barrett, his left arm out the window, his hand on the wheel, his cargo shorts. He's wearing his "drive-on rag"—an olive drab bandana—around his neck like a kerchief. He explained to me earlier about the use of the drive-on rag in the Ranger battalion. It can be used to soak up sweat, to tie something, as a napkin or a snot rag, or to dip in water if you're hot. He did the latter when we finished the ride and he changed out of his sweaty tank top. I look down at Barrett's T-shirt. It depicts a police officer wearing body armor and a gas mask, charging toward the world with a big rifle. "Hurdle the Dead, Trample the Weak" is emblazoned above the image.

Barrett and Rick are exchanging good-byes. Rick gives me a bland "Nice to meet you, ma'am." No eye contact. I feel a wash of irritation for still having a wilted smile on my face, for still wanting to please. As we pull out of the parking lot and drive the short distance to the freeway on-ramp, Barrett grabs the white paper bag, extracts his food and a hot sauce packet, rips the packet open with his teeth, squeezes the hot sauce onto his taco, crunches a big bite, and takes a big swig of his diet Coke. All while driving with one hand. Then he glances over at me. "Hey. Your chow's getting cold."

I've been in this predicament before. Not exactly the same, of course, but there's always been a point in my past relationships when I felt a cold splash of alienation, felt terrifyingly apart from my lover. I assumed that feeling of distance meant there was something terribly wrong with the relationship. But I never want to let go. I want to find some way to scramble back to safety, to connection. I know what to do. I need to get the other person to change, and in order to do that I am willing to contort myself into all kinds of knots. For example, when Nathan didn't want to have sex, I resolved to not have sex either, anticipating he would eventually come to the realization that he was missing out. Or when another beau wanted to be nonmonogamous, I dated someone else with the hope my original lover would become terribly jealous and change his mind. The beauty of this is you can keep trying. If you get brought up short, you can just resolve to try harder.

I ask Barrett, "What's a four-fifteen family?"

"Domestic dispute."

"So what did he mean, 'You had to handle your business'?"

Barrett sighs. "I had a caper the other night where I had to arrest this drunk guy, and, well, he didn't want to be arrested. Long story short, I ended up using a palm strike on him, and his family didn't like that. They've filed a complaint, and Internal Affairs is investigating."

Doubt jolts me again. A palm strike? Is that a euphemism for whacking some guy upside the head? I feel like I am being pulled underwater. I can't get enough air. Here we go—police brutality. In my epistemology, people involved with police brutality are menacing, gray bloblike entities. They don't have divots on their legs from when they were four. They didn't knock themselves out accidentally running into a parking meter while playing tag with their younger brother.

So now I am at sea. Who *is* Barrett? I can so easily picture someone like Rick beating the shit out of a drunk guy. But Barrett? Is he one of them, too? His demeanor seemed to alter slightly when Rick was around, his language changed, got more clipped. Maybe when he's at work, it creeps into him, the angry evil blob, the bully, the brute.

Could he be cold and heartless like the cops in my past? Like the ones at the Stanford "Out of South Africa" protest? The ones who had hoisted my upper arms behind my back and bent my hand over in an excruciating wrist crunch? Who'd yelled at me, "You're hurting yourself, ma'am. Stop hurting yourself!"

When I decided to participate in the protest, sitting down cross-legged on the cold linoleum floor of the student union, I thought I knew what to expect. The other, more experienced activists had told me what would happen. We'd be carried out by the police and then cited and released. It sounded pretty simple. I assumed I'd be finished in time to go to the theater with my mom later that night. I wasn't worried by one activist's breathless, last-minute advice: "Just in case they take you to jail, remember—cops lie. They always lie, don't believe anything they say."

Afterward—after my mom had bailed me out of jail, after the incident spurred the largest protests for divestment in a decade—Stanford conducted an investigation into the use of the pain compliance techniques at the Old Union protest. The report found that while not illegal, the "means of carrying out the unresisting students was wrong and unjustifiable." The president of the university sent me a personal letter of apology. It wasn't enough for me. I called the report a whitewash. I wanted all those cops fired.

I feel myself wishing again that he hadn't said he was falling for me. If Barrett hadn't said anything, maybe, just maybe I could have embraced the challenge of sparring with him. I could have imagined myself as his teacher. But now the "This is such a lark" attitude is no longer available to me. We have crossed into a realm where I now feel a great responsibility for Barrett's attitudes and beliefs. Love, after all, means supporting your partner, does it not? And what if your partner represents something you don't believe in? Then it just doesn't work, right? I have never been married, but I think I know some of its basic requirements. There's a reason people talk about their partner as a "soul mate" or "their other half." There is supposed to be some gut-level, cell-level recognition of the other person as deeply familiar. Isn't there?

To be with someone as different as Barrett would require changing myself to a degree that's too big even for chameleon *me* to contemplate. I roll down the window and look away from Barrett at the brown hills dotted with windmills. I try to find the old way I felt about him. He's easy to be around. He makes me laugh. I try to shape these memories into solid bricks to make a dam against the torrent of despair in my chest. This is doomed. And it's my fault. I shouldn't have let it get so deep. I should have known better. I am pathetic for letting this happen. What should I do? Should I tell him everything I find disturbing about how he views the world and that therefore I can never see him again? I play with that possibility for a while. And that's what finally brings me back in touch with the old Barrett. When I imagine saying good-bye to him, then I can remember being in his arms. Although the weight of what I see in Barrett's T-shirt, in Barrett's world—guns, body armor, gas mask—is making me sink into weeds and muck,I realize if I let go of the weight now I will shoot to the surface and get the bends bad.

Barrett slides his hand across to my thigh and smiles at me. I look down at his hand. Sometimes he has grabbed my hand to cross the street, or jerked the dog's leash, and he just does it too hard, like he doesn't know his own strength. I wonder if when he hit the guy with the palm strike, he didn't realize how hard he did it. In order to ease the storm inside me, I have to signal to him that our relationship is probably not going anywhere.

"Did you tell Rick I was your girlfriend?" I say.

"Huh?"

"You called me your girlfriend."

He looks over at me, puzzled. And also, I realize—the knot in my stomach tightening—hurt. "Aren't you my girlfriend?" he says, pulling my hand over to his mouth and kissing it.

I am trapped. I feel sick. I pull my hand away and bring it to meet my other one, which is tucked between my legs. I hunch over and rock while rubbing my hands together. "I—well...I don't...I just think it's a little early for that," I mumble.

We ride along in silence. As we pass the sign for Camp Parks, Barrett looks south and does a mock salute.

"What are you doing?" I ask.

"Just saying hi to Koons and Powell, those poor SOBs."

"Who?"

"Koons and Powell, you know—the LAPD guys who arrested Rodney King. They're in there—in the federal prison next to Camp Parks. I saw them once, when I had drill, the two of them walking together in the exercise yard."

"Do you mean the guys who beat up Rodney King? You can't possibly be defending those guys!" It relieves the tension in my chest to be speaking, to be arguing. "I saw that video, I couldn't even look at it more than once. It was absolutely horrifying! Those guys were so clearly out of line!"

I hear in my voice a trill of anger, which I try to control. Barrett has no such problem. He says calmly that he believes the officers were just doing what they'd been trained to do, that King might have been on PCP. He says they never show the whole video; King didn't respond to a Taser, wouldn't comply with the officers' repeated commands. Summing up, Barrett says, "That video just showed what most people would rather ignore—that we pay cops to do a job regular folks can't deal with."

If I still had a shred of hope about squeezing Barrett and me into some form of soul union, it is squashed by this new evidence. I saw that video. It was obvious. Those guys were callous, inhuman. I say, "That's what they're trained to do? That's sickening. There must be something extremely wrong with LAPD if that's how they're trained."

Barrett says he has a lot of respect for LAPD, that Daryl Gates is a damn good leader, the father of SWAT, and someone who does the best he can for his troops.

I cannot believe what I am hearing. "Oh, great," I say. "Let me get this straight. You *admire* the guy who said, 'Casual drug users should be taken out and shot'? He's a freakin' lunatic. *I'm* a casual drug user, for chrissake, and so are virtually all of my friends. Do you want *me* shot?"

Barrett looks over at me. "Aw, he wasn't serious. The guy just says whatever pops into his head." He laughs affectionately, the way a parent might about a mischievous child. "Hell, his own kid's a tur—I mean, a drug addict. I'm sure he doesn't want him shot."

"I can see why his kid's a so-called turd," I say, "with a father like that!"

Surprisingly, it is a relief to argue with Barrett, to give voice to my separateness. It's delightful to talk about cops and drug users instead of Barrett and Sophia. I let the pressure of my confusion come out in my voice. I accuse Barrett of defending rotten cops, of supporting cops who beat people up, who choke people and lie in court.

"Look," he says, "some guys are off the hook and I don't defend them. But a lot of cops are just trying to get stuff done, they're just sick of watching the same turds—ones they *know* are rotten—get off time and time again. They really want to make the neighborhoods safer for the good people who live there."

"But cops can't take the law into their own hands!" I say, watching my hands fly up in the air as if of their own accord. I point out that our justice system is set up to make sure the innocent don't get unfairly punished, and to be sure of that, we tolerate a certain amount of guilty folks going free. I elaborate. I give examples. When I argue like this, I am calmed by my own dispassionate and authoritative voice. This is all very far away, my voice declares. In matching the rhythms and intonations of my professors in college and graduate school, my voice declares my separateness from Barrett.

Barrett nods. "Yeah, well that's great in theory, but it's a little harder to take out on the street. The sad thing to me is you take a good cop, a hard-working cop, who's motivated to put the bad guys in jail, and he gets caught on some videotape, and do you think anyone's giving him any credit for his efforts? They string him up."

Professor Sophia points out that cops like he's talking about are resolving a contradiction that policymakers should have to face up to. "They should push back," I say, "make political leaders confront the trade-off!"

Barrett shrugs. "The world just doesn't work that way. The politicians aren't going to admit it if it costs them votes. Cops who don't want to get their hands dirty just end up in the building getting fat."

I'm trying to define the problem here so I can recommend the policy solution. That's what I do to get control of a situation I don't like. I apply the eightfold path I learned in policy school: define the problem, assemble the evidence, construct the alternatives, select the criteria, project the outcomes, confront the trade-offs, decide, then tell your story.

I will need some time to think about this, I think with relief. I mustn't rush to a decision. This will take time. Poorly thought-out policies always have perverse consequences. Like rent control. I'll need some more time with Barrett while I consider this more fully.

When we pull up to my house I am glad. I want to be in my world again, to see the modern art portrait of my father that makes him look like Lenin, the "Die, Yuppie Scum" sticker plastered to my filing cabinet, the Mapplethorpe poster of the muscular naked woman in my bedroom. Barrett puts the truck firmly in park, then points at Jaime's truck. "Hey—I've got that present for Jaime, remember? Looks like she's home!" and he jumps out, coming round to my side to offer his hand as I clamber down.

Barrett's already let Jaime try on his shoulder holster. He's chatted with her about her truck, inquired how often she changes the oil, and admired the way she's rigged up a cozy sleeping platform in the back. Jaime in turn has tried to be friendly. In fact, she started out enthusiastic about Barrett, and I was hopeful they would hit it off and become buddies. After all, when Jaime and I go on a beach outing with multiple vehicles, she loves more than anything to take radios and use mock-police language. She insists we all have code names. Hers is Petunia, mine is Dragonfly. In the early days of my courtship with Barrett, she used to get excited about Barrett's arrival and say things like "Hey, is Mr. B-Bravo, A-Alpha coming over tonight?" But he would point out—albeit gently—that she shouldn't say "Check check over" after she finished saying something. She should say "Check" to confirm someone else's transmission and "Over" when she was finished speaking. It just took all the fun out of it for her.

"Where could Dona Juana have gotten to?" Barrett asks, looking around the house. "Does she have a friend over?"

Barrett is in awe of Jaime's love life, and I suspect a little bit jealous of it, too. Jaime is tall, slender, athletic, with short hair: boyish without being hard, not pretty exactly, but definitely attractive. She wears soft flannel shirts and cutoff jean shorts and flip-flops and a baseball hat backwards, and she has tempted many straight women over to the other side. Barrett doesn't get it. I do.

"Shhh," I say as we step into the kitchen. "Don't let her hear you call her that. She'll be embarrassed."

Just then, we hear the clattering of footsteps coming up the back porch. Jaime pushes the door open with her foot. She's holding a tray with the remnants of breakfast on it and holding the door open with her body, to allow Dave the dog and a pretty woman to pass by.

Barrett rushes to help with the door.

"Don't worry, big guy, I got it," Jaime says.

Barrett holds the door anyway. He looks at Jaime's guest and says, grinning, "It's no problem. I can see you got your hands full." Then he switches to using his foot as a door prop, and sticks out his hand to the visitor. "Hello there, I'm Barrett McAllister. I'm Sophia's boy—I'm a friend of Sophia's."

The visitor's name is Melanie, and when she finishes shaking Barrett's hand, she looks sidelong at Jaime, and I know from that little exchange of glances that they have been talking about—and probably making fun of—Barrett. They barely know each other, and yet I sense they share the view that Barrett is different, an outsider. I feel a momentary spark of anger, a brave little flame of indignation, but it is squelched by a wave of shame. We all stand there in silence. It seems like the moment will not let us go. We are snagged on it.

"Hey, Jaime," Barrett finally says, "I got a little present for you." Jaime starts unloading the dirty dishes from the tray into the sink. Barrett brandishes an oval white patch trimmed with red, and hands it to her. He has noticed that when she does work around the house, like sanding and painting old furniture or cleaning the basement or changing the oil of her truck, she dons a pair of blue coveralls, like an old-fashioned service mechanic would. Recently, when we were at the Post Exchange at Travis Air Force Base picking up Barrett's new lieutenant colonel uniform, he spied the patches. "Jaime needs one of these for her handyman outfit," he said. I was touched he'd thought of something for her and hopeful it would help them become closer.

"What's this?" Jaime says, surprised. "For me?" She takes the patch and looks down at it. It reads "Jaime" in red script.

"It's for your coveralls."

"Hey. Wow." It's absolutely perfect for Jaime. It's just the kind of thing she loves. I know she really likes it, and I realize with dismay that this fact is making her really uncomfortable. She doesn't *want* to like Barrett. She doesn't know what to do. She gives him an awkward chuck on the shoulder. "Hey, thanks, Barrett."

"No problem," he says with his little-boy grin.

"Okay, then...well, see you guys later." Jaime looks at me as she says this, then she grabs Melanie's hand and tugs her out of the kitchen.

The first time I break up with Barrett I do it at a waterfront park on a sunny afternoon. We sit together on a concrete bench, my bare leg touching his cargo pants. I cry as I deliver the message Jaime helped me prepare: What we are doing is a waste of time; we should get the breakup over with; it will never work. He holds my hand and listens. I talk and talk in circles. You and I have nothing in common. We don't believe in the same things. We aren't interested in the same things. I point out that he always eats meat. He never buys organic. He doesn't recycle. People who are meant to be together shouldn't have doubts like this.

"But we are happy being together, aren't we? There are some things we both like, right?" He draws his finger along the inside of my thigh.

I put my hand on his and say, "But c'mon, your whole life is centered around violence and crime, around battling enemies, cops versus turds. You wear T-shirts with these scary guys on it that say 'Trample the Weak'—as if that's a good thing! While I—I believe in helping weak people, I don't believe in trampling anything. I believe in nonviolence while you consider those brutal LA cops who beat up Rodney King your brothers. That's just—just contrary to everything I stand for! I try to think about, participate in activities and thoughts that bring about love and kindness to the world. Maybe it sounds corny but things that are *exalting* to the spirit. Spirit lifting, if you will. But your whole world is...is..."

"Spirit dampening?"

"Yes. Exactly!"

"Spirit dampening" is so perfect. Barrett has this way of both letting me know he understands and making things a little lighter at the same time. I am amazed at the power of being understood, of simply being heard. We are still obviously very different. We still don't agree. Yet how is it that I feel so close to him?

For a good while, we just sit holding hands. I start to feel the pebbles in the bench making indents in my thighs.

Finally he says, "So, are we breaking up?"

I have never been with anyone who was so calm about breaking up. This in itself would ordinarily make me think the other person doesn't love me. In my mind, someone who truly loves me should be completely falling apart at the idea of letting me go. And yet I believe him when he says he's fallen for me. And here's the oddest thing: I believe he will continue to care about me even if we do break up. And yet he's not drowning, he's not crumbling, he is just sitting solidly next to me.

"Don't you think we should?"

He replies, "Look, I don't care if you like the same things I do, or think the same way I do. You're beautiful. You're smart. You really care about people. You care about *me*. You're good for me and I like being around you."

What tempestuous heart can resist such calm? Relief bubbles in my body, the weight in my gut softening, effervescing.

"I can stop wearing that T-shirt if you want," he adds.

This is the confusing thing about Barrett. He calls suspects "turds." He defends Koons and Powell. He calls people he doesn't like "communists." I have been imagining that I could help him, show him how to be more compassionate and more loving and more accepting. And yet now *he* is the one accepting *me*.

Granted, I still have doubts about us as a lasting couple. His ideals as a warrior and my ideals of transforming the world with love still seem fundamentally in conflict. But sitting next to him, holding his hand in mine, it's easy to push that worry away. It's not like we are getting married or anything, I tell myself. Why shouldn't I continue to be with someone who is so kind to me?

A little longer, I tell myself. We'll stay together a little longer.

Jaime casually pokes her head into my room.

I am just finishing up a session on the bike trainer I have set up in my bedroom. It's a good way to get a quick workout.

"Hey, doin' anything tonight? Wanna go see Rebecca Riots?"
Jaime asks.

I unclip my bike shoes from the cleats and gingerly step down.
"Mmm...maybe...where?"

"It's over at the Sweetwater." She looks at the floor, then quickly
adds, "And uh...it's a benefit for Copwatch."

I remember one of my favorite lines from Dante's *Inferno*, "Oh
how time hangs..." I don't know what to say. Over the last month
or two, Jaime has gotten really interested in Copwatch—a local
group that hosts a Web site where it posts pictures of local cops
accused of brutality. Before I met Barrett, I would have thought
nothing of going to see this band, hanging out with Jaime and her
hip lesbian friends and railing against the power structure. And I'm
sure that there are probably plenty of rotten cops out there, inse-
cure bullies on a power trip, but now I also know that when we hear
about any incident involving a cop, and we analyze it and think,
Gee, why'd they have to do that? Why couldn't they have shot him
in the leg? we're not realizing that the cop is out there night after
night, dealing with people on their worst behavior, and that the
cop might work really hard, and might be really good at keeping
secrets, and might not freak out when his girlfriend tries to break
up with him...But I know how Jaime will take this. Jaime will take
this as me selling out. She will take this as a betrayal—not only of
her, but of myself.

Carefully, I begin, "Jaime, gee, I dunno..."

I see her flinch as I begin to speak, see the combination of hurt
and anger in the compressed line of her mouth. "Jaime," I say, "of
course I am against police brutality, but..." I tell her I am beginning
to understand the police perspective better, that sometimes things
are more complicated than they may appear.

Of course she gets hopping mad. "You just aren't the same person anymore. You've completely changed. And for what? For some
guy!"

"You know," I say, my jaw tensing, "you don't even make an effort to understand why I like Barrett. *You're* the one with the whole
agenda about who I should be."

"That's not true. I just think you're making a mistake."

"The thing is, as different as Barrett and I are; I still get to be me. *He* doesn't put pressure on me to be anyone else. *You're* the one who's always disappointed."

Jaime extends her hands in front of her in a surrender position and shakes her head. Then she takes a slow step backward, saying, "I just don't get it. Honestly. I don't think I ever will."

FIVE

Individual Liberties

When in difficult country, do not encamp.
—Sun Tzu, *The Art of War*

I T'S BEEN SIX MONTHS, AND BARRETT and I are doing all the steady-couple things. We spend our weekends at alternate houses and a couple of nights a week together at my house, which is closer to both the Police Administration Building and the community development bank where I work. We have our favorite restaurants and take care of each other's dog. As long as I don't think about how different we are and what it means for our future, my time with Barrett flows easily. During the good periods, I forget to play my typical girlfriend role. I don't pretend I like the same things as Barrett, I don't contort myself to make the relationship work. And it works anyway.

Then inevitably, there comes a jolt:

ME *(reading the paper)*: Wow, it's been five years since they killed Rosebud. It seems like just yesterday.
HIM: Who's Rosebud?
ME: The political activist who was killed by the Berkeley campus police. I remember when it happened. I was in policy school.
HIM: Are you talking about the gal with the machete in the chancellor's bathroom?
ME: She had a machete?
HIM: It wasn't Berkeley police, it was Oakland.
ME: No, I'm pretty sure it was campus police.

Hɪᴍ: No, I know. Because it was my buddy.

Mᴇ: Your *buddy?* Wait a minute. Are you saying a *friend of yours* shot Rosebud?

I don't know how to express to Barrett the despair this conversation triggers in me. It seems to me that its very existence means we can't be together. And it reminds me of other problems with Barrett and me, like that I can't figure out how to get him and Jaime to get along better. I don't know how to say, "Barrett, I love you and I love Jaime and I want to live with you both but don't think I will be able to." So instead I just let the question spill out, asking him while he is heading off to work, casually, like it's not important, "What do you think about you and me living with Jaime someday?"

Barrett looks at me. He starts to speak, stops. Then he just starts laughing.

"C'mon," I say. "I know it's been a little rocky, but maybe after a while, I mean, you both like trucks, the outdoors—her dad was in the Foreign Service like your dad. I mean, really, you have a lot in common."

Swinging his heavy duffel bag into his truck, Barrett says, "Babe, if we were in combat, I'd worry that she was going to shoot me in the back."

Days after, Nathan writes that he'd like us to be friends, that he misses me and wants me in his life. He comes to see me one day at my house, attentive and full of self-reflection. He's been talking about me in therapy. He realizes he got scared. We end up hugging for twenty minutes in my kitchen. Just standing there, me with my back to the sink, holding each other. I feel that heady rush. The bond feels so powerful it brings back that old anxiety: can I get this deep a connection with someone as different from me as Barrett?

Of course I tell Barrett about seeing Nathan, giving him the news while we're having breakfast at my favorite place, Lois the Pie Queen. I am relieved that Barrett does not seem hurt. He just nods and doesn't ask any questions. He calmly orders the Reggie Jackson special (steak and eggs), while I order the tofu scramble and grits. Then he looks up from the newspaper and says, not anything about

Nathan, but "I can't believe how much these people pay for *art!*"

"Don't you like art?"

"I don't have much use for it."

I've never met anyone who would make such a bald assertion without shame, without apology. Unaware that he is deliberately provoking me, I fall right into his trap. I say, "But art is the highest form of human expression! Art can be redemptive, transformative; why, it can even put you in touch with the Divine."

I wait for his response while straightening the fork next to my plate. I am slightly embarrassed. I know I am overstating my own interest in art and that I sound like a pompous ass. But still, is it possible he will be sheepish? I look at him with anticipation. He finishes his mouthful of egg, raises his paper napkin to his lips and dabs gently before pronouncing, "You can't eat it. You can't shoot it. It doesn't even *smell* good."

I invite Barrett to go on a sea kayaking trip in the Gulf Islands of British Columbia. I look forward to being out in the wilderness, away from politics, away from Internal Affairs and all the reminders of the different worlds Barrett and I inhabit. I want a vacation from worrying about my tenuous future with Barrett. I also want some time away from trying to make sense of the most recent note from Nathan, in which he said, "Part of me wants to ask you to run away to Vegas right now and marry me."

We get off the ferry at Sturdies Bay, on the brown flanks of Galiano Island. Then we take a taxi through the forested hills to Montague Harbour Marine Park and pick up our kayaks. While I am the more experienced kayaker, Barrett really shines when it comes to the camping logistics. In no time at all, we transfer all our gear to dry bags, buy ice for the small cooler, pack the kayaks, and set off on the three-hour paddle to uninhabited Sphinx Island for our first night's camping. When I start to flag, he teaches me Civil War–era marching songs to cheer me up:

> *Oh, it's not the pack that you carry on your back or the*
> *Springfield on your shoulder*
> *Oh, it's not the sight of those khaki-colored lines that make*
> *you feel your limbs are growing older*

And it's not the hike down the long highway that wipes
away your smile
It's not the socks of sisters that raise those bloomin' blisters
It's the last long mile!

Clad in our bulky life jackets and spray skirts, we really feel the blazing sun, and even dipping my hands in the icy water doesn't cool me off enough. Once we've pulled our kayaks safely onto the shore, I immediately strip and dive in. The cold water feels like millions of tiny needles poking into my skin, waking up every cell. I jump up and down in the water, exhilarated. "C'mon!" I shout to Barrett, "jump in!"

He probes the water with his neoprene-clad foot and shakes his head. "Babe, don't you think you should put some clothes on?"

"Why? There's no one around. C'mon in! It's wonderful!" I shout. "Take your clothes off!"

"Unh-unh. No way."

I have nearly reached my limit in the cold water, so I take one last plunge under, then emerge nose first. I love the way my hair slides back on my head as I come up. I hoot again, then jump-run my way onto the shore. Barrett comes to meet me with a towel and my clothes. "Here, now dry off and put these on."

"What are you so uptight about? There's no one around."

"You can't be sure."

"I'm sure enough. I don't really care if someone sees me. I love swimming naked. It feels so natural. Don't you think?"

"I don't know. I've never done it."

"Never? Not even in a hot tub with friends?"

"Nope. And don't intend to."

Wow. I can't count how many times I've been naked outdoors—in waterfalls and secluded beaches in Hawaii, swimming holes in the Sierra, hot tubs in Berkeley or Tahoe, in both winter and summer. Poor Barrett!

We pitch our tent on a knoll overlooking the water, and Barrett has the stove set up in no time. We cook up a stir-fry dinner, then Barrett washes everything with a miniature sponge and some camp soap he brought. He rinses the dishes with clean water and dries them with a camp towel and packs them neatly away. When it starts to drizzle, Barrett sets up a "hooch"—a little shelter—with a tarp and some parachute cord. We sit underneath it in our camp chairs and sip hot drinks and look out at the straits and the islands around us. Soon it starts to get chilly, so Barrett moves our gear under the hooch and we climb into the tent to play cards and snuggle.

We have planned for five days of kayaking. The first two days are glorious; hot, calm days, crisp nights, and smooth water. It is early September and we are on the cusp of autumn weather in the Northwest, which could bring rain and wind. But so far, summer still reigns. In the mornings, we eat breakfast, pack up camp, and paddle for a few hours before stopping for lunch and tea or coffee on some gentle shore. I read to Barrett from the guidebook, noting that the Gulf Islands are one of the few remaining pockets of Garry oak ecosystems. When we start to paddle again, we point out eagles' nests in the high trees along the shore, and twice we see the eagles themselves, swooping and gliding. It's a couple more hours of paddling to our nighttime destination, where we set up camp, read, eat dinner, and crawl into our sleeping bags exhausted and happy.

On the morning of our third day, we have to make a channel crossing. Mostly we like to hug the shores of the islands, but if we want to have lunch on Salt Spring Island and camp on South Pender Island, we need to break out into the open water. As we cross, the sun is still blazing, but there's a stiff wind making the water choppy. About two-thirds of the way across, my arms are leaden and my lower back aches. I see a tiny island where we can stop and rest. But as we approach I realize the island has no gentle sloping beaches, only a rocky edge. Barrett yells that he thinks we should keep going. I notice a spot where we can slide in among the rocks. I yell back to Barrett, "We can get in here! Follow me!" The wind is whipping up and the waves are pushing me in too quickly. I back-paddle furiously to slow my approach. Barrett's kayak is bumping into mine. "Back-paddle!" I yell to Barrett.

I can't stop my onslaught into the rocks so I stick my paddle out to the side to soften the impact, then jump out and pull the kayak through a slot. I am struggling with the kayak and I see Barrett back-paddling furiously, a panicked look on his face. He is yelling something to me, but I can't make it out in the wind. "It's okay!" I yell. "Use your paddle!" I haul my kayak up onto the shore and run out in the water to help him in. His boat bounces against the rocks and he curses. "Through here!" I yell and grab the front of his kayak. He jumps out and slips on the slippery rocks below, almost turning the kayak. I pull the nose of the boat up onto shore and he clambers up holding the back.

"Whew!" I say. "That was a little dicey."

He says nothing.

"Are you okay?" I ask.

"Why did you stop here when I said we should keep going?"

"Because I saw a place we could get in and started in, and then I really couldn't stop."

"It's all rocks. We could have put a hole in one of the kayaks. Then we'd be stuck out here!"

His mouth is set in a thin line, and he is looking at me, his eyes squinty and hard.

"Look, I've kayaked more than you have. I stopped on an island like this the last time I came up here. The kayaks are tougher than you think."

He doesn't answer and I hope the matter is settled. We rest for a while, then set off to finish the channel crossing. The wind is even brisker now and we are in "following seas," the waves pushing us forward from behind. It sounds helpful, but it's actually scary; as novice paddlers, we are uncomfortable surfing the swells. Finally we get close to Salt Spring Island and see an inlet where we can make our way into the marina and have lunch at the restaurant. As we approach, Barrett yells something to me that again, I can't make out. I yell back, "Can't hear ya!" and shrug my shoulders. We see some other kayakers exiting the inlet as we enter and I wave to them, grinning at the dog in the prow of their boat. He is their masthead, but unlike the traditional torso of a mermaid, this masthead has its mouth open and its tongue flapping. Barrett yells again, a garble, but I make out that he is asking me if I saw the dog. I yell back yes.

The marina restaurant is dark and it feels odd to me to be around people again. We order fish and chips. A TV in the corner plays a Sunday news program, one of those "If I can shout the loudest, I must be right" types of program that makes me cringe. I sit with my back to it and study my placemat, a map of the southern Gulf

Islands. Barrett looks up at the TV, then remarks, "That motor-voter thing is such a dumb idea."

I jerk my head up. "What?" It has never occurred to me that making voter registration easier by coupling it with your driver's license or photo ID would generate even the slightest controversy. "Isn't it a good thing to make it easier for more people to vote?"

"If they're too lazy to register to vote, why should we help them?"

I look up from the map at him. His opinion seems to be motivated by pure meanness, pure spite.

I ask him if he realizes how difficult it is for some people just to feed their families. To keep their car running and get the groceries on the table. I say maybe registering to vote is just one more thing and they can't get to it.

Barrett's voice is low and strained. "You are so naïve. You don't see what I see. People watching TV all day and sucking off the government tit. Even your buddy Clinton wanted to clean up welfare. Even he saw the laziness, the people taking advantage."

I tell him he is lumping all welfare recipients into one big category. My God, can't he have some compassion? I point out he doesn't know what it's like to be poor.

"Don't I? You think my mother wasn't poor growing up? Or that she wasn't poor when she was a single mom raising three kids? You think it was fun being the only kid eating peanut butter and butter sandwiches? Getting beat up because I was the one of the few white kids in school?"

Something in Barrett's tone makes me shiver. This is a new kind of shock. There is something ugly in his voice, something hostile toward me. It's as if he has suddenly realized that I am different from him, and now he hates me.

"Well, so, you know it's hard, so why don't you have any empathy?"

"You liberals! Living your comfortable lives, singing 'Kumbaya,' with no sense of *reality*. So we were poor. You didn't see us dealing drugs, or getting welfare, or asking for a leg up from the government. You work hard, study hard, pay your dues. That's how you get ahead."

The waitress brings our food. I can't touch mine. My face is burning. There have been many times before that Barrett has said something that made me think it was impossible for me to be with him. But he has never been angry with me. It wouldn't have really surprised me if this had happened when we'd first met, but now it catches me off guard. In fact, now it seems downright unfair. Was he not paying attention before when I told him what I believed? This is a hell of a time to figure this out, when I'm stuck with him for days.

I stand up and mumble something about going to the bathroom. The bathrooms are outside, down a plank deck. They have blue and white life preservers on them. I march past the one that says "Buoys," past a public telephone, until I find the door that says "Gulls." I turn on the tap. As the warm water flows over my hands, I start to cry. I look in the mirror at my contorted face. What is the deal with men and me on vacations? I think about Nathan's card and the part about wanting to elope to Vegas. As usual, thinking about the card gives me a brief little lift of triumph, of vindication. Maybe I am meant to get back together with Nathan. Maybe that's where this is all leading.

When I imagine my relationship with Nathan, it feels like I'm swimming in a murky pool, whereas Barrett has felt like swimming in cool clear water. Only now a shark has just emerged from a hiding place. The suddenness of Barrett's hostility makes my stomach burn. He has known where I stand; it's not fair to suddenly get mad at me about it.

The telephone is just outside. I'll tell Barrett to go to hell, and I'll call my brother to come get me. Although we're a very long way from California. And what about the kayaks?

My brother answers after four agonizing rings. I sob into the phone, explain the situation. "Aw, Soph," he says, "I'm so sorry to hear you're having a rough time."

"What am I going to do? How could I be so stupid?"

"Listen, this is just a bad moment. You can't let it define your whole relationship. Things will shift. If you liked Barrett before, there's gotta be some good in him. It's just a couple more days. Just finish up the trip and then see how you feel."

After hanging up, I go back in the bathroom and splash my face with cool water. Maybe my brother's right, maybe I shouldn't give up. Besides, I don't have much choice at this point; it's just not realistic to abandon the trip here. I walk back to the table, my legs a little wobbly. Barrett is eating and doesn't look up. When I see his crew-cutted head leaning over his meal, anger wells up in me. Even though we are arguing on vacation, I don't feel pathetic like I did with Nathan. I just feel pissed off. Which feels a whole lot better—at least I have some strength.

We kayak in silence to South Pender Island. According to our guidebook, there is a nice beach to land on and a good hidden campsite in the trees, just up the hill. We pull the kayaks high on shore and tie them to trees just in case of a high tide during the night. Then we "hump" our tent, the sleeping bags, the stove, and our food bag up to the campsite. We've done this enough times that it doesn't require much communication.

When everything is set up, Barrett suggests we go down to the little spit of beach we can see from the campsite. The earlier rough weather has calmed and now the water is gently lapping against the shore.

"You go ahead," I say. "I'm going to stay here and read."

"Ya sure? You could read out there. I could take the stove and make you a hot chocolate."

He is offering me a white flag but I refuse it. How do I know when he will decide to lash out at me again? "No," I say, avoiding his gaze, "I just want to stay here."

"There's a lot of skeeters up here."

"I'll be fine."

"They really like to bite you."

"I've got the repellant."

He stands there looking at me a little while but I ignore him, pulling my books out of a dry bag. Finally he grabs his camp chair and starts down the trail to the beach.

I lie down in the tent with Lao Tzu's *The Way of Life*. For a little while I just stare at the ceiling of the tent and try to rest in solitude. Lying on my back, I flutter the pages of the thin paperback. My favorite thing on trips like this is to open the book to a random page, read the morsel of wisdom, and see how it applies to my life. I settle on poem 76. It speaks of the unbending quality of the dead, whether plant or animal, and contrasts that rigidity with the inherent suppleness of the living.

I hear Barrett shout, "Soph! Hey, Sophia!"

Emerging from the tent, I look down toward the sound. Barrett is standing on the sandy beach, waving up at me, wearing nothing but his neoprene booties and a goofy grin.

When I grab my own camp chair and clamber down the hillside to the beach, he is sitting in his chair reading, still naked. He looks up at me. "Hey this nudie thing ain't so bad."

"I guess 'we liberals' do have some good ideas."

"Hey—I'm sorry about back there."

"You seemed so angry, like you hated me. Do you really think motor-voter's such a bad idea?"

"You know what, I don't really give a damn about that. I was just kind of mad at you because it seemed like you were ignoring me earlier."

"What? When? I wasn't ignoring you."

"I yelled to you a couple times, and you didn't answer, and then I made up some nonsense about the dog to see if you were really paying attention, and you said 'yes' and I knew you weren't really listening."

"Babe, I just couldn't hear you. I wasn't ignoring you."

I remember Barrett's face when he was trying to get into the rocks. The way his eyes were wide and his mouth was pulled together like a stitched scar. He was plain scared. I have never seen him afraid before. It's amazing how easily fear transforms into anger. It hadn't occurred to me that Barrett might be nervous. But when I think about it, despite all the dangerous things he does—the SWAT team, the jumping out of helicopters, the chasing bad guys—he is always incredibly careful. I guess that gives him a measure of control, whereas out here, he's had to let me be the leader. Still, it wasn't exactly fair to pick a fight with me over politics.

Then there's a sudden release in me, and I laugh. How many times have I done that when I was mad about something else? It took guts for him to admit it, and it took maturity to realize what was really behind it. Sometimes I don't know exactly why I am angry. And he is not only apologizing, but offering me something else besides, the gift of his nakedness.

I tell him that I'm really sorry he thought I was ignoring him. I propose that he just ask me next time if he suspects it.

"That might be better, huh?"

"Yes, that would probably be a good policy for both of us."

"Okay." We sit quietly for a bit until he says, "Do you want to take your clothes off?"

Soon after we get back from the kayak trip, on a weekend morning at my house, I emerge from my bedroom to make breakfast for Barrett and me. Barrett is still in my room, rustling in his duffel bag. My housemate Jaime and her friend Sasha look up from the breakfast nook. "Hey," I say.

"Hey."

They look at each other. Sasha nudges Jaime, "Go ahead. Tell her."

Jaime looks at me, her brows pulled together into an upside down V. "Hon, it's probably no big deal, but I thought you should know..."

"What?"

"Well..." She's stalling.

"C'mon!"

"All *right*..." She sighs then says in a rush, "Sal ran into Nathan on a Jewish singles' hike yesterday. He asked out one of her friends. We thought you should know."

I feel a stab under my ribs. But he said he wanted to run away with me and get married! A little voice in my head chides myself: *Don't be a fool, remember what he really said, he said "part of me."* I guess the other part is still looking for a nice Jewish girl. That was one of Nathan's objections to me—that I wasn't Jewish.

Barrett comes out of the bedroom and into the kitchen. He's hiding something behind his back and grinning. "What are you gals talking about?" Then he says, with a snort, "Who's going on singles' hikes?"

Sasha and Jaime exchange meaningful looks and skedaddle.

I am torn. I don't want to be upset in front of Barrett. I don't want to hurt his feelings, but I'm taking a gut punch.

Barrett presents me with a small white box. "Here babe, I bought you some *art*."

Inside is a coffee mug, black, with two multicolored dolphins cavorting. I examine the mug in great detail, buying time, not sure how to react.

"It's you and me. We're the dolphins," he adds.

I look up. His lips are pursed in a struggle not to smile. Then I get it. I've underestimated Barrett. The mug is an inside joke—poking fun at my pretentiousness about art, his hillbilly pose, and the two of us together.

I want to erase my thoughts of Nathan by doing something silly, something outrageous, just Barrett and me. "You know what we should do today?" I say. "Let's go to the Museum of Modern Art!"

Barrett doesn't really want to go; he only goes because I want to. He doesn't like cities, feels nervous in crowds. When I ask then why on earth did he become an inner-city cop, he smiles ruefully and says, "I guess it's different when I've got body armor on." We drive over in Barrett's new truck. Barrett has never once been on BART, San Francisco's regional subway, even though local police officers ride for free, and he doesn't want to start now. He prefers the control of having his own car. He has already taught me not to pull up so close to the car in front of me when I'm stopped at a traffic light. "Always leave an escape route," he cautions.

We hit traffic on the Bay Bridge. Barrett looks for street parking for about ten minutes before grudgingly pulling into a lot. The first exhibit we see after passing through the glass doors is the Picasso portraits. Barrett gets glassy-eyed. "I don't really get modern art—what's the point?" He perks up when he sees the display of a Jaguar E-3. Looking at it, he tells me that at Presentation Brothers College in Cork, Ireland, where his father took the three boys after their mother's death, Barrett studied elocution. "My fahthah's cahr is ah Jag-u-ahr. Drives rahthah fahst," he demonstrates, then: "Have you communed with art enough yet?"

"Oh, c'mon, we've hardly gotten started!"

"We could still go fishing if we left right now."

"Let's just look upstairs."

Barrett morosely follows me to the elevator. But upstairs he spies an exhibit of the best photos of the *New York Times* over the last hundred years. He is transfixed. "You know who that is, don't ya?" he asks me.

"I know he's a president."

"That's LBJ!"

"Oh, right, of course."

He quizzes me on others. I can't identify Trotsky, Mussolini, Houdini, Jesse Owens, Lee Harvey Oswald, Stalin, George Wallace, or Calvin Coolidge. I've never even heard of Eamon de Valera. I do get Hitler, Nixon, and Einstein. Frida Kahlo is the only one I know that Barrett doesn't.

Even though Barrett seemed to enjoy the news photo exhibit, he is tense and irritable as we exit the museum, walking a half pace ahead of me. He heads directly back to the parking lot.

"Do you want to grab some tea and some lunch first?" I ask.

"Let's just get out of here."

The parking attendant gives Barrett an up-and-down once-over, and his eyes narrow. I am surprised, but in the future it will become something of a pattern. Barrett's off-duty outfits tend toward khaki cargo pants and untucked plaid button shirts to cover his gun. Sure, he's got the "high and tight" haircut and a taut, no-nonsense demeanor, but he doesn't seem that out of the ordinary to me. But certain people—always men, always not-quite-upstanding citizens—will take one look at Barrett and smell cop. You can see the hostility rise in them. I don't know if they sense Barrett's disdain for them, how he takes in the stubble on the face, the stains on clothes, the less-than-prompt service; or if they assign him the role of the Man, but they use their small power to dig at Barrett as if making payments on a large and very old debt.

In this instance, the parking lot attendant, a stout Sikh, begins to pay an exaggerated amount of attention to his cash register. He makes piles of quarters on the ledge of the register. I am trying to come up with an excuse for the parking lot attendant's behavior. During the whole outing I have been resisting the tension emanating from Barrett, cheerleading instead for the great time we are having. But I can see this guy is being a jerk. I give Barrett the hand-and-arm signal he has taught me for "Get your head outta your ass," holding my right fist in my left hand and pulling it out theatrically.

Barrett gives me a halfhearted chuckle, then says in a falsely cheerful voice, "Hey, Chief, here's my ticket, what do I owe ya?"

The attendant looks over at Barrett and frowns. "Just a sec," he says. "Can't you see I am not ready?"

Barrett says, "Listen, we're in a hurry. Can you please tell me what I owe you?"

The attendant emerges from his little booth and takes the ticket out of Barrett's hand, but instead of going back inside the booth, he takes the long way around the back of our car. In an exaggerated fashion, he pulls sunglasses from his pocket and stares at the register.

"Five bucks, ten bucks, what? Come on!"

"Five dollars."

Barrett has been holding out a five the whole time. I am indignant, too, but I don't want this interaction to define the whole day. Barrett throws the money toward the man and I hear the gravel crunch underneath our tires. "Goddamn raghead!" Barrett fumes. "Fat fuckin' raghead."

"Barrett, stop it. Jesus, don't talk like that!"

"What? Didn't you see that? That prick was deliberately ignoring me."

I let my disappointment swell. The day's ruined. There will be no amazing transcendence of our differences today. "I saw him," I say, "and I agree he's an asshole. I understand why you're angry. So call him an asshole, call him a prick, I don't care. But don't call him a raghead—it's racist. Jesus, you sound like such a redneck!"

"I *am* a redneck," he mutters as he accelerates on to the freeway.

When we get back to my place, Barrett starts packing up his duffel bag before heading to work. I feel queasy. I can't contain it. I begin, "Barrett, you know how much I like you, but...but...we have *very* different values."

"Are you talking about the 'raghead' thing? Look I was just pissed off and tense from being in the city. You know I didn't really want to go to that museum. When I'm angry I go for the jugular, for whatever weak spot I can find."

"I don't like that. And it's not just that—it's everything. It's how differently we think. It's...look, I need to tell you I was upset this morning when I heard about Nathan going on that hike. I—I—still think about him." I tell Barrett about the underlying common ground that Nathan and I had. That even though Nathan's family is Jewish and mine is Catholic-gone-secular, our views of the world overlapped. There were so many things we didn't even have to talk about. Of course it's okay to be gay. Of course we both supported diversity. Of course we didn't eat a lot of red meat. Of course *we were not rednecks*. "Whereas you and I, Barrett..." I continue, "It's like we come from different cultures; even though we're both American. You and I are so different, I think...maybe, *too* different."

I stop, suddenly aware of the direction the conversation is taking. Am I ready to break up with him? "Oh, Barrett," I say, "I really like you. I like you *a lot*," feeling suddenly in my gut how true this is. I don't want to hurt Barrett. I'm not even really mad at him. I might even...*love* him. But isn't our relationship just impossible? Aren't we just *too* different?

I put my hand on his. "Barrett, am I—am I hurting your feelings by telling you about Nathan?"

Barrett shakes his head. "Look, babe, I'm not jealous of that guy."

I stare at him. "You're not?"

"Sophia," he says, and sits me down on the bed, holding my wrists. He kneels in front of me and looks at me steadily. "Look, if you want to talk about problems with you and me, that's fine. I can't help it if you are still hung up on this flaky Nathan guy. But listen to me. I'm not jealous of him. Hell, you've told me what he's like, how he bailed out on you while you were traveling, how he didn't see how sexy you are. Look, I'm sorry, but I cannot be jealous of a guy who goes on *singles' hikes!*" He laughs for a second then looks at me sternly again. "I'm not someone who blows his own horn a lot. But you can count on me. I—well, I have a lot of heart. I may not be the smartest guy in the world or the best-looking. I'm sure not the richest guy in the world, but I make an honest living. I guess what I'm saying is...you could do a lot worse than me. You really could."

I am floored. I look at Barrett, so surprised that it takes me a minute or two to think through what he's just said. If I were in his situation, listening to my girlfriend say she still had feelings for someone else, I would feel so *diminished*. I would think, she likes someone else better, and that would be all it took for me, I'd assume that other person *was* better. But here is Barrett, in front of me, not really fazed at all. His sense of self is completely intact, despite what I've just said.

The tight ball of dread in my chest dissolves and is replaced by a sense of expansiveness, of possibilities, like Barrett has just wiped a clear patch for me in a foggy window. What if *Sophia Raday* were to hold herself with the confidence and poise that Barrett does? What if I were to stop turning to Nathan, or to Jaime, or to anyone else, to validate my choices? Why should one man's fickleness completely crack my self-image? My God, Barrett's right.

With Barrett looking at me earnestly, I realize it isn't that Nathan has deep commitment issues or that I am fundamentally unlovable. Neither of us is fatally flawed. We simply had a dynamic in which my fears played off his fears and neither of us could find our way back to a place of safety. Nathan was great to be with in many ways, and the way we mirrored each other at times made for a profound sense of familiarity. But at other times, our similar self-doubts made our relationship volatile and unsteady. *So maybe being alike isn't the path to true love.* Wow. Like a film slowly rewinding a scene of a shattered mirror, I feel the shards of my self-confidence begin a slow journey back toward an intact whole.

I take a deep breath and slide off the bed and sit cross-legged next to Barrett. "Okay," I say, "then let's talk about you and me. I hate that when you see a slow driver you say you bet they're Asian, and I hate the way you assume the women cops will have trouble with firearms training. You know how you are so proud of being a guardian of freedom? How you say that people like me are free to imagine a world of nonviolence only because there are guys like you willing to give their life to protect us? Well, freedom means something to me, too. It means being allowed to be whoever you truly are, without someone assuming that you're going to be angry because you're black, or you're a bad driver because you're Asian, or weak because you're a woman."

I explain to Barrett that if you bring preconceived ideas to an interaction with a person, you are *taking away that person's freedom.* It feels so great to say this, to get this off my chest, and I pause for a minute to catch my breath. I see the mug that Barrett gave me with the two dolphins on it. I hear myself say, "We all need to give every person the freedom to be whoever they truly are, don't fill in blanks with some idea you already have." And it hits me. What I am saying isn't just something *Barrett* needs to learn. It's something *I need to learn.* I think I'm so open-minded, but what about how I think about Barrett? Barrett's not just part of the faceless, amorphous blob that are all the things I'm opposed to. And when he does something I don't like, it doesn't negate everything else that he is. He's not *just* a cop, or *just* a soldier, or *just* a redneck. Not one of those labels captures Barrett as I know and love him.

Next to me I hear Barrett say softly, "Well, I guess I can say *hoo-ah* to that."

The next day I buy a journal. Lying on my back in my grassy back-yard, I write in it all my doubts and concerns about a long-term relationship with Barrett. I coach myself not to push my doubts away. We may have issues to sort out; we may be vastly different. But I resolve that from now on I will face up to them, not sweep them under the rug by telling myself this is not serious. I will do it because it's so clear to me now that it's the only way to make this—us—work.

I am an archaeologist digging into myself, unearthing a musty internal compass. I am going to have to make the decision about Barrett alone. After all, I'm the only one who can really know. I can ask friends and family what they think, but they can only help if they somehow help me uncover how *I* truly feel. Otherwise, it's just noise. In realizing this I have two simultaneous feelings. The first is a scary open space in my ribs, the vastness of what I've just decided to take on. But the second is an unfamiliar current of power.

SIX

Constructive Engagement

Energy may be likened to the bending of a crossbow;
decision, to the releasing of the trigger.
—Sun Tzu, *The Art of War*

W E SHOULD BOMB *THE FUCK* OUT of Libya," Barrett
mutters as we sit down with our foil-wrapped burritos at
Gordo's, my favorite neighborhood taqueria. Barrett has been edgy
since he picked me up at my house, impatient with the line at the
taqueria, annoyed by the workers watching the soccer match as they
made the burritos. I have made stabs at the usual small talk, asking
about his day, but despite his distance I am startled by the violence
of his comment.

"What?"

"I said," Barrett repeats himself slowly, expelling each word
through gritted teeth, "We. Should Bomb. The Fuck. Out of
Libya."

Easy now, I tell myself, just breathe. Try not to picture the bombs
exploding. Don't think of small dusty villages, livestock, chickens,
old men pushing carts, women holding children's hands, *boom!*
Keep breathing. Don't throw your burrito at him. Don't scream
it's over and how could I have ever thought I liked you, anyway?
Don't tell yourself you're a crazy fool. Just stay calm. This is the
type of situation we have started couples' therapy to deal with. And
also to give me a chance to fully explore my doubts. I can feel my
body tensing, my thoughts starting to come in a torrent, rising like
a choppy sea. I tell myself to remember what our couples' therapist
taught us. We are like tuning forks. When one person is upset, the

other person starts to vibrate at the same frequency. Resist it. You are separate from Barrett. Breathe. We are not one and it is okay, it is good.

"So—you're very angry about Libya?" I finally venture.

"You're goddamn right I am; that place is lousy with terrorists. They're pushing us, and we've been letting them get away with it for too long. They need to be taught a lesson."

I pick at the foil tamped into one end of my burrito. Remember, we are two individuals. We don't have to achieve spiritual unity. Our therapist says it's a common mistake for couples to think that the initial "honeymoon" phase of constantly being in sync, of feeling like the two of you are almost the same person, should last. This thought is my life preserver amid my roiling emotions. In fact, our therapist went further, and said that the healthiest relationships are those consisting of two fully realized—and separate—individuals. I think my mouth fell open with half disbelief, half relief when she first said that. Really? I don't have to feel responsible for the things my boyfriend says? I don't have to worry if I don't feel a cosmic oneness like he is my long-lost twin? A lead weight was lifted.

"So you are particularly upset with the government of Libya, as opposed to say, average families: moms and babies? You don't necessarily want to bomb them?"

I am making my typical active-listening mistake. I am trying to teach him something with my question, trying to ease my own feelings, when I should just be exploring his. I make this mistake over and over again in our couples' counseling sessions, but the therapist assures me I'm not unusual. It is incredible how *hard* it is to explore another person's feelings without bringing your own reactions into it. The technique we're learning is called "I-to-I." Barrett and I take turns being the Initiator, the person who brings up something that is bothering him or her, and the Inquirer, who listens and helps the Initiator deeply explore his or her feelings about the topic at hand.

Barrett has swiftly ripped the foil off half of his burrito and is taking purposeful bites. He eats the burrito mechanically, like his job right now is to eat a burrito, so that's damn well what he's going to do. He looks up at me, gesticulating with a chip, "Of course not! Just the terrorists—the ones who would kill you or me if they could. Without thinking twice, just because we are American."

Oh *them*. I guess I don't have so much sympathy for those people, either.

Heeding our counselor's voice coaching me in my head, I stop myself from pointing out that that is very different from bombing the fuck out of the whole country of Libya. *Go deeper. Go to where the emotion is.* We have explored various scary topics in couples' therapy. So far I have talked about my concerns about Barrett's lack of excitement and creativity when it comes to our future, and Barrett—at the therapist's suggestion—has explored his feelings about duty and work and what those concepts mean to him. The results have been amazing.

When Barrett talked about what duty meant to him, he reminded me of my very favorite part of *The Sun Also Rises*, when Hemingway writes about *afición*. Hemingway never defines it, speaking of it only as something that the Spaniards in the novel recognize in Jake, the protagonist. It seems to stand for authenticity coupled with passion. And after Barrett talked about how heart is what gives a warrior the strength to do his duty, to lead and to sacrifice, to keep going in the face of adversity, to commit himself to something bigger than himself, to be part of a team that does dangerous things for the common good, I realized that what Hemingway called *afición*, Barrett calls heart.

In another session, Barrett listened and really grasped why it upset me when I asked him his plans for the New Year and he said, "Make money."

I said, "What about me? Am I included in your plans?"

He responded, "Make money for me and Soph."

I explained that I wanted him to have ideas of things he wanted to share with me—his favorite books, starlit nights, crystal-clear pools. And Barrett got it, he really understood. Of course—that understanding doesn't necessarily mean that he is going to start surprising me with rose-petal-strewn baths. But still, the tight balloon of anger and frustration in my gut released.

"So you're angry about terrorists in Libya?" I say. "Can you say more about that?"

"I'm angry about people thinking they can push us around. I just feel like popping one of those rag—one of those terrorists."

I've hoped that with counseling, Barrett and I might be able to get through the rare but intense moments of alienation that punctuate the otherwise easy periods of our relationship. If I can find some way to tolerate the jolts and the shocks of what he says sometimes, then maybe there's hope for us. The I-to-I process offers some hope, challenging as it is to suppress my own distress at the *way* Barrett is expressing himself, in order to find the authentic emotion underneath. I say, "Wow, you're really frustrated. Can you tell me more about it?"

He answers eagerly, "It's just so infuriating. Here I am, a well-trained American soldier, ready to go and fight for his country, but these goddamn politicians are such candy-asses, such wimps..."

"It sounds like you feel sort of powerless, is that right?" I can tell I'm on the right track when Barrett stops playing with his chips and looks up at me. Something is shifting in him and when he next speaks, the edge in his voice is gone.

"Yes! That's it! Like they won't let me do my job! And it's the same thing at the police! The leadership is always running scared. You know how hard I work, how seriously I take my job, and now when I need them to back me..."

"Back you in what?"

"You know—in that Internal Affairs thing."

"So did something happen?"

"Yeah, something did."

"What?"

He takes a deep breath and pushes his chair away from the table, then looks up at me. His eyes have gone flat, guarded.

"Please. Tell me." I whisper.

"Okay," Barrett growls. "It's those scumbags at IA. That asshole Cunningham. They recommended I be sustained—sustained for excessive force."

I feel my stomach curling at its edges. Of course we had to come back to this. Stay calm, stay calm. I have been trying to forget about Barrett's being investigated by IA for that palm strike, but haven't really been able to. Jaime is lingering in the corners of my mind. She has her arms crossed on her chest and is frowning. I have had so many imaginary arguments with her in my head. That's not all there is to him! Don't you see how he runs to open the door for older people and mothers with kids? Why, he saved an elderly gentleman who had stumbled at the bottom of the escalator at the airport. He's a hero! You don't know him! I say, but even as I imagine protesting, I feel like Jaime has the trump card. She holds it up. "Police Brutality," the card says.

I've been watching Barrett ever since he told me about the IA investigation. And he really squeezes my neck too hard during a massage. But at the same time I've been surprised at how disciplined he is, how much restraint he shows. When someone flips him off driving, he doesn't respond. In fact, once while I was driving with Barrett on the freeway, a jerk in a jacked-up truck started tailgating me. I started to slow down and Barrett chided me, "Don't antagonize him. You never know what people will do." Sure enough, the guy whipped in front of me and stopped short. I wanted Barrett to do something, like flash his badge, but instead he told me to go into the slow lane until the guy got bored. I couldn't believe it. I said, "Barrett, what's the point of being a cop if you can't nail jerks like that! That's the *whole reason* I'd want to be a police officer, to have the power to make that guy suffer!"

But he just shook his head. "It's not like that. It's not like that at all. You lose your cool and you can be out of a job. We have to be even more careful than the average Joe."

I wonder, what if—what if Barrett really did use too much force on that drunk guy that day? Maybe he did. Maybe he didn't. But what if he *did*? If I go on being his girlfriend, if I go on loving him, does that mean I condone it? Does that mean I am somehow saying police brutality is okay with me? For the first time I look at this question squarely. And my answer is, I don't think it does. I don't think it has to. I can say this because, for one thing, I have a fuller picture of the challenges that Barrett and other police officers face. But perhaps more importantly, I have a fuller picture of *Barrett*, beyond that one palm strike. I'm not saying that cops are always right or perfect. Far from it—some cops are really angry. Presumably all cops make mistakes, and clearly they go overboard some times. But it's still okay to love Barrett. Because he is more than that one incident, whatever happened, justified or not.

In the back of my mind, I know that this means I will have to rethink some of my own past interactions with the police. I will have to recognize the humanity of, say, Mark Cochinard, who arrested me in Nevada. But I note with relief how angry Barrett is at Cunningham. He doesn't like the guy in the role of the cop, either! It's just natural, and yet it's important to realize that there is more to each police officer than any particular interaction.

"Are you going to freak out now about how spirit dampening my work is?" Barrett asks.

Here's the other amazing thing that's happened in couples' therapy. Those moments of understanding—of seeing into the other person's heart—they have formed a little buffer of understanding that seems to be softening our bumpier times. And that buffer, coupled with our growing history of good times together, is creating an intimacy that's fuller and deeper than the sporadic dizzy highs of closeness with Nathan.

I reach over and cover Barrett's fist with my hand. "No, babe, I'm not freaking out. I'm sorry about IA. You work harder than anyone I know. I know it hurts for the department to criticize you after you have been so loyal. I just want you to know—I'm very proud of you."

"You're proud of me? The guy about to have excessive force on his record?"

"I'm not saying I'm proud of that specifically. Look, honey, I can't say if that palm strike was justified or not, that's for you to decide in your heart. It just doesn't matter to me. Everyone makes mistakes. I am proud of who you are, of how much you care about doing a good job, and in your own way, how much you try to make a difference."

When I invite Jaime out for dinner at Barney's, our local burger joint, she gets all excited like a little kid. That's one of Jaime's many charms: her love for life's simple pleasures. Her enthusiasm is a reproach, one more lash across my heart about what I have to tell her. If she suspects any ominous reasons for the invitation, she doesn't let on. She scoffs at my Greek salad and orders a veggie burger, curly fries, and a beer.

I want to get this over with. "So listen, hon, I've got something to talk to you about."

She looks up, surprised and confused by my tone. She grabs the edge of the table and rocks onto her chair's back two legs. She wants distance but is trying to be casual about it. "What? What's up?"

"I know you're not Barrett's biggest fan—"

"It's not *that*. It's just I think you deserve someone who—who *gets* you."

I start to tell her that actually things have been going really well with Barrett lately, and that's when it starts to hit her. She lands her chair back on its four legs and looks at her plate, then up at me warily. "Are you telling me you want him to move in?"

Eras don't really end in an instant, but later I will recognize this as the moment I lose Jaime. Not completely, of course—when Dave the dog will die unexpectedly a few months from now, Jaime will still go with me to throw dog biscuits into the sea. Even as months become years, we will have enough history to keep in touch, send birthday e-mails, get together once in a while. But this is the end of something—I hesitate to say it, but perhaps it is my youth—the end of our single, happy-go-lucky, not-yet-settled-down period.

My "Yes" comes out as part of my exhalation. I know Jaime thinks that by making a choice for the future that includes Barrett, I have abandoned her. And I guess in some ways I have.

Of course, this dinner conversation has been a long time coming. Jaime's long since stopped advocating my breaking up with Barrett and I've stopped confiding my doubts to her. She's already started cultivating other friends. We've become less buddies and more two people who simply share a house. That's why she was so excited about the dinner out. She was hoping for a return to our old camaraderie. We both want to find a way to keep things from changing between us.

And we continue even after she moves out—just up the street with three single women—to try to recapture easy times together. When Barrett is working swing, I spend many of my evenings at Jaime's new place. I become friends with her roommates, do yoga with them, go to movies, hang out as they read profiles on Match.com.

"Look, this guy's hilarious! He says he likes to go squirrel hunting on weekends!" exclaims Patty.

"Maybe he really does," I venture.

"No way! Don't you get it? He's being *ironic*! I'm going to e-mail him. I need a guy with a wry sense of humor."

"And they have to be good dancers," adds Lisa. "I can't imagine being with someone who's a dork on the dance floor."

I sit and listen to them talk about the vital characteristics in a mate, and I want to say, none of it matters, don't you see? Here's what matters: will he see you in your moments of weakness and still love you? Will he understand when you call him crying because you've seen a dead dog on the side of the road? Even though he sees dead dogs all the time and has even had to shoot a few himself, will he turn down the police radio anyway? With a voice that calms you, that pulls you to earth, will he say, "Hold on, babe, I'm pulling over"?

On a spring hike in the Berkeley hills, picking our way through the mud puddles, I tell him what I hope for the future—to create harmony through building a loving family and community, to contribute to peace in the world by starting from within: within me, within my family, within my community. To find a man that will share household and parenting responsibilities, someone who will do crossword puzzles at night with me, make good food, help me create a healing, nurturing space. Barrett nods at me earnestly. In our last few couples' therapy sessions, I have brought up my concerns about his lifestyle, how virtually all his energy, all his life force, goes into his work. I am worried that I am always the one who makes sure we spend time together, that I am the caretaker of our intimacy. Shouldn't that be shared? Barrett agrees to take turns planning our dates, even as the therapist points out that not every responsibility has to be equal as long as overall there is a sense of balance. Perhaps Barrett safeguards the finances while I plan the good times. But I am skeptical. At this point I make nearly as much money as Barrett, and still I plan all our weekend ski getaways, our dinners out, our barbeques.

After each therapy session, we sit in the car, quietly holding hands. This is one of my favorite times, an afterglow not unlike the sweet lull just after sex. In one of these moments, relaxing into my seat, I marvel at how much being heard lightens differences. We don't even have to agree, but somehow the landscape between us softens. Just then, Barrett looks over at me and says, "I'll quit the military. I'll retire. Just as soon as I get my twenty-year letter. I'll leave. That'll give us more time together."

A ray of excitement shoots through my rib cage. This is progress, this is change, this could be the beginning of his becoming...but I stop myself. I know how much it means to Barrett to be a part of the military, how much he regrets leaving active duty, how he lost his sense of family. Once he confessed he'd never felt more alone than when his last box of MREs (meals ready to eat) left over from active duty finally ran out.

It's amazing that he would offer this. It means so much more than just freeing up an extra weekend a month. He's willing to give up the military for me, for our future together. He's saying our relationship is the most important thing in the world, more important even than his identity as a soldier. He's saying he doesn't need the military to be his family anymore because he's got me. I'm his family now. So what does it matter if I plan our time together? It's just my strength, just like his is staying calm when I am being moody. As long as I know our relationship is the top priority in his heart, that's enough.

Not long after this conversation, Barrett kneels before me in front of our fireplace and asks, "Sophia, will you marry me?"

"You ever heard of Jimmy Cliff?" I say, while turning up the air conditioning. Barrett and I are driving up to Sonoma in the hundred-degree heat to finalize menu details and to stock the refrigerator with ten cases of wine, a dozen cases of beer, and an assortment of soft drinks.

Barrett shakes his head, so I tell him about riding in the back of a police car on my way to the Elmwood county jail in Milpitas, California, after being arrested for protesting Stanford University's investments in South Africa. The police car smelled of stale bodies and cigarettes, and grime was etched into the vinyl seat.

"No kiddin'. I've never set foot in the backseat of my car," he says.

I was wearing only shorts and a T-shirt, I continue, and it was cold, so I shifted my legs up and down and listened to the sucking sound as the plastic peeled away from my thighs. I learned later that if you think you might get arrested, you should have a support team in place, ensure that you are not alone in jail (I was the only woman), and probably cancel your plans for an evening at the theater with your mom (I thought we'd be cited and released).

"Wow," says Barrett after a while. "But I'm confused."

"What about?"

"What's this got to do with Jimmy Smits?"

"Jimmy Cliff."

I tell Barrett about Jimmy Cliff's song "Peace Officer," which famously questions whether police officers are indeed instruments of peace, suggesting instead that they are warmongers. Listing the typical equipment a police officer carries, the lyrics liken police officers to aircraft carriers.

I wanted, I explain to Barrett with a grin, to reach out and help the officer rethink his role in an oppressive society, so I sang the song to him as he drove me to jail. Through the mesh barrier, I could see only the ruff of his blue utility jacket, the pink of his balding pate, and an occasional wink of his glasses in the rearview mirror. I am building up to the part I know Barrett will like best. That eventually it became clear to me—to my great annoyance—that I was providing the police officer with high entertainment.

"So let's hear it," Barrett says.

What the heck. I have changed a lot since I was at Stanford. I sing to a different policeman, this one the man I am going to marry. It makes him laugh, too, but this time I laugh along.

On the Thursday of the long wedding weekend, when our forty or so guests arrive at their simple cottages, change into their bathing suits to jump in the pool or have a glass of sparkling water in the shade of the hundred-year-old adobe, the temperature shifts to the mid-80s after two weeks in the 110s. The magic is more than the perfect weather and the iridescent blue dragonflies darting about poolside, more than the white tablecloths, the cobblestones, the twinkling lights garlanded among the grapevines. It is more even than my cousin George's video montage of Barrett's and my family photos, George's voice cracking when he gets to the part where Barrett's photo trail ends at his mom's death.

It is June 2000, a presidential election year, when the biggest

controversy on the campaign trail is who should get credit for—
and what to do with—the budget surplus. The Green Party (which
Jaime supports) is plastering local buildings in Berkeley and San
Francisco with an image of one head with two faces: Bush's and
Gore's. There's no difference between these clowns, the image in-
sists. While I find this intensely irritating, and argue at length with
Jaime about it, it is a good indication of the *gestalt* of the time. Little
do we know how ridiculous it will shortly seem.

I am marrying a police officer, a soldier who is soon to leave the
military. Might I be forgiven for believing on this day that Barrett
and I represent a coming together, that we personify a possibility of
change, that we are part of a wave in which the people of the world
learn to get along more peacefully? That our union demonstrates
that understanding might someday triumph over conflict?

When I was studying at Stanford, the theory of international
relations most in vogue was called "structural realism." First ad-
vanced by Kenneth Waltz, it held that because states operated in a
world of anarchy, each one had to vigorously pursue its own security. At Stanford in 1983, my professor Stephen Krasner summed
it up as "Détente shmetente; in a bipolar world, the two poles are
inevitably in conflict." Another of my Stanford professors once said
in class, "Every time I speak, whether at a university or to a community group, never a Q&A goes by without someone in the audience
asking—"and here he adopted a high-pitched tone—"'But when,
Professor, when will the arms race stop? When will we learn to live
in peace?'" The professor became agitated as he told us what he
always wants to say, his head tipping back so that his well-groomed
forelock lifted and then flopped vehemently down as he shouted:
"*Neh-ehver!*"

Can I be forgiven for thinking that maybe now, with the peaceful dissolution of the Soviet Union, with the cold war over, with
a flush of new prosperity, that Barrett and I will work together to
build a peaceful life on the cusp of a new millennium that will prove
my Stanford professors wrong? After all, while almost two years
ago, a little-known terrorist named Osama bin Laden claimed responsibility for the bombing of our embassies in Nairobi and Dar
es Salaam, the destruction of the Bamiyan Buddhas have yet to
bring the Taliban into the consciousness of many Americans. We
are still a few months away from the attack on the USS *Cole*. The

Dayton Accords have been in effect for five years, bringing George and his soldier wife Mindy home from Bosnia/Herzegovina. Was it totally crazy of me to think that perhaps this gathering of cops and activists, of hippies and soldiers, might coincide with a fresh start for America?

On Friday, "Activity Day," our guests shoulder shotguns and blast at sporting clays. They taste wine, have massages, hike or swim. At the women's gathering on Friday night, friends present me with poems, dance hulas, and roast me about my past with ditties set to the tune of *The Brady Bunch* theme song. When it is her turn to speak, Mindy puts her arm around my waist, saying, "When George told me about his liberal cousin Soph, I wasn't too sure if I was going to like this—this hippie girl." She grins and looks at me. "But Soph, you're all right."

On Sunday, the day of the wedding, I get up early to do sun salutations. Then I am scheduled for a massage, hairdresser, makeup artist, and the Wedding Dress. Missey, a dear friend, is my maid of honor. She runs into Barrett about the time I am settling into the hairdresser's chair. She asks him how he is doing. He says, "I've cleaned all the shotguns. I've checked all the fluids in my truck. And it's only noon! When do we start? I'm ready."

When the ceremony begins, a six-foot bagpiper plays "Marney's Wedding," a traditional Scottish gathering tune. The little girls in attendance lead the gathering in, scattering a path of pink, yellow, red, and white flower petals for the crowd to follow. I stand above on a hillside with my brother and my mother and watch my husband-to-be below with his brothers. The men in the wedding party wear tuxedos like Humphrey Bogart wore in *Casablanca*, smoking cigarettes among the ferns and redwoods. The music, aching and joyful, feels a part of my skin, my cells. How could I ever have wondered whether this was right? I've been to many wonderful weddings but this one is the most magical. And it hits me that our differences are what make everything so full, so special. It is *better* this way.

At the end of the ceremony Barrett and I jump a broom. This symbolizes passing from one phase of life to another and, specifically, crossing the threshold of domesticity. A photo will show me leaping over, both white sandals at least sixteen inches off the ground. Barrett, holding my hand, is crossing with a formal march step.

Barrett picked the menu for the wedding dinner: prime rib, jambalaya, coleslaw, and corn bread. I added a vegetarian alternative, then put Jack Daniels in the wedding cake as a consolation. When George makes his toast as best man, he says, "Sophie came to me a few Christmases ago, complaining that she couldn't find a *real* man in California! And I said, well I know *one* real man in California. And the rest is history!" Barrett's military friends yell "Hoo-ah!" A couple of my friends roll their eyes.

Aunts, uncles, children, friends waltz to the zydeco band. Luminarias twinkle, the full moon comes up. Tattooed former Marines dance among tattooed lesbians in the soft midsummer evening.

Barrett and I collapse in bed that evening around midnight, after hours of dancing and laughing and cake, cigars, and port. I am exhausted, every fiber of my body crying for the earth, for down, for respite. My face throbs from smiling. Barrett and I curl our bodies together in bed. I rub the bristly sides of my husband's head, then the softer crown on top.

As I fall asleep I am looking forward. We will get pregnant right away, have our second child whenever we feel ready, and renovate our house to accommodate our growing family. Finally it is all coming together for me. I can't wait for our future to begin.

SEVEN

Allegiance

Tell me what you love, and I will tell you who you are.
—Pope John Paul II, *Speeches That Changed the World*

I FIND OUT I AM PREGNANT JUST a couple of months after the wedding. Barrett and I go out to dinner at a bistro near our house to celebrate. He is excited, especially at the prospect of having a little boy to take to baseball games and on fishing trips. On the night we conceived—just before Barrett was to leave for a three-day SWAT team competition—we made love because I calculated I was about to ovulate. I teased Barrett that it was too bad he had to leave because by having sex before the egg is released, a girl is more likely to be conceived: while "girl" sperm may swim slower, they last longer than "boy" sperm. Barrett held me to him with renewed vigor, saying with a laugh, "Aah—but it's *not* going to be a girl."

I laughed back. "How do you know?"

"I just know. The man determines the sex, and I have very masculine sperm," he said. Then he invoked his favorite male figures as we made love. "Teddy Roosevelt!" he cried as our bodies moved together. "Chuck Norris! George Patton! John Wayne!"

I blush at this memory as Barrett tells the hostess we would like a corner table by the window. As usual, he pulls out the near chair for me, thereby reserving the chair against the wall for himself. The waitress introduces herself and goes over the specials. I move the bud vase with its single African daisy from the center of the table so I can grin over at Barrett. In my lap I am holding my saltines. So eager to be pregnant, I already feel a little dizzy, a little queasy, although it's been only a couple of days since we saw the second pink line. I will find out later that the nausea generally doesn't begin for at least a couple more weeks.

Nonetheless, I feel light-headed, and I have to keep myself from giggling aloud. I've longed for a baby for the past few years. I sense that there is a kind of connection I seek that only a baby can bring. Some way to shed my sense of standing out, of unease, of not quite belonging. I imagine that fully belonging to a particular group must feel like putting on a warm cloak. The closest I've come to that feeling was when I was as an activist. There was something magical in those moments when my friends and I marched side by side crying, "Divest now!" or "U.S. out of El Salvador!" in unison. Some sense of safety, some dissolving of our individual burdens and worries, some ability to be fearless together. And yet this freedom in the embrace of a group was ephemeral, undone for me by the fruitlessness of our actions. This is what soured me on protests in my twenties. So I went to policy school, and afterward rolled up my sleeves to change people's lives. I taught low-income women how to start businesses. I ran a loan fund to finance their plans. Then I joined a national bank that supported new business models that benefited poor communities: worker ownership, nonprofit social ventures, community ownership. I enjoyed my work but it didn't ease the emptiness I felt inside, mirrored by so many people suffering in the world. For a long time I imagined it was a soul mate I needed. And finding Barrett has helped quiet the ache, my hunger for connection, but it hasn't eliminated it entirely.

I think the answer is a baby. I am tired of taking on the world's problems. I want to create a tiny oasis in the world's desert of discord: a sweet little house and a loving family. I want to build something beautiful, no matter how small: a bulwark of peace. A baby will give Barrett and me a joint focus, toward the hearth, toward each other. Barrett is such a doer; he is not happy unless he is checking tasks off a list. He's coined a phrase, a "McAllisterful day," and likes to say, *Are you having a McAllisterful day?* meaning a day when you knock out a long list of tasks. And yet Barrett's tasks are focused on work. He needs to organize the training tapes at the department; he should write a protocol for the firearms portion of the next academy; he should go to the latest training at Gunsite Ranch. On the weekends he is often tense and restless. "Sunday anxiety," a friend called it: he is uncomfortable without the focus of work. A child will change that, won't it?

I lean across the white tablecloth toward Barrett. "What color should we paint the baby's room? I'm thinking yellow—a sunny yellow. What do you think?"

Barrett is studying his fork, twirling it between his thumb and forefinger. His brow is furrowed, and he doesn't respond.

"Hon? Are you okay?"

He looks up at me. "If I ever call you by another name, if I ever call you Sheila or Sally or any other name, that means you should grab the baby and run away as fast as you can. At least half a block away. And then you call 911, do you understand?"

Perhaps it is a testimony to how much I've come to understand Barrett's worldview that I know exactly what he is thinking about. There was an armed robbery a few years back at a restaurant down the street. Barrett is trained to be ready, to imagine dangerous scenarios and then envision his own appropriate reaction. Now Barrett is imagining himself as a father. And fatherhood to Barrett means another person he will have to protect.

Sighing, I look up at his worried face and tell him yes, I do understand. We sit for a while in silence. I want to talk about putting up a swing in the backyard, or building a playhouse for our little one to play in. I want to talk about places we will go as a family, how we will swing our child between our arms as we walk to the aquarium or the museum or the ice cream store. I want nothing to intrude on our joy.

It doesn't occur to me that in Barrett's scenario, danger divides our family. That Barrett has just told me that if peril presents itself, he wants the baby and me to run away from the threat while he presumably runs toward it. It doesn't occur to me that most people might expect their mate to stay with them and the children. Instead, amid the heavy mood that envelops us, I feel a familiar rush of tenderness—he is so gallant, so true. He will be a wonderful father.

As I watch him from the bed, Barrett packs up a large cooler with yogurt, crackers, cheese, fruit, and salami.

"There you go, babe, lots to eat and drink. Water's here on your nightstand. Do you want more books?"

Sixteen weeks pregnant, I've had an amniocentesis just yesterday, offered to me routinely because I am just over thirty-five years old. Barrett went with me, squeezing my hand while the doctor inserted a long thin needle just under my belly button. After withdrawing the amniotic fluid, the doctor looked up Barrett and proclaimed, "There now, all set," instructed me to stay prone for another ten minutes, shook Barrett's hand, and headed out the door. After the ten minutes were over, I gingerly stood up. I felt a trickle down my leg. Then another. And another.

We drove home with me reclined in the passenger seat. I knew that my water could break and I could go into premature labor and lose the baby. But my OB, while appropriately concerned, was reassuring. Total bed rest until it stops, she said, no more than one pillow, no TV unless it's mounted on the ceiling, and don't get up except to go to the bathroom. She said she was confident it would close up within three or four days.

Barrett leans over, grabbing his coffee mug from the nightstand and kissing me on the cheek in one swift motion. I grab his arm. "It's hard to read lying flat like this. My arms get tired. What I really want is company."

Barrett sighs. "Babe, I gotta be at this patrol rifle thing. Look, it's going to be okay. I know it is. And if anything happens, I'll come home right away. Did you call Jaime?"

"Jaime's not my husband."

"Look, the guys are counting on me today. I just can't let them down."

"And tomorrow? It's Thanksgiving! Do you *have* to work on Thanksgiving? With me on bed rest?"

"Soph—if I'm going to take three weeks off—"

"A month!"

"If I'm going to take a bunch of time off after the baby comes, I need to get Jacobs and the other guys squared away to take over the quarterly training."

He leaves. For a long time I stare at the ceiling, at the dark wood of the exposed beam under the gable of our bedroom roof. There is a spider in its web in the one of the corners. For a long time I watch it, wondering if it is dead, then in the dim corner light, I see the web tremble with the slight movement of one of eight legs. It is so much more patient in the stillness than I.

I am on Barrett's side of the bed. Slapping my hand around his nightstand, I pick up the closest thing I can reach, some papers stapled together. Holding the papers above me, I see that it is one of Jeff Cooper's *Commentaries*, a rather dated one from March 1997. Barrett is a great admirer of Colonel Cooper. He sometimes buys *Guns & Ammo* just for Cooper's column and he regularly prints out his *Commentaries* from online to read before bed. The *Commentaries* are a collection of Cooper's somewhat random observations about the world, focusing a lot on shooting, the NRA, and personal defense. Barrett has circled one of the snippets and I see it is about the infamous (among police officers) robbery at Laurel Canyon in North Hollywood. The police were caught off guard by the robbers' high-powered rifles and homemade body armor. During the ensuing gun battle, several officers and civilians were wounded. The incident was resolved when LAPD SWAT arrived and killed one gunman and the other killed himself.

Barrett started the department's Patrol Rifle Program as a result of Laurel Canyon, and was later awarded a departmental Medal of Merit for his work. Cooper writes:

> We have received a flurry of exasperated comment from people all over the country complaining about the shooting at Laurel Canyon in California. The wrathful question is *"Why can't these people shoot better?"* I believe the answer is that they can but they don't.... To maintain control under conditions of lethal stress calls for a warrior mentality, and that is something that cannot be simply inserted into a police officer in the course of a training session.
>
> Of course, it is obvious that one rifle of even modest power in one of the police squad cars would have brought that action to a conclusion immediately.

I move my legs around slightly, tighten and relax them. *Lethal stress calls for a warrior mentality.* And what does creating a peaceful world call for? What does creating a nurturing home call for? My body aches from not moving. And to think there are women who spend weeks, even months, of their pregnancy on bed rest. How is it possible? I twirl my ankles in circles, clamp and unclamp my fists. To distract myself, I think about how Barrett and I can change our work schedules to accommodate taking care of our baby. If Barrett works the weekend, he can surely get the day shift in the next draw. That way I'll take care of the baby on the weekends and Barrett can take over at least two days during the week while I work. The key will be balancing work and family and sharing the load equally. I don't want my child to have the revolving door of babysitters that I did, that ever-present feeling of loneliness. And yet I know I'm going to want a professional life.

Finally Jaime arrives. She hands me a Tetris Game Boy for later, when she has to go. Then she sits on my bed and chats with me until the shadows spill across the room.

A few weeks later, I have gotten off bed rest, the amniotic fluid has stopped leaking, and the baby appears to be fine. It is Christmas Day and Barrett and I are opening our most exciting present: the wrapping a plain white envelope with a return address of "Peninsula Ultrasound Mammography & Radiology." Barrett and I sit in our bathrobes, thigh to thigh, and giggle. When we pull out the paper, I see the writing through the back of the sheet and gasp. We turn the paper over and read the blue ink together:

"Congratulations! It's a boy."

In the early morning of January 12, while I am sleeping the relatively comfortable sleep of the second trimester, the phone rings. Barrett receives many late-night pages and phone calls, usually SWAT call-outs for which he jumps out of bed, dresses quickly, and kisses me good-bye. I always get up and go to the door with him, make sure I catch his eye before he leaves. "I love you. Call me when it's over." Then I watch him drive away with a familiar tape playing in my mind: *Will this be the last time I kiss him? Should I throw a fit? Not let him go? Is this the moment I will always regret?*

The alarm clock on the nightstand reads 3:25 a.m. Barrett is not jumping up. In fact, Barrett is not here. Groggily I remember Barrett is already out on a call-out and that he should be home by now. Just don't let it be Mike or Walker, they're the ones I put on the form the department sent me, the one that asked—who would you like to have contact you in case of your husband's injury or death in the line of duty?

I answer the phone cautiously. "Hello?"

I have an imperfect method for dealing with the anxiety I feel whenever Barrett is out on the street. I try to pre-feel everything that might happen, just so it won't be so shocking if something does. I pre-feel one of his friends arriving at my door, telling me Barrett's been killed. I imagine the friend hugging me, telling me everything will be okay. My mother and my brother coming over to the house, hunched in my living room, hands dangling between their knees. I picture myself like Jackie Kennedy at JFK's funeral: beautiful, stoic. This is about the time when I realize pre-feeling is totally ridiculous. For starters, I would not be stoic. I inhale deeply. *This is what he loves. This is who he is.* I focus on my breath and imagine my thoughts drifting away as little puffy clouds as I breathe out. Don't think, I tell myself, just breathe.

To my relief, it is Barrett himself calling. "Babe, I—I'm going to be late."

But there is unfamiliar gravel in his voice. "What's wrong?" I ask. "What happened?"

"It's...it's...my friend Pete. He's been shot. I'm going to the hospital. I'll call you later. I gotta go."

Pete is on the SWAT team with Barrett. He is part of the group, including Barrett, that has recently won a Northern California SWAT competition. Barrett uses a photo from the event as his screen saver: six guys in Hawaiian shirts holding up plastic beer cups as if toasting and grinning broadly. A bulb of anxiety in my chest abruptly awakens, its roots clutching my gut, tendrils sending the taste of bile to my throat. I shuffle back to bed, shivering under the covers. I don't turn out the light. I call Oscar over, pat his soft head from the bedside. *Ohmygod ohmygod ohmygod. Please let him be okay. Hold tight it might be okay. Let him be okay.*

I want to do what is right in the situation. Should I cry? No, no, not time yet. My body is wide-awake, screaming for me to take action: get dressed, plunge my car through the darkness, do something to help. Should I go to the hospital? Call someone? I have never met Pete or Pete's wife. Barrett doesn't socialize that much with the other officers, and yet he has an ease with them that he can never come close to with my friends. We've been to a few cop parties where I struggled to find people to talk to. It was a typical work party where colleagues only talk about work, only worse—these guys (and a few gals) have their own language and an experience we family members really don't share. No. There's no one to call. I can only sit perched on my bed and stare out into the heavy night, beckoning to numbness.

At 5:30 I hear Barrett open the front door. I go to meet him. He is in his black SWAT uniform, black army boots. I don't want to ask anything yet, and he lets me lead him to the kitchen nook, where he sits down and slumps, his head in his hands. I sit across from him and put my hand on his wrist. After a second or two, he looks up and says, "It took so long for the ambulance to come. Maybe we should have taken him in the squad car. They tried to resuscitate him, but it was too late. He died. Pete's dead."

Barrett is in front of me, but I don't see him. I am looking somewhere inside my own head, trying to process this information. I squint my eyes quizzically at the dark mist. Dead? Pete? Someone we know? Red flashing lights in the darkness, a stretcher, a sheet over a face. No. It can't be. Today is January 12, the anniversary of the day Barrett and I met at Café Mondo five years ago. We are going to have lunch together later to celebrate.

Barrett emits a guttural choking sound. His body is not used to crying; he sounds like a rusty machine. The noise pulls me back into my own body, where my throat is constricting and my lungs ache.

"Wait," I say. "Are you sure? I mean, there's no way—no way they can save him?"

"He's gone," he says. "Pete's gone. I saw him."

My eyelids clamp shut, trying to keep the truth out, the tears in. It is no use.

We sit for a few minutes in silence. Then Barrett sighs and stands up. He walks to our liquor stash on top of the fridge, pours himself a shot of whiskey, and throws it down his throat in an angry jerk. We lie down in bed, me in my bathrobe, him in his boxers and T-shirt. Holding hands, we lie together silently for about a half hour. Then Barrett says we might as well get up. I call work and tell them I'll be late. Barrett and I go out to a local diner for breakfast. I pick at my two poached eggs and listen to Barrett talk on the cell phone to the lady at the union who takes care of these situations. Barrett will arrange the bagpiper; Barrett will ask for a military color guard. Barrett will find out if the family wants presentation of a flag.

A day or so later, we drive the forty-five minutes to Pete's house, in a nice new subdivision where the houses take up almost all of the lots. Many cops prefer to live on the outskirts of the Bay Area, where the houses are cheaper and people they've arrested in Oakland are unlikely to show up in line at the grocery store. When we arrive at the house, there is a cluster of cars outside it, and three men standing in the driveway.

For several weeks there will be a police officer outside the house twenty-four hours a day, just in case the wife or children need something: a quart of milk, a shoulder to cry on. The men stand with arms crossed, shuffling their feet. When we get out of the truck, they look up from the ground to nod to Barrett. As usual, the officers—all male—barely acknowledge me. I've come to realize they don't mean to be rude; it's just that they are awkward around someone like me, an outsider. The bonds between these men—like those of soldiers—are forged in a crucible of adrenaline and fear and pain, and now through the loss of a comrade. When I first met Barrett he explained that he joined the police force because he missed the solidarity of the military, missed the bond that comes from working in dangerous conditions. Unlike me, he doesn't feel a connection to another person by sharing ideas and common experiences at, say, a social gathering. Relying upon each other to survive binds these men together. And it's only when the job's realities slash through to the private family life that the wife and family become part of the club. Then there will be police officers standing in the driveway, twenty-four hours a day, mostly mute, just so the family knows they are not alone. As for words in this situation, what good are they?

"You on now?"

"Yeah, we're on till twelve."

"And then?"

"Jones. Then McGee."

"Then I'm out."

"Okay."

It's cold with a bitter wind, so after the greetings, Barrett and I get back in the truck. Pete's wife has a three-year-old boy and a nine-month-old baby girl. I am five months pregnant. I've never met her but I try to picture her in the house. Is she in shock? Is she walking around mechanically? Is she wailing? I shift my weight in the truck seat and look around me. Barrett's truck has gray vinyl seat covers and heavy-duty rimmed plastic footwell mats to hold mud or snow that might come off your boots when you step in. When we drive in it, we sit up high and kind of float above the rest of the traffic.

Sometimes at the oddest moments, like when we are driving to get more propane for the grill or going to Costco for gas, I will look over at Barrett and feel a surge of joy. The feeling throws me off balance, like a gust of wind that rips my hat off and makes me chase after it. It's in those moments of unexpected exhilaration when Barrett threads himself through me. But what happens when you've entwined yourself with another and your beloved dies? You can't pull down just one single vine climbing up a sunny wall. If you pull one down, the whole web comes down together.

After an hour or so, the widow sends word that we should come inside where it isn't so cold, where there are food and drink. Barrett and I file into the house through a phalanx of friends and family members. I take a seat in the sunken den, where the football game's on with no sound. Everybody talks in low voices. Above the TV, on a shelf, I spy a large framed portrait of Pete's youngest child. In it, the baby peeks out from under an American flag.

I hear a voice from the stairwell talking in a tone as if to a child, "Don't you even worry about that. We've got that all taken care of now. I'll be back first thing in the morning. I'm five minutes away if you need me before then. You just rest now." I recognize Rich, a friend of Barrett's from the force: Pete's best friend. As Rich descends the stairs, his gaze falls to his feet, and it's as if he has forgotten the people downstairs watching him. The bouncy warmth dissolves and Rich looks haggard, his face full of worry and exhaustion. Then abruptly he collects himself, strides across the room, and speaks tersely to Barrett and some of the other men.

I wish there was something for me to do, that I wasn't superfluous here. But Barrett is my husband and this is his world and I want to share in it. Barrett and I have argued several times about the funeral. He feels adamantly that I should not go, that it will be too long and too emotional for me. So all I can do is sit here, be a part of the process through my presence. It feels so inadequate but at least it is something. We leave about an hour later. I never meet Patricia, the wife. She stays upstairs with the baby.

On the day of the funeral, I walk down from my office and stand on the curb looking down Broadway, the main thoroughfare of downtown Oakland. I watch as hundreds of police cars, police motorcycles, and fire vehicles slowly pass me on the way from the funeral to the burial. Of course I see dozens of cars with insignias from the Bay Area: Oakland, San Francisco, Berkeley, Hayward, San José, but there are also cars with insignias from as far away as Grass Valley, Fresno, Bakersfield, even Reno. For about fifteen minutes, I watch the men and women in uniform, the many different municipalities sharing the shape of the shield, seeming to say: We are brothers and sisters. We are here for each other. We stick together. With office workers bustling past me on all sides, I stand watching, alone on the sidewalk with my hand over my heart.

Niko's skin is translucent, tinged with yellow. On his forehead, I can see a large blue vein running south, like a river on a map, its tributaries spreading out over the bridge of his tiny nose. At five days old and just over six pounds, he is not a large baby. He seems to want to sleep more than eat. The doctors say he must nurse every five hours no matter what. This is harder than it sounds. Sometimes we have to wipe him down with a cold washcloth to get him to awaken. Having tried my third breast-feeding position, I still haven't gotten him to latch on properly. In "the football carry," Niko's head rests in my hand and his legs dangle by my elbow. But just like in the crossover carry, and in the lie-down position, it's not working.

"Goddamn it," I mumble. Barrett appears beside the rocking chair and kneels down so his face is close to sleepy Niko's. "Wake up, Dr. Folliculious," he says in a singsong voice. "Dr. Folliculious, time to report to booby!"

This morning we took Niko to the pediatrician so he could evaluate whether the jaundice was improving. The doctor reassured us Niko would be fine, shaking his head and smiling sadly, saying he wished he could ease the anxiety of first-time parenthood. But everybody just has to go through it. Niko is improving. He doesn't need to go back in the hospital for light treatment. Just keep nursing.

Barrett looks up at me. "Okay," he says, "get ready, and when he opens his mouth, I'll push him firmly on." He cups his hand under mine so we are both holding the baby's tiny head. "Okay, get ready, wait...wait..."

When Niko's mouth opens like a little trout's, Barrett cries, "Now!" and plasters the baby's mouth up and around my nipple. I gasp. At first there is just lashing pain. I hold my breath. But soon I feel a telltale pull that indicates at last the baby is really on my breast. Barrett grins at me then down at his son, who is suckling noisily. And in just a few seconds, the pain lessens. I let my shoulders relax, drop the baby's minimal weight onto the nursing pillow.

I settle back in my chair and pick up *Leaves of Grass* from the windowsill, flip through it. I remember ruefully that Bill Clinton gave this book to Monica Lewinsky, which will make it completely suspect in Barrett's eyes. He voted for Bush in the last election, out of party loyalty more than anything else. I'd challenge him, "But you don't believe in prayer in schools, do you? You're not antigay, you're not antiabortion!"

"I know," he'd said, "but I'm a Republican."

I chance upon a passage in "Song of Myself":

Stop this day and night with me and you shall possess the
   origin of all poems,
You shall possess the good of the earth and sun, (there are
   millions of suns left,) You shall no longer take things at
   second or third hand, nor look through the eyes of the
   dead, nor feed on the spectres in books,

You shall not look through my eyes either, nor take things
    from me,
You shall listen to all sides and filter them from your self.

Yes, that's it, I murmur. I am beginning again right here, in this moment, with this child, this sun. Niko is cocooned atop the floral horseshoe nursing pillow, asleep at the breast. His skin, underneath the receding yellow, is beginning to show its luminous pinks and blues. It's true—what the other mothers say—the agony of the birth fades. I remember the feeling of being on a rocket, a rocket moving so fast that for hours there was no stopping to reflect, there was just getting through the raw *now.* Then, after the narcotic, a moment's respite. A laugh, a joke with the nurse; can't she give me more? Then just when I thought I'd gotten through the worst of it, had finally dilated to ten centimeters, the rocket sputtering, all momentum falling away. Freefall. Nothing and nothing and nothing. Except white hot pain.

There was a pediatrician next to the incubator. He was standing holding a hospital blanket open, expectant, like a mother waiting with a towel for a child to get out of the bath. Now I see him as a symbol of me, of the world, waiting to welcome my child, waiting for the focal point of my life to arrive. A reason for the struggle. A reason to create peace.

Niko's lips are moving on my breast. His tiny hands clench and unclench. I don't care anymore how long we had to wait. He is here. I hope Barrett can forget the difficulties of the birth. Afterward he told me all that I couldn't see: the doctor sweating, struggling with the suction, muttering under his breath, cursing. When the power to the heart monitor blinked off, Barrett could only stand there. He is not used to the spectator's peculiar trauma, the helpless watching and waiting. That's usually my role. Sometimes I wonder if it's even harder than being the one in danger.

Niko's lips purse into what seems like a smile, into a soundless laugh that seems to take over his body. I run my finger along his ears, already full of earwax, along the valley rifts between his hands and his forearms, on to the pudgy forearm. I remember the doula guiding Barrett's shaking hands to cut the umbilical cord. Barrett's stubbled face came next to me. The pain and the fear were already fading. I wanted to tell Barrett not to worry, not to cry. It was his son's birthday, and there was a whole new world ahead of us. As I began swirling into sleep, I wanted to say, Barrett, we have our baby and there is a new me and a new you and we are all that matters.

On an early morning in September, the phone wakes me up. It's Barrett. I am sleepy but happy to hear from him. Since Niko's birth, he calls me regularly throughout the day, my hello followed by one of three questions: "Are you all right?" "Is Niko all right?" or "Is everything all right?" But this time, after my hello, he says abruptly, too abruptly—"Are you listening to the news?"

I've barely woken up and already I'm irritable. As if I have time to listen to the news! He knows I hate television. He knows I hardly sleep, that I'm up twice a night to nurse the baby, and once more in between feedings to pump. Because without a stockpile, I'll run out of breast milk around dinnertime. Then four-month-old Niko screams while we take turns pacing the kitchen with him.

"Two planes have hit the World Trade Center. They think it's a terrorist attack."

I hear Niko's cry and walk numbly, automatically, to his room. Pinching the phone between my shoulder and my cheek, I pull Niko up out of his crib with both hands and snuggle him against my chest with his head over my shoulder. My body tenses, something like armor settling around me. I don't want ugliness to intrude. I am holding my baby. He smells of lavender and pee like every morning. He has lost the wrinkly red face and now, at four months, smiles at me when I make raspberries on his belly. I am wearing my white chenille bathrobe like every morning. The baby's room is just as it was yesterday: yellow walls, three mobiles, one of which I made myself from shells and driftwood and pretty beads. There is the dresser I painted the week before he was born, blue frame with yellow drawer fronts. The pulls are little multicolored farm animals. What does Barrett mean—*terrorist?*

Barrett is always hyperaware of the potential for conflict in the world—both locally and internationally. He is always on the lookout for problems. I have a running joke with him. When we discuss politics and he foresees some major political conflict. I'll say, "Here we go again, on our way to Armageddon!" Granted, this is not the way he usually imagines the conflict starting. He usually focuses on some problem with China, so this terrorist business gives me pause. Yet it's possible that he is somewhat exaggerating. I finally respond, "Are you *serious?*"

"Yes. I'm serious." His voice is firm, emotionless. It is his army voice. Then it softens and it's the note of concern that terrifies me. He says, "Babe, I'm sorry to tell you this, I'm sorry, but turn on the television."

"What—what channel?"

"It doesn't matter. And sweetheart, sit down."

I don't want to turn it on. Until I turn it on it won't be real. The baby should nurse first. There's laundry to do. Barrett is saying that it looks like they hijacked commercial flights and deliberately flew them into the World Trade Center towers. That one of the towers has collapsed. They thought it was an accident at first, and then another one hit the other tower.

I can't process his words.

I turn the TV on mute. And I see it. Over and over again, the soaring building, the billowing smoke, the fire, the people hanging out windows, the tower shuddering and falling. Giant, impossible plumes. Then the second tower, the same thing.

Sometimes when I am dreaming, there is some weird cue, something that just so profoundly doesn't make sense, that while still asleep, I realize I'm dreaming. And I try to wake up. In my dream I pinch myself, jerk myself, and sometimes I think I've succeeded in waking up—but it's always into another dream. Could this be one of those times? It has that same impossible feeling. I want this to be a dream. Not just because this is too horrible to imagine. It is, but also because if this is real, what other unimaginable horrors might happen? What else might I wake up into?

I stare down a tunnel in my mind, trying to find familiar landmarks, the comforting touchstones: I am my parents' daughter. I am newly married with a beautiful baby. My husband and I are building a life together. We love each other and we love our child. That love protects me. Protected me. It meant that although Barrett is a police officer and faced danger, our world was still secure. Niko's world was secure.

It doesn't make sense any longer. I am a new mother, holding a tiny vulnerable little baby. And everything has changed. I am not sure of my way; the terrain of the future is completely foreign. But it's not unfamiliar to Barrett. As a police officer in Oakland, Barrett is intimately aware of the bad things that can happen to individuals and families. And as a Reserve soldier, he prepares war-games for other Reserve units, so they can practice military operations under numerous different scenarios. Barrett is a warrior always on the lookout, always anticipating potential attack. You could almost say he was waiting for this moment, preparing for it, all his life.

"We have to be strong now, babe," he says. "We have to be ready." Barrett's voice has steel in it, steel and rock and earth. He pauses and I wait for him to speak again, to give me something solid to stand on, my next foothold.

He says simply, "It's started."

EIGHT

State of Alert

On the street, let no stranger take your hand.
To allow a potential assailant a firm grip on your right
hand is to give him a possible fatal advantage. Use your
eyes. Do not enter unfamiliar areas that you cannot
observe first. Make it a practice to swing wide around
corners, use window glass for rearward visibility, and get
something solid behind you when you pause.
—Jeff Cooper, *Principles of Personal Defense*

WHEN BARRETT AND I SIGN OFF from our many daily
phone calls, we sound like a lot of couples—*Okay, bye, love
you*—that sort of thing. But Barrett often tacks on *Remember, stay
in Condition Yellow*. Barrett has studied Colonel Jeff Cooper's self-
defense maxims for years. He's done this since long before 9-11
and long before the Department of Homeland Security established
the color-coded threat-level system in March of 2002. Telling me
to stay in Condition Yellow is Barrett's way of reminding me to
remain on guard against the many potential threats he perceives
all around us.

Before 9-11, Barrett's watchfulness often got on my nerves. If
Barrett and I were outside—in front of our house, say, or at a sidewalk café—it frustrated me when he would break eye contact to vi-
sually sweep our surroundings. If we approached a lone young man
as we were walking the dogs, Barrett would slide his hand along the
edge of his safari vest, pulling it back to provide better access to his
holster. I would question him. "That guy? C'mon, what was suspi-
cious about *that* guy?"

"He's wearing a winter jacket and it's August."

I'd think of harmless reasons to wear a warm coat. I'd say, who knows, maybe the guy has a fever. I didn't like that Barrett was choosing to perceive what could be innocuous behavior as something potentially scary. There are two reasons I objected to the way Barrett visibly tensed: first, I thought it made Barrett's life full of fear, and second, I thought that sometime Barrett would inevitably be wrong, and in those times *Barrett* was creating an injustice. A small one, perhaps, but nevertheless a hurt in a world too full of hurt. Basically I believed it was important to telegraph a sense of openness, of trust, and—dare I say it—love to the world. I believed that if you did, then *largely,* you got pleasantness and love back. If, on the other hand, you communicated suspicion, you got hostility.

But then 9-11 hits. And it ignites a war inside me. Maybe 9-11 is an extremely scary but also extremely unlikely occurrence, and my ideas about giving people the benefit of the doubt still make sense. But *maybe, just maybe,* 9-11 means something else. Maybe it proves Barrett's philosophy right. Attacks can come anytime, anyplace, often from unexpected quarters, from people who don't give a damn that I am kind, smile at homeless people, rescue stray animals, and work to give low-income people more opportunities. Mohammed Atta's neighbors thought he was a nice guy. So which of my nice-seeming neighbors might turn out to be evil? How many "sleeper" cells are out there? And in what ingenious way will terror be wrought next? First it was airplanes and then it was anthrax. Suddenly plastic knives, box cutters, manicure scissors, shoes—are all potential weapons.

Just in case, Barrett and I stop going to San Francisco when we get a rare date night together; we don't want to be separated from Niko should the bridge go down. Each time I step onto a BART train, I momentarily hesitate, wondering if there will be a bomb on it. The West Coast seems like the obvious next place to hit. Will it be the Golden Gate Bridge? Or the "Hollywood" sign? After the anthrax scares, I agree to be careful with the mail, to avoid touching anything, especially a parcel, that comes from someplace I don't recognize. I no longer protest when Barrett warns me never to wear headphones while running because I can't hear an attacker approaching. I don't object when he tells me not to look down at my watch if someone asks me the time because he may be trying to distract me prior to an assault. I nod when he says not to open the door to someone I don't recognize even if they are screaming for help. It could, after all, be a ploy to get me outside.

In the months after 9-11, as the United States invades Afghanistan, I spend many nights home with the baby while Barrett works late. He is now the safety coordinator for the Training Division and also one of the lead firearms instructors. He runs the department's Patrol Rifle Program and of course he is on the SWAT team, so there are many night shoots and call-outs as well as plain old preparation for teaching keeping Barrett working long hours.

Increasingly, I imagine intruders hovering just beyond the penumbra of our front porch light. When I hear a knock at our door one evening, I mimic Barrett, evaluating the intruder through the thin edge of light between my window frame and the shade. Stranger. Male. Big. Night has fallen. Oscar is asleep on his dog bed, his hearing starting to go. The stranger pushes the doorbell again and the loud clanging sounds aggressive. I know Barrett would not want me to open the door. In fact, when Barrett is home he motions me away from the door and approaches it with his hand on his gun.

Most people would think that's an overreaction, but Barrett doesn't. True, it's probably not going to be an assailant, but if there's any chance it could be, why not be ready? And yet I am aware of a shift in my own trust in the world that troubles me. I still essentially ascribe to nonviolence from a practical as well as an emotional perspective. In political struggles, violence often just doesn't work—it continues a spiral of pain, humiliation, and anger. I sincerely believe the Palestinians would have far greater success in their quest for statehood if they were to pursue it through Gandhi-like satyagraha instead of suicide bombings. And I believe in bringing compassion and kindness to everyday interactions as well. But if I imagine—as I increasingly do—a violent assailant or assailants coming after me or my family, then there's a rub. In the long term we must work toward peace and justice, but in the short term I'm going to protect my family.

I run to our dresser drawer and pull out a loaded pistol (safety on) which, again mimicking Barrett, I tuck in the back waistband of my pants. Barrett's off-duty dress consists of tan "BDUs" (tan versions of the standard-issue military fatigues) with a thick leather belt. Whereas I am wearing yoga pants. As I approach the door, the gun slips from my waistband down next to my thigh. I drop to the floor so as not to be observed and wrestle the .38 out of my pants. By the time I've recovered it and my composure, the intruder's walked to the next house. The back of his T-shirt reads "Students for CALPIRG," a well-known California consumer research organization.

In early February of 2002, just a week or so after President Bush makes his famous "axis of evil" comments in the State of the Union address, Barrett and I take nine-month-old Niko on a hike in the hills bordering the eastern edge of Berkeley. It's a beautiful California winter day, the air fresh after a rain. Barrett has finally finished training the latest police academy class. I am determined that we will have some quality family time. I have quit my job to take full-time care of the baby and I love being with Niko. His first six months brought me moments when time itself seemed to sparkle, Niko and I laughing at nothing at all, at just being together, the purest joy I have ever felt. I believe that communion is what the world needs to heal. It's what Barrett needs. It's what I need.

Sometimes at night, standing Niko on his lap, Barrett will begin a countdown: "Five, four, three, two, one..." Letting his lower lip rumble, Barrett creates the sound of billowing rocket engines. Niko is the rocket, rising in a straight line, then arcing over Daddy's head. At the apex the sound effects change from blastoff to a *Wheeeeeeee!* Then as Niko comes down, Barrett gently shakes Niko's shoulders and whispers, *Juggah-juggah-juggah.* This is the point where Niko's eyes dance, his mouth opens in a great O, and they both laugh. I gobble up these moments as if I am malnourished. But all too soon, they are over; Niko and I are alone again, and I'm hungry to share something with Barrett that I can't quite name.

Niko sits in a pack on Barrett's back as we hike down a steep muddy trail that tunnels through poison oak, blackberry vines, and eucalyptus. At the bottom we dawdle along the creek bed before heading up into the open green hills dotted with wildflowers. Red-tailed hawks float on the thermal air currents high above us. When Niko starts to fuss, Barrett points to a hummock with a few flat stones on it. I sit down to nurse, Barrett beside me. The air is so clean I think I can see the individual molecules dancing in it. Barrett's thigh is warm next to mine. I feel his arm around me and his lips grazing my cheek as our baby nurses happily. *Don't miss this,* I think. *This is a perfect moment: feel it, breathe it in.*

Is it the sluicing of the long green grass against fur that causes me to look over? A dark mass hurtles toward me and the baby. The dog's mouth is open, its pink jowls gleaming. Unconsciously, my body reacts. I drop forward on my knees and arc my torso over the baby. The dog thumps against my back. *What the—?*

When I hear the dog's sharp gag, I look up to see Barrett jerking a big bucking pit bull by the collar. Barrett shouts, "Get this dog away from us *right now!* I've got *a gun* and I'll *shoot* it!" A man on a mountain bike—braking too hard with his front brake—pitches forward, briefly flying. The bike continues solo, bumping and finally crashing into a bush, while the man scramble-runs toward the dog saying, "Okay, sorry, man. I got him, I got him."

In high-stress situations, Barrett has explained to me, time becomes distorted; you lose your peripheral vision and also much of your hearing. These phenomena are known in law enforcement and to self-defense experts as time dilation, tunnel vision, and auditory exclusion. In order to optimize his reactions, Barrett must mentally rehearse various lethal confrontations and his own successful response to them. In his rehearsal, he practices looking right and left so as not to miss additional attackers. He imagines the scenario in slo-mo and acts without the auditory clues of gunshots or shouts for help.

When Barrett releases the pit bull to its owner and starts back to where I am still sitting with the baby, I try to catch his eye. I want to return to the tranquility we all felt before. But Barrett is looking at the ground and shaking his head.

Grabbing his arm, I try to laugh with him to release the adrenaline. "Wow," I say, "did you see that guy cartwheel off his bike?"

But Barrett is berating himself, "That dog could have killed Niko, or bitten you. *Christ,* I didn't see it coming, I didn't see it, how could I have been so completely in Condition *White!*"

"But you did great, you got him off us and we're all okay."

"*No.* I let my guard down. Something could have happened to Niko and it would have been my fault."

"But sweetie, we're in about as mellow a place as can be. It's okay for you to relax once in a while."

"I can't relax when Niko could get hurt."

So that perfect moment we just shared, that beautiful glorious healing moment of connection—that's *Condition White?* We're not allowed to have those anymore?

After the pit bull incident, Barrett asks me not to take Niko anywhere where dogs might be loose. When June 2002 rolls around, my cousin George is deployed to Kuwait to take command of a battalion there, and a heat wave hits the Bay Area. To escape the heat, my mom-friends take their children and their dogs to a nearby spit of old landfill now covered in art and California poppies, jutting into the bay. We call it our town's beach. When they invite me to go, I hesitate. I want so badly to go. I think it will be okay, but how do I *really* know? How do I know *for sure* that it's safe? Barrett has seen the results of dog attacks on other animals. He has heard stories from other officers about dog attacks on children. It seems unlikely but not completely impossible. I don't feel certain enough to go against Barrett's wishes. I decline, and Niko and I swelter alone in the backyard. My friends report having had a great time, that the kids and dogs frolicked at the water's edge, enjoying the cooling breeze off the bay.

Shortly thereafter comes a weekend day, still broiling, so I ask Barrett if we can go together to the spit. "Look, one of us can keep an eye on the dogs and the other can watch Niko," I reason.

"I don't like it."

"So how about *you* come up with a good way for us all to keep cool?"

We go.

When we get there, I shoulder the tote bag filled with a blanket, sand toys, the Frisbee, swim diapers, snacks, and drinks, and we set out from the car. Barrett glances around him. "Okay, there's a big Akita and a German shepherd on this end, let's go to the other end.

Also, I want to stay high so I can keep an eye out while you take care of the baby."

"So you don't want to toss the Frisbee around?"

Barrett emits a snorting noise. "Absolutely not."

I hold Niko's hand as we start down to the water's edge for the good wet sand. Niko has just started to walk in a wobbly way, but the sand is too unstable for him to navigate without the tether of mommy's hand. A black lab is boinging up and down around his person, who holds a large stick. Barrett manifests beside us. "That stick could hit Niko. Stay away from that dog." He watches as the dog sprints past us after the stick. Another dog starts wrestling with the black lab for the stick. Their circular wrestling dance is coming closer to us. When the dogs momentarily drop the stick to concentrate on wrestling with each other, Barrett grabs it. Because Barrett lifts it up, the dogs notice the stick again and come running toward us. In his zeal, one of them knocks Niko down. I grab my son and hug him until his sobs stop, then look at his father's face. Accusation is etched in the bear trap of his jaw, the rocky stare, the clenched fists. In silence, we walk back to the car and drive home.

Outside the house, we sit in the car for a few more moments. I feel weighted into my seat. I don't even take my seat belt off. I know that pretty soon Niko will start to squirm in his car seat, but I don't have the energy to propel myself out, sling the tote bag over my shoulder, unclip the five-point harness and haul Niko out. Barrett finally says, "Why do you make me go to places like that?"

"Make you?" I cry. "Make you? I'm just trying to have some fun! I keep assuming one of these days you'll be able to relax, and you'll see what it's like to be *happy* for a change."

Barrett seems genuinely perplexed. "I can't *have fun*. What if Niko gets hurt?" he says. "I have to be in Condition Yellow."

I can't bring myself to say what I am feeling. Looking at Barrett's worried face, I can't say to him, Don't you see that you *caused* the dog to hit Niko? That if you had just relaxed it would have all been *fine*? Don't you see that you are having tunnel vision right *now*? That you are so obsessed with danger that you can't even relax with your family?

Instead I say, "Babe, the problem is you only focus on danger and you don't see the beauty that is all around you. Yes, we need to keep Niko safe, but we *also* need to show him how to be joyful, to recognize beauty. Being aware of the beauty that is all around us—that's *my* Condition Yellow."

Barrett is glancing around the car, assessing the landscape. Nothing appears amiss on our quiet tree-lined street. But we Americans now know death can fall from the bright-blue sky on a day that looks like any other. It's so hard for us to stomach the fact that despite our country's economic, technological, and military strength, there are things we can't control. It's just contrary to the American "can-do" spirit. We want to regain control. President Bush said three days after 9-11, "The conflict was begun on the timing and terms of others. It will end in a way, and at an hour, of our choosing."

None of Barrett's military training—not the years at West Point, the years in the Ranger battalion, or even his participation in the invasion of Grenada—has prepared him for the stark vulnerability of fatherhood. Finally Barrett gets up and pulls Niko out of his car seat. I open the hatch of our Subaru and grab the tote bag out of the back. As I come around the side of the car, Barrett says, "Yeah, I guess you're right." Then he holds Niko out to me. "Can you take care of him now? You know, you never know when we could have an earthquake. I should...I'm going to go strap his dresser to the wall."

NINE

Preemption

And, as a matter of common sense and self-defense, America will act against such emerging threats before they are fully formed.... In the new world we have entered, the only path to safety is the path of action.... The United States will, if necessary, act preemptively.

—*National Security Strategy of the United States*, September 2002

MY MOM HAS BEEN SPENDING MORE time at our house, keeping me and the baby company. If Barrett is home at dinnertime, she engages him in conversation about the United Nations and the confrontation with Iraq.

"Let the inspectors do their work!" she exclaims as I struggle to put Niko in his booster seat.

I want to agree with my mother. After all, I was appalled by Bush's refusal to sign the Kyoto Protocol, by elements of the Patriot Act, and more recently by the administration's attempt to erode the legal definition of torture. And yet something stops me—an uncomfortable twitch of fear in my belly whenever I think about 9-11 and my baby boy, and the fact that they exist in the same universe. What if Saddam *does* have weapons of mass destruction? I feel hamstrung by the administration's logic: we can't wait to see if he really has them because we may find out the answer through death and carnage. And 9-11 proved one thing to me: more people than I'd ever imagined hate the United States. Islamic militants recently killed hundreds of people in Bali. In *Bali*, a place that traveler friends once described to me as one of the most peaceful places on earth.

So all I say is, "Barrett, can you grab a maraca for Niko while I get the chicken out?"

Barrett calls hyper-analytical people "stupid-smart." He's never said it about me, has always boasted to his friends of my accomplishments. But I've begun to wonder if I am stupid-smart, full of airy-fairy ideas of peace and love but oblivious to the exigencies of the here and now. I don't know. I'm no longer sure what we should do. And I *hate* that. I'm accustomed to confidently looking out at the world and coming up with helpful suggestions for improving things: from my mate to the country's foreign policy. Normally, I would embrace a complicated analysis of the roots of 9-11, an explanation that involves poverty, humiliation, powerlessness, voicelessness. But the commensurate solutions—requiring a deep knowledge of history on the part of our policymakers, reduced dependence on foreign oil, education, cultural exchange—they don't quiet my anxiety. Barrett recently gave me a gas mask. Holding it up in front of me, I looked at the sinister alien visage and asked Barrett if they came in infant sizes. We laughed sadly as I tucked the gas mask under the first-aid kit and the flares in the back of my car. The political solutions I have always embraced seem to take too long, seem too fraught with complications. Lately it's been easier for me to retreat into a world where I *know* what's best—taking care of my son, my family, my dogs, my household.

Barrett gently tosses an egg-shaped maraca up and down in his palm to get Niko's attention. I remember another time when he made that same tossing motion, during an incident that happened before Niko was born, before 9-11. Only instead of a maraca, he tossed a quarter. It was a sunny Saturday and I heard an engine roar outside our house. I went outside to see if I could glare at the driver, perhaps motion for him to slow down. Barrett stood at the foot of our driveway with his arms crossed. To my surprise the car—a beat-up red Mazda—was accelerating in reverse. Then right in front of our house the car screeched to a stop, its windshield shattered into ice crystals.

Two young men with shoulder-length hair sprang out of the car, leaving the doors wide open. I started down the steps, not sure what I was going to do. They yelled something to each other and stalked toward Barrett. Barrett strode toward them. There was a controlled fury in the way he walked, like he knew he had to bring at least as much force to the situation as they did. I stopped at the bottom on the steps, uncertain of what to do. There were two of them and only one of Barrett. Barrett reached the edge of our driveway before they did and stopped, punching his index finger toward them as they approached and bellowing, "You were driving *way too fast!*"

The young men slowed their approach, dropped their fists. I could see them sizing up my husband, taking in the high-and-tight haircut, the military cargo pants, the army boots. During the momentary pause, Barrett pressed his advantage. "You were going over sixty miles an hour! On a residential street! That's reckless driving!"

The driver stuttered, bewildered, "Our windshield, man, did you—"

Barrett spoke in a low, clipped voice, almost a growl. "You. Need. To slow. *Down.* I suggest. You. Get back. In your car. And get. Outta here. *Slowly.*" He waved his cell phone at them. "Unless you'd rather I call the cops? And have you arrested for violating California Vehicle Code twenty-three one-oh-three?"

Eyeing Barrett for another second, the driver dropped his hands to his sides, palms up, in a gesture of surrender mixed with supplication. His partner followed his lead, and we watched as they got in their car and left.

"What the heck is going on?" I asked Barrett. "Did something happen to their windshield?"

Barrett drew his hand from his pocket and tossed the quarter up and down. "Who knows?" he said, looking at me sidelong. "Somethin' musta hit it."

"Did *you*—?" I began. "You didn't—"

I stopped and looked at him. In certain matters we both know to adopt a "Don't ask, don't tell" policy. He does the same when it comes to certain of my friends, their parties, and controlled substances.

" 'Course I didn't," he said. "That wouldn't be right." Then he flashed me a mischievous smile. "Would it?"

Afterward, I pondered Barrett's question. Say he had tossed a quarter gently into the air at just the right time, a quarter that might have done little damage if it hit a car traveling at twenty or twenty-five miles an hour, but could shatter the windshield of a car traveling at sixty-five miles an hour. I couldn't suppress an intense feeling of satisfaction. It would have taken tremendous calm, precision, confidence. But underneath my glee was a sliver of uncertainty. Was it really right? The driver might have lost control and crashed. Of course, I remind myself, the reckless driving also may well have hurt someone if it hadn't been stopped.

I wonder at this memory as I spoon the chicken over noodles.

"Fine," Barrett says in answer to my mom. "But at some point Saddam may need to see the U.S. demonstrate its military might. He thinks we're cowards. He needs to see that he can't play with us any longer."

As I distribute the bowls, I glance over at Niko. "Barrett! He's spilling the applesauce!"

Barrett retrieves the bowl of applesauce from beneath Niko's elbow.

"But Barrett," my mother protests, "the dirty politics that Rove is playing, the way they smeared that Vietnam vet in a wheelchair!"

I continue to think back to the speeders on our street, marveling at the proportionality of what Barrett may have done, the aikido-esque way he may have used the force of the speeders against them. It reminds me of something I've read somewhere—that if you yourself are at peace, your reactions to conflict will be naturally appropriate. You will bend when bending is what's necessary and stand firm when that is called for. The problem is that most of us are not at peace with ourselves, especially not when we are engaged in a conflict. Instead it is amid pain and grief and fear and anger that we respond.

"I know, I don't agree with that," Barrett says. "But that doesn't necessarily change the fact that we should have taken Saddam out in 1991. If we don't stand up to him, he will just continue his deception."

Niko's maraca falls to the ground. He places a chubby hand on the high chair tray. Trying to lift himself out, he sends a plastic plate of macaroni and tomato sauce shooting onto my lap.

"Help!" I yell, grabbing Niko as I feel the warm sauce on my skin.

Barrett stands up, ready to take action, his chair screeching as he pushes it back. Then he looks around him. Then at me. He wants to help; he just doesn't know what he should do. "Hand me a warm washcloth to clean up," I say. "Then finish your food and you can take him afterward while I eat."

Barrett nods. The truth is that when Barrett's home, he tries to help me. He makes animal sounds or he picks up a baby book and tries to entice Niko with it. But his movements are slightly awkward. He doesn't know which are Niko's favorite toys, doesn't know that "tuppy" means television. So just as I've begun to retreat from political discussion, he has begun to retreat from baby care.

On a sunny weekend I take Niko to Lake Anza, a pretty lake in the hillside park above our house. Barrett is working as usual. Today he is at the Army Reserve. He has taken a new position, at the division level. I have asked him if he thinks he may get deployed, but he assures me that they don't want Reserve soldiers at his rank, that his skills aren't up to those of active duty colonels. But I am still nervous.

At eighteen months, Niko can walk long distances, and the two of us spend each afternoon and evening exploring the neighborhood. His favorite destinations are the Laundromat, to watch the suds in the washing machines, the car wash around the corner, and the elevator at the library. Bored with our regular haunts, I have brought him to this small lakeside beach and have been rewarded with a rare moment where Niko is still. Tired from his recent explorations of the water's edge, the snack bar, the sprinkler for hosing off sandy feet, and the grassy area in the back, Niko sits in the sand facing me. Surrounded by sand toys his face is alight with a giant smile. I am blowing bubbles and he is laughing as he reaches out a hand toward one.

Familiar thoughts come to me as I survey the buckets and shovels, the rejected sippy cup, the baggie full of goldfish. Gone is the office with a view, the strategy meetings, the public speaking. I am no longer part of any coordinated effort to make the world a better place, to bring housing, or schools, or more businesses to low-income neighborhoods. My sense of inner power, of leadership, is shriveling up inside me. Between having our baby and September 11, something has shifted in me and my marriage. Whereas I thought both Barrett and I would be deeply in tune with our son, and that joint attunement would bring us into a kind of natural harmony, instead we have been pushed into very discrete, and rather traditional, areas of responsibility. Barrett is all action and work. He is the public figure, the leadership figure. I am the caretaker, the manager of our household, the one behind the scenes. My work is unheralded and—let's face it—occasionally tedious.

Sometimes I don't care; the moments of connection with Niko are enough to fill me. Like now, as he joins me in the shade of a low-hanging branch. Treating me as half jungle gym, half giant doll, Niko pushes my knees up, opens them out, steps on my stomach, sits on me and bounces, and finally lies down on top of me. We laugh and hug and wrestle. He bounces on me, his horsie. And just beyond him, the branches of the willow against an electric blue sky.

After righting myself, I dip the bubble trumpet into the soapy mixture and look around at the other families enjoying their lakeside picnics. Do they all have what I am seeking? They are "intact": one husband pulling a bottle out of a diaper bag, another helping at the grill, a third tossing a ball with a gaggle of kids. Everywhere around me, happy families enjoying the sunshine. I feel a hot surge of despair. I wonder how Niko and I must look to them, like we are missing someone, missing a limb. It doesn't occur to me that I am falling back into an old pattern, looking to my partner to fill a void inside myself.

They are right next to us, but living in a different reality. In their world, they watch the saber rattling about Iraq as it were a football game, a spectator sport. They plan multifamily trips to Costa Rica or parent getaways to spas in the wine country. It's not that they don't care. Many are passionate in their outrage at the Bush administration, some in their conspiracy theories about how the right wing secretly planned 9-11 so that the United States could invade an oil-rich country. But the potential invasion of Iraq doesn't impact them the way it does my family. It doesn't make them worry *anew* that their partner is too different, that they can't have the family life they planned, the shared sense of purpose.

I catch a bubble on the end of the bubble trumpet, bring it to Niko to pop.

· · ·

We go back to therapy.

I try to explain the emptiness I feel. That I am lonely. It's not just that he works a lot; it's that so much of his energy goes toward work. I want Barrett to move more in rhythm with the baby and me. I want him to share some of the baby care and the household management so that more of my energy can be directed toward other things.

The therapist asks Barrett to respond. He leans forward, his elbows on his knees: "My family is the most important thing in the world to me."

The therapist points at me. "Talk to Sophia," she says gently.

He looks at me. "You—you and Niko—are the most important thing in the world to me. It's just that I see myself as the protector. I do my thing so that you can enjoy yourselves. You and the baby can play while I provide overwatch. I'm like a—like a lion on the hill."

I tell Barrett I don't want a lion on a hill. I want Barrett to connect with me as an equal and to co-parent Niko. I say there is a Spanish word that expresses what I want: *convivir.* It means to live together, but the connotation I am talking about has an active, celebratory sense: to spend life together, to share life. It could be translated literally as to "co-live." We talked about this already, I say, we addressed this before we got married. Doesn't he remember? We've been through how I want him to focus more of his creative energy, his thoughts, his ideas toward the family. Doesn't he remember he'd planned to leave the military to make more time for us?

Barrett cocks his head at me, surprised. "*Leave* the military? But I can't leave the army *now*," he says, "now that we've been attacked. Now that we're *at war.* I'm a soldier. I have to do my duty. If the country needs me, if they ask me, I'll go."

The air is too stuffy in the little room. I sit on the left corner of the loveseat, Barrett to my right, not touching. There is a weight pulling on my lungs. I am trying to suppress how hurt I am. I am trying to stop myself from thinking, *It's like he was already married. He was married to the military and he promised he would leave her and marry me; only now she's snapped her fingers and he's going running back.*

Part of me knows I am letting my insecurity turn everything into a test. Part of me knows that my partner can't erase all my own feelings of inadequacy through his devotion. But I can't stop the feelings from coming. I am second in his heart. I come second. I thought things were different with Barrett, but they aren't. Do I tell him how much this hurts me? My breath is short. I let out an indignant "huh," and move to open the small window next to me. I look at the door, our therapist's ottoman. I look at the floral print of the loveseat, the bland watercolors on the walls, anything but his face. Because if I look at his face, I will start crying. Everything is so staged in a therapist's office, the couch facing the therapist's chair, the white-noise machine, the tissues strategically placed at arm's reach. We are in a *therapist's* office. Isn't this where I am *supposed* to confess my fears, rational or not? When my hear myself speak, I am surprised at how bitter I sound. "I can't believe you just said that. As if you are a free agent. As if you don't even have to consult *me.*"

"Don't you see? I have to do my duty. Otherwise I couldn't look myself in the mirror in the morning."

"What I see is that the military comes first and your family comes second. What I see is that you think you can just up and leave and everything will be taken care of. Can you imagine *me* saying something like this? Can you imagine me saying, hey, the people in East Timor need my help? They are one of the poorest nations on earth; they just became independent, and they need my help to help build their economy. I have studied antipoverty strategies all my life and this is a great opportunity, so if they need me, I need to go. Good-bye, Barrett! Take good care of Niko! See you later!"

Barrett is leaning into his hands, his elbows balanced on his knees. He is looking down at his black army boots where his blue police utility pants are bloused, commando-style. He puts the palms of his hands to his eyes briefly, then looks over at me. His eyes are wet. "But I do it all for you. For you and the baby. So you will be proud of me."

It occurs to me to ask Barrett if he made a promise when he became an officer, before he met me, before we were married. He looks over at me, dumbfounded. "Of course I did." And recites from memory:

I, Barrett McAllister, do solemnly swear that I will support and defend the Constitution of the United States against all enemies, foreign and domestic, that I will bear true faith and allegiance to the same; that I take this obligation freely, without any mental reservation or purpose of evasion; and that I will well and faithfully discharge the duties of the office on which I am about to enter, so help me God.

So he *was* married already. I say, "Wow, Barrett, maybe you should have mentioned that before the wedding."

I try not to see the hurt in his eyes. I know September 11 rekindled something Barrett has been searching for—a greater mission, a chance to be part of history, an enemy to battle. It has given him direction. Whereas it has somehow *dwarfed* me, made my personal hopes and dreams silly and naïve. Barrett has an opportunity to defend his country against a ruthless enemy. How can I be upset that he doesn't spend enough time with me and my son? I am being so petty. He should forego a sense of purpose so we can go on more picnics?

My cousin George has already deployed to Kuwait. He leads a battalion training at New York Kabal five miles from the border of Iraq. The *kabals* in Kuwait were established after Operation Desert Storm as bases for U.S. military personnel to train for desert warfare and, if necessary, to defend Kuwait. They are remote tent cities several miles wide with ten-foot high walls of sand surrounding them. After 9-11, the kabals were renamed after the states most impacted by the attack: New York, Pennsylvania, Virginia, and New Jersey.

George wrote in August that the temperature can climb over 130 degrees, that the wind is picking up. He wrote of the nightly IVs of cool water to keep his core body temperature down. He and his troops wait for orders to cross the border into Iraq, braving whatever stockpiles of mustard gas or other chemical weapons Saddam has, or the WMD he is reputed to be hiding. Saddam has threatened dire consequences if Iraq is attacked, saying, "The forces of evil will carry their coffins on their backs to die in disgraceful failure." After this comment, George was interviewed on a national nightly news program and asked about his fears of combat. He said without a flinch, "If it comes time for George Csonka to fight, he will go."

I imagine George's wife Mindy as the perfect military spouse, resolute in the face of sacrifice. "Tough as woodpecker lips," George says about her admiringly. I want to be tough as woodpecker lips for Barrett. Isn't that what he deserves? I want him to feel that unwavering support. I have learned enough about his world to know that one of the triumphs of the American military is the way soldiers are taught to work together, to rely on one another. I am supposed to provide the backup for Barrett. If I don't "stand tall," as they say in the military, I will set off a chain reaction of letting people down, starting with Barrett. But I'm guessing Mindy and I feel very differently about the war. Based on our past political discussions, I sense she feels some personal fulfillment in being part of this fight. Whereas I don't. I am not sure how to both honor my own ambivalence and support my husband. I say, "Honey, I know that you try to be the best person you can be, so that we will be proud. And I want to support you. But I'm not Mindy. It's just not—"

I stumble. How do I explain? That I had an idea about what marriage and family meant that was different, different from the often-lonely march it has become? That I thought we would have a sort of healing communion, we would create a kind of joy that dances between family members like sparks above a warm fire? That it's not just picnics or laughter on the beach, or planting vegetables and watching them grow, or painting bright colors on our walls, or part-time work or writing for me, it's what all those things add up to. A filling of the soul, a kind of wholeness in connection.

But how can I stand up for these flimsy ideals in the face of war? How can I keep him from participating in this struggle, when he has prepared for it for so long?

My rational side recognized the Bush doctrine of preemption as radical as soon as it was announced. It was too one-sided. I even laughed, saying, "You don't *announce* a policy of preemption. It just makes no sense. You preempt in exigent circumstances for a specific threat, but to *announce* a policy of preemption is like announcing that you've decided you have carte blanche to attack whenever you feel like it! That your feelings of insecurity outweigh everything else!"

But here in the therapist's office, preemption takes on a different meaning, a personal meaning. It's my ideal of love and marriage, my belief in nonviolence, my hopes to "think globally, act locally," that are being preempted.

The therapist says, "You'd really like to support Barrett."

I say, "Of course I would."

She says gently, "It's hard for you that you are not like Mindy?"

"Yes. I love Barrett and want him to get the support he needs. It's just that..."

"You want to be the perfect wife."

I stare at her. "Doesn't everyone want to be the perfect mate to their partner?"

She says some women might simply say, "This is who I am and this is who I'm not."

I can tell that the therapist is encouraging me to take a stand. She's telling me that it's okay to say that this isn't what I expected. But the heavy thump of my heart signals something else. We are on a march to war, whether I like it or not. I am the drafted one, grumbling and reluctant. I'm not a true believer, but still. George was asked on TV if he would second-guess the mission when he started to lose troops in combat. He said, "The important thing is accomplishing the mission. Because we are nested within something much bigger. If we don't accomplish our part, we jeopardize other soldiers."

Is this really a time for me to worry about my individual dreams? It's not what I expected my marriage to be like, and that's hard, but so what? My life isn't so bad. We have enough money. I have a beautiful son. We would like two children and perhaps I will get pregnant again soon. It's a little hard for me to imagine how I'll be able to take care of two children alone, but we'll hire help. I just need to be stronger, more like Mindy. One of the only times George ever saw his wife cry was when she kissed him good-bye as he left for Kuwait, saying, "We'll never be able to get Alex and Emma now." He reassured her he would do everything he could to keep the legal adoption process moving while he was deployed. She cried, but still she didn't waver. Could I be that strong? Maybe my husband works a great deal and I am overwhelmed with domestic duties. Maybe when he is home he is tense and distracted. So *what*? We're a nation *at war*.

After a deep breath, I tell Barrett that he and I are partners. Life partners. That means we make decisions that affect the family together, not individually. If he feels strongly that he needs to stay in the military, we need to make that decision together. Of course I will try to support him to do what he feels is right. But we need to talk about it as a family.

Barrett nods. He takes my hand. "Please understand how important it is to me to do my duty, to see this through. I'll leave when this is over, I promise." Then he considers his boots again, adding, "Besides, it shouldn't take that long."

In only a couple weeks, Barrett finds out he is being called up. *You are ordered to active duty beginning January 30, 2003, for 365 days.* He will be based at nearby Camp Parks. He can come home most nights and we will see him on the occasional weekend when he is not traveling. His unit does training, and while Barrett cannot tell me details, it is clear to me that he is getting troops ready for an invasion of Iraq. Also a "stop-loss" is announced, which means that Barrett cannot retire from the military even if he wanted to.

To ring in the New Year, Condoleezza Rice makes her famous comment on Iraq's presumed possession of nuclear weapons: "We don't want the smoking gun to be a mushroom cloud." A week later, Barrett discovers his name has come out on the list of lieutenant colonels approved for promotion to colonel. He didn't apply for promotion, but some of his friends at the unit put in a packet for him.

Colin Powell's speech to the United Nations on February 6, 2003, convinces Barrett, me, and even my mom, like so many other people, that Saddam has WMD. (Although my mom still doesn't think we need to invade.) Colin Powell seems everything a soldier should be. Like Barrett, he is calm and steadfast, with an air of warmth, a sadness that suggests regret about the tragedy of war. My faith in him was recently buoyed because of his opposition to the administration's stand on Guantánamo. In his presentation to the UN, Powell confirms Barrett's impressions that Saddam won't stop until we make him. He also deepens my resignation that war is inevitable. At the dinner table that night, my mom insists we are rushing things, that there are other avenues we should pursue to contain Iraq's WMD.

Barrett responds, "Well, the situation is all the fault of one man."

"You mean George Bush?"

"No, I mean Saddam Hussein."

Later Barrett tells me he would like to stay in the army three more years to get the retirement benefits at the colonel level. He says it will be worth it because it will give our family more financial security. We argue about it, but leave it undecided. Even though he is not being sent into combat, we go to a meeting where he prepares a will and a power of attorney so that I can manage all our financial affairs. I get a little plastic-bound pamphlet called a family readiness packet.

A couple of days later I pull out Barrett's giant red army binder of important military papers to file away the new will and power of attorney. Sitting on our bed while Niko naps, I leaf through my family readiness packet. Cover page, purpose page, table of contents, and then the first page of actual content. It is entitled "The Prayer of the Army Spouse":

Dear God, I am proud to be wed to one who defends freedom and peace. My challenges are many and I pray for your love and guidance to meet them.

Special to me are the symbols representing my religion, country, community and home. I pray for the wisdom and grace to be true to their meaning.

You are the symbol of my religious beliefs and the source of my strength. Because my life is full of change I cherish the solid and constant spiritual foundation that you provide. Help me Lord, to be an example of your teachings.

My national flag represents freedom. Let me never forget, or take for granted, the hope it shows to the world. Bless those who have made sacrifices for freedom.

My wedding ring represents eternity and never ending love. Let me celebrate all of the joys of our togetherness and find comfort in them during times of separation. I pray also we are spared the ultimate sacrifice of duty to country.

My house is a symbol of our family and its unity. It is the place where we share memories of the past and build dreams of the future. Make willing my heart and hands to do even the smallest tasks that will make our house a better home.

Thank you God for daily being with us as we live in the Army. Please grant us your continued blessings, increased strength, infinite guidance, as we live to your honor and glory. Amen.

I sit perfectly still, stunned. My hands are cold, my feet threatening to fall asleep in my cross-legged position, but I can't move. Do they think they know my innermost feelings and beliefs? Or worse, that whatever my innermost thoughts and values are, they would like me to embrace these instead? I don't know where to begin, what thing to protest first. I toss the packet aside and pull out my computer.

I begin to bang away at the keyboard, writing out all my objections. They assume they know what I hold sacred. They assume that I accept their implication that U.S. military action is always about "defending freedom and peace." As I type, I feel energized in a way that I haven't in a long time. Why, by the way, has the war on terror come to "preempt" every other political issue? Why have concern for global warming, women's issues, China's growth, regional conflicts in Africa all virtually disappeared? They seem to think I don't know anything about history. They imply that I'm some kind of fifties housewife, happy to be in the shadows, doing the *smallest* tasks!

I consider telling Barrett there is no way I can do this and that I want him to get out as soon as he can. I pick up the will and the power of attorney, stuff them in plastic folders to go in the red binder, and leaf through it to find their spot. The binder has all Barrett's orders, his promotions notifications, his awards, his reviews. A line catches my eye: "A superb performer!" it reads. I read a few more: "My best Lieutenant Colonel," "exceptionally intelligent and resourceful," "embodies the complete professional officer." The comment section of each review all end with "Promote immediately!"

I swallow. I am not going to be happy doing all the *smallest* tasks, but neither can I ask him to quit because I object to some spouse propaganda. The personnel and matériel are piling up on naval ships in the Gulf, and troops gather at the Kuwait kabals. Many Americans sit eager for something to reassure us of our power in this new world of terrorism. Just as our invasion of Iraq appears imminent, it is becoming clear that I will become a military wife. But what I won't do is let the army dictate who I am and what I believe in. I have been looking for a focus for my writing. Well, here it is. I will chronicle an outsider's experience of military life. I will write out of self-preservation.

A few days later, on the evening of Barrett's last day at the police force, he comes home after telling his police buddies good-bye, thinking he'll be trading in the blue uniform for a camouflage one for quite some time. But just a few hours later he is summoned with the rest of the SWAT team to contain a riot on the Oakland streets. It is Super Bowl Sunday, January 27, 2003, and the Raiders have lost. As he leaves the house, the sun is dipping below the horizon. I know we are on the brink of something chaotic and uncertain, so as Barrett gets in his truck and pulls away, I hug Niko tight. Together we watch stripes of pink appearing in the sun's wake, rising against the darkening sky like welts.

TEN

Casualties

Ours is a world of nuclear giants and ethical infants.
We know more about war than we know about peace,
more about killing than we know about living.
—Omar Bradley, as quoted in *The Military Quotation Book*,
by James Charlton

I SIT AT MY NEW DESK in a corner of the bedroom, looking out the window at my winter garden. All is gray and brown, the dead papery vines of my cucumber plant cracking under the weight of the yellowing fruit. I want to cut it all back, all the fallen branches, all the upstart weeds, the brilliant pink chard, the poppies and dead seed heads of the maiden grass. Today at 2:00 p.m. I go in to get the results of my fertility blood panel. I will find out if I am still the brilliant midsummer dahlia—or the brown-edged rose, just starting to droop.

I ask my ten-hour-a-week babysitter to take Niko out so I can let the quiet of the house wash over me. To simply stop—stop tending to my baby, my husband, my dogs, my home—and just stare out the window and think, to weave the thoughts together, slowly, languidly, letting one build off the other, is yoga for my mind. Next to the monitor I have taped a note to myself, inspired by the ideas of the poet Ann Carson. "Go as far as you can in a thought or sentence and then go around the corner to try to find some pocket of it that hasn't been apparent yet, in faith that there is going to be one there."

But today I feel more like I am trying to untie a tangled web of thoughts, trying to find the one loose end where I might enter into the dense knot of my inner conflict. How do I reconcile myself to two seemingly opposing realities: my pride in the dedication and courage of soldiers like my cousin George and, of course, Barrett, and my feeling that this war is wrong? It is somehow exhausting work and often I take breaks and let the spaces between my thoughts be a resting place.

Back in the spring, I armored myself for the war, told myself it was inevitable. I felt awe at George and his wife Mindy's courage as he prepared to lead the 1-41st Mechanized Infantry Battalion into Iraq just as she planned to pick up their adopted children in Russia. In early March, George flew from Kuwait to meet Mindy in Russia for forty-eight hours in order to appear at the final court proceedings. Then Mindy stayed on in Russia for a week, completing the remaining paperwork and taking care of Emma and Alex. This act of faith, assuming the mantle of motherhood just as her husband was going into mortal danger, demonstrated a strength that still makes my jaw drop. On March 14, 2003, Mindy and the kids arrived in the United States on their way to Fort Riley. Less than a week later, on March 20, 2003, George and his unit crossed the berm into Iraq.

Shortly thereafter Georgie was featured on the news for a second time. He was shown speaking to his men: "We're *not* going to stain the reputation of one-four-one and the American people by indiscriminately killing civilians!" Watching the American troops on television those first few days of the war—being met with flowers, Iraqi children reaching to touch their uniforms, the people dancing jubilantly at their arrival—I thought perhaps we were actually doing something good. On April 23, 2003, Lieutenant Colonel Chris Hughes defused an explosive encounter with an angry mob by ordering his men to point their weapons toward the ground, "take a knee," and smile. He transformed the situation with a smile, with the most basic human-to-human communication. Now *there* was an American military operation even an admirer of nonviolence could support!

But then later the same day, Barrett told me something that changed everything. He was talking about the Third Infantry Division, and mentioned, tangentially, how their confidence was thrown when they blew up a van with women and children in it. He said this deadpan, like he was talking on a police radio or discussing the weather. My stomach clenched.

"What?" I asked. "They killed a family?"

"The van didn't stop. It ignored warning shots. There'd just been a suicide attack at another checkpoint. The soldiers had to blast it. Turns out it was a whole family, like twelve of 'em, in the car."

I tasted something bitter in the back of my throat.

"Honey, I'm sorry," Barrett said. "I thought you'd heard about it. It was all over the news."

From the *Washington Post* I learned that an unidentified vehicle carrying fifteen people came toward an army checkpoint at high speed. There was some confusion as to whether warning shots were fired or not. Eventually an army captain just screamed, "Stop it! Stop it!" and the van was bombarded with twenty-five-millimeter cannon fire. Ten out of the fifteen people died, including all five children. One unharmed woman didn't want to leave the van because the bodies of her two children were still in her lap. American soldiers paid the survivors an unspecified amount of money "as compensation."

It has become clear to me in recent months that there are no WMD in Iraq, that the justification for the invasion was manufactured. In addition, the planning for "post hostilities" was virtually nonexistent. How could I have written e-mails to friends saying I saw no other choice but to invade? How could I have been so stupid?

I feel a chasm developing in our country, with the deepest part of the crack running right through my heart and my marriage. It is a gulf that runs roughly along the same fault line as Barrett's and my differing opinions on capital punishment. Whenever the topic comes up, he always asks, "But how would you feel if someone you loved was kidnapped or killed?"

I always say the same thing, that I understand the desire for vengeance. I always concede that yes, I would want to kill the perpetrator myself. But I add that those urges don't come from the best part of me, the part of me I am most proud of, the wisest part of me. The conversation always ends at an impasse, Barrett and me arriving at a familiar box canyon.

Barrett has begun to check up on me a couple of times a day, calling me by one of his many complicated nicknames. "Mo-Squeevlius," or "Boweevely One," or "Pie-Peeno," he begins, "I'm doing a health and welfare check on you; you sounded a little sad earlier."

His concern warms me even as I feel us pulled in opposite directions: he wants work and duty and not to question or feel, and I want to get back to the place where I knew what was right, when I knew this invasion was out of the question, when war was the absolute last option. When I was in touch with the fact that whatever the invasion may achieve in the short term, the cost is too high. War—for both the soldiers and the civilians affected by it—blasts the vast fearful spaces wider, leaving them raw and cavernous with sharp edges.

Just the other night, like many nights, I lay in bed thinking about that woman in the van whose two children died in her lap. Next to me, Barrett read a book called *On Killing*. No one else's husband—that I know, anyway—reads books with titles as bald as that. This on top of the *Cooper Chronicles*, *Guns & Ammo*, and the newsletter from the *Gelatin Shoot Association*.

"That is *so* horrible," I said.

"Spirit dampening?"

"Exceedingly."

"Actually, it's about how people have a natural aversion to killing, how only 15 to 20 percent of soldiers in WWI shot to kill."

"Really?"

"But modern armies have figured out how to overcome the resistance and now we have more like 90 percent shoot-to-kill ratios."

"Super."

"No, seriously, the book talks a lot about how important it is for the killers to be welcomed back into society, to be approved of. Otherwise they go off the deep end from guilt. It's what happened to a lot of the guys in Vietnam."

The light in my room has shifted and the blank computer screen in front of me jogs me out of my reverie. A light rain has begun to fall and I watch the droplets pooling against the window. I have not typed anything in twenty minutes. My therapist has begun gently suggesting drugs. But we are hoping to have another baby. I can't take antidepressants while I'm trying to get pregnant. Why should I take antidepressants anyway? I've got my reasons to be blue.

It's wintertime and we're at war. It's raining, everything's dying in the garden, Barrett's at the army base most of the time. I just got my period, again. I'm not pregnant, again. I have been wrong about so many things.

December 8, 2003

I thought a baby might provide me with a path back to tender-
ness. Is that a dream from which I will be slapped awake? Some-
times I don't recognize a belief has shaped my world until it is
gone, and suddenly the sun shines sideways, the grass grows out
of the walls, and there, at the corner of the horizon, the clouds
are falling down.

When we arrive, the Kansas City airport is quiet and clean, almost peaceful. Around us glass and steel and wide empty corridors gleam. Barrett remarks that Kansas City is known as one of the airports with the lowest security. Once we exit the glass-enclosed cluster of six or so gates, we are out in the public sphere. We load Niko into a backpack on Barrett's back and start toward baggage claim, past the Kansas City Marketplace and the CNBC Newsstand. Rounding the Cinnabon's, we see George coming toward us, a child on each side. "There they are!" I yell. "George! Hey!" I start, but suddenly I feel shy. George's adopted children don't know me, and they are just getting the hang of English. I note that they are really little for their age: at ages five and five and a half, they are no bigger than two-year-old Niko. I contain myself as I approach, then smile at them and kneel down. "Emma, Alex," I say, "I'm Sophia. We're so happy to meet you finally." Alex extends a hand solemnly and Emma peeks out from behind George's leg and gives me a timid smile.

"Sophie! Gaz!" George calls Barrett by a nickname he gave him at West Point, releasing Alex's hand to clap Barrett on the shoulder. Barrett gives the kids high fives as hellos. I hug George. It's been eight months since he got back from Iraq, but it's the first time I've seen him since he got home from the war and began parenting his adopted children. I close my eyes briefly, and a tightness I didn't even know was in my chest releases. George is home. He is safe. The same man who crossed the berm into Iraq not knowing if he was going to get hit with mustard gas or worse. He's right here, holding the hands of two beautiful children.

George is high-fiving Niko when his cell phone rings. "Yes, hon, I got 'em, and we're on our way. Okay, Mindy says it's time to move out!" He looks around quickly for Alex, who is fingering a plastic package of cookies. "Alex!" he bellows, "grab your ears!" Alex reaches for his earlobes and scurries awkwardly back to George to grab his hand. "Okay, son, at ease," George says, "but remember the rules. No touching."

We pile our bags on a metal luggage cart and head down to the parking garage. While Barrett unloads the bags into the car, Alex and Emma clamber into the backseat and George climbs into the driver's seat. I adjust Niko's car seat while George yells, "Okay, kids, are you Redcon One?" Emma gives George the thumbs-up sign from the back, indicating she has secured her car seat. In the army, there are four readiness conditions indicating a unit's preparation and alert level for combat operations. Redcon One is the highest level of readiness, fully prepared to move or engage in combat. Alex finishes with a buckle and yells, "Redcon One, Dad!"

"Geez, guys, you didn't need to come all this way, we could have rented a car," I say. I'm thinking about how Niko would react if he had ridden for an hour and a half in the car, then walked through the airport for a few minutes holding his dad's hand, then promptly gotten back in the car for another hour and a half.

"You kiddin'? No way. We wanted to come get you," George says.

This is the way George and Mindy are. When Niko was born, they drove up—four hundred miles—from George's sister Molly's house in Los Angeles to see Niko. They stayed at our house for a couple hours and then drove four hundred miles back. And Barrett is like that too—tough, able to endure. I'm the oddball in this group. Me and Niko.

During dinner George does most of the talking. Niko has gone to sleep early, and the rest of us listen to George's stories about Iraq. He tells us about his brigade following the Third Infantry Division across the line of departure (LD) into Iraq. The order to cross came about twenty-four hours earlier than expected. Because the units were loading their food and water last, many of them crossed the LD without the requisite five days of water. Many of the supply convoys carrying food, water, and fuel never could quite catch up.

"So that's why the convoys were so vulnerable?" I ask.

"Yes!" exclaims George. "The thing was, we knew the *fedayeen* were retreating from standard warfare and regrouping as insurgents, and would potentially threaten supply units." George uses his knife and fork to demonstrate routes and positions as he tells us how his battalion recovered the surviving members of the 507th Maintenance Company, Private Jessica Lynch's group, who had been ambushed after trailing its convoy and making a wrong turn in Nasiriya. After George debriefed the 507th's company commander to figure out what went wrong, George had his troops stop each convoy on Route Boston to make sure they had maps, that their GPSs worked, and that their weapons were locked and loaded. "They just weren't prepared to operate in an asymmetric environment," he mutters.

"There were a number of planning failures in this war, don't you think?" I say.

George glances up at me for a second, and pauses. "Yes," he says slowly, "there were definitely some planning deficiencies."

His face is flushed and he talks quickly, telling story after story. Eventually he begins to talk about his battalion's battle to liberate As Samawah, and his demeanor changes slightly. As Samawah straddles the Euphrates, so the army needed to cross the river in order to control the city. After a few days of planning, the troops got permission to cross the Euphrates, with George's battalion in front. In preparation, George tells us, he sent a scout unit ahead to reconnoiter alternate routes for the battalion's supply convoys in case the enemy bombed the bridges after it crossed. George's voice drops to a whisper as he says, "I lost one of my scouts that day, Jeff Benton." George looks away from the table for a moment and closes his eyes, and when he opens them again I see something raw in his face.

"Oh, George—" I begin. But at the sound of my voice, he re-squares his shoulders and cuts me off, skipping details of the battle to describe how within hours of the attack, hundreds of people swarmed out of As Samawah to laugh and swim in the river. He adds, "We called that mission 'Operation Stalwart Benton.' And no one can deny we didn't achieve something profoundly good that day. No one can say Jeff Benton died in vain." He is leaning forward now with both hands flat on either side of his plate, like he is ready to spring forward to attack anyone who would counter his assertion. "No. One."

My legs and shoulders are taut in response to the adrenaline emanating from George. "You guys did such a good job," I venture warily, "such an amazing job, I just wish..."

His eyes flit over to meet mine, and he exhales impatiently. "It's not over, Sophie, and you can't believe all this tragedy the liberal press is spouting. People who have never heard a shot fired in anger, they don't understand what it is like. The media only cover the bad stuff and none of the progress that is being made."

Barrett uses that same phrase—"never heard a shot fired in anger"—and it always provokes me. It's a handy way of disregarding the viewpoint of anybody outside the military. And I know that George himself has been frustrated with the poor planning of the invasion. I want to know how that jibes with his defense of the overall effort. I say, "But George, the whole WMD thing, the way we didn't provide security, infrastructure...somebody's gotta be held account—"

George is telling his kids to eat a little more vegetables and a little more meat before they are excused. When he turns to me his voice has an edge. He says we needed to take the fight onto Arab soil. He points out there have been no more terrorist attacks here. He suggests that this was Bush's intention all along, that the threat of WMD was just a ploy to get the public in support.

I am surprised that George and I seem to be at this familiar place of tension. I hadn't meant it to happen tonight. In fact, I am careful not to say what I am thinking: that George has fallen into a logical error, believing that we must continue with something because of all we have already invested: in this case, the blood of our soldiers. And I can't argue with the fact that there have been no more attacks here. There could be something to that; I don't know. I would like to be persuaded that the war in Iraq is not an enormous tragedy, not a ghastly waste, that our leaders didn't betray us. But I'm not convinced. So, as gently as I can, I give voice to my doubts.

I point out that we were already fighting on the enemy's home turf, in Afghanistan. I say I am concerned that we risk failure there by invading Iraq. I ask why we couldn't focus resources on building democracy in Afghanistan.

George pounds his fist on the table. "People like you—" he shouts, "you just don't understand how dangerous the enemy really is! Don't you get it? Radical Islam is opposed to everything we believe in. The jihad is about restoring the caliphate. It's about theocracy. These people are ruthless. They want to destroy the American way of life. We *had* to take the fight over there. The fight's not in Afghanistan; it's in Iraq! If you want to deny the foundation for the caliphate you do it nearer to the Kush, nearer to Mecca and Medina, closer to the cradle of the Assyrian civilization, you do it from *Baghdad!*"

I begin to try to explain myself, to say that I don't mean to take the threat lightly.

"No! I am sick and tired of you people! You! And my sister Molly! And all you, you MoveOn types! You people piss me off!"

I stare briefly at George, then drop my eyes to the tablecloth, to the bits of bone on my plate. My face is burning. I stand up stiffly and begin to help Mindy clear the table.

After dinner, a classmate of Barrett's from West Point comes over to visit, along with his wife. I am relieved to have other people to talk to, so that I can avoid George. The couple is talking about their teenage children and the wife asks Barrett if we have kids. He tells her about two-year-old Niko asleep upstairs and says that we hope to have another.

"Wow," she says. "Going for some kind of record as the oldest parents ever?"

It's turning out to be quite a night.

After everyone retires, Barrett and I lay in bed on a lumpy mattress, Niko sideways between us. Barrett says, "My sliver is very comfortable, how 'bout yours?"

I turn my head toward him. "Did I say something wrong at dinner?"

"Naw. George is just a little touchy. It's combat. It changes you, makes you less patient with people who have never been through it."

"I would think he'd be even angrier than I am about all the incompetence in handling the war."

"He can get mad about the details, but he's never gonna say that the overall mission was a mistake. You have to understand, George went to visit that soldier's parents. He had to look at that young man's *mom* and try to give her some small comfort. Just like I had to do after Grenada. There's nothing harder." He props himself up on his elbow, then goes on, "Anyway, you gotta feel some pride at the way we kicked those Iraqi asses in a couple of weeks, after all the time they were fucking with us. Because they *were* fucking with us."

"I don't know," I say. "All I can think about is the children getting bombed. My hairdresser has this picture of herself with her new baby in a sling, and she's holding a banner that says, 'Don't bomb Iraqi children. Iraqi children are our children.' And when she showed me the photo, I started to cry."

Barrett puts his hand on mine, and a few minutes go by. Then he says, "Yes, there is a downside to war."

"You're intellectualizing."

"Perhaps."

"If our child was killed by a bomb, no amount of intellectualizing would ever make you feel better."

Silence.

I poke him indignantly. "Are you sleeping?"

"No," he says, "I'm not sleeping. I'm thinking about what you said."

"Pips, come here!" Barrett calls. It's another of his nicknames for me. It's May 2004, an evening just before dinner. I am putting away Niko's baby toys in storage boxes to make room for the new gifts he received at his third birthday party this past weekend. Niko is watching *Dora the Explorer*. When I set up the TV to play a videotape, I do it in a precise set of motions to ensure that Niko (and I) don't unwittingly see the news and the inevitable shot of the hooded prisoner with the electric probes attached to him. The Abu Ghraib scandal broke just a couple weeks ago. I tape simple puzzle pieces to a board. "You won't believe this!" Barrett says.

"What?"

He points to an e-mail with the subject heading "Army War College" on his computer. "Sir," it reads, "A resident seat has become available. Please contact me immediately to let me know if you want the seat." A degree from the War College is a prerequisite for anyone aspiring to the rank of general. Like the vast majority of Army Reserve colonels and lieutenant colonels, Barrett was signed up to complete the Army War College training through correspondence. He has never heard of anyone in the Reserve being invited to the residence course.

"Wow," I say warily.

"Must be some mistake," Barrett says.

I say nothing. Barrett and I have been arguing about how much he works, how he didn't slow down after he was demobilized. He is the rangemaster at the police department along with his Army Reserve G3 duties, *and* he has been saying that he will need to start studying ten to fifteen hours a week for the War College correspondence course.

Barrett is speaking softly, casually, but there is a hum of excitement in his words that he can't contain. He speaks while looking straight at the computer, half to me, half to himself. I gather up multicolored rings that fit together in a stack, and place them in the storage box.

"They say it's supposed to be a gentlemen's course. It's meant to give army colonels a midcareer break, some time to rest and spend time with family, an opportunity to get medical issues resolved. Some people even call it a country club."

Finally he turns and looks at me. "You'd have lots of support— you know how the army is—you wouldn't have to worry about who will help you with Niko. You know, when the baby comes?" He says this last bit uncertainly, like he is floating out a balloon and waiting to see if I will puncture it.

I am about eight weeks pregnant. As during my pregnancy with Niko, I am tired and slightly nauseated, but not crippled. With the baby due around Christmas, somehow my anxieties about my marriage, about Barrett's overwhelming work hours and my own restlessness have changed somewhat. While I am worried about managing two children and the house, I am nevertheless giddy at the idea of a baby. With Niko turning three, I'd begun to feel restless at home, wondering about working again. But a new baby

changes all that. I *want* to be home with an infant, for at least the
first year.

I ask how much time we have to decide. Barrett shakes his head.
He doesn't know, doesn't think we have much. We decide to go
out to dinner to discuss this further. As I pack up Niko's bag of
small toys, Barrett calls the student contact the War College provided in its e-mail. Then we walk to Barrett's favorite neighborhood restaurant—the smelly Korean place with the kimchi platter
that reminds him of his tour at the DMZ, the demilitarized zone
between North and South Korea. At dinner Barrett tells me that it's
not to further his military career that he wants to go. Yes, he will
be agreeing to serve for at least three years afterward. But it's for
later, for when he gets out of the military. The prestigious degree,
the contacts he'll make, will help his career when he leaves law enforcement. It'll make us more solid financially. There's a very good
childcare center on post, he adds. Tons of kids on post: "Passels of
'em runnin' around, kid heaven," Barrett quotes the colonel from
Alabama whom he spoke to over the phone, complete with southern
accent. Numerous playgrounds, a great commissary, a health clinic,
a cleaners, a movie theater—all right on post. Everything I need
within walking distance, he tells me.

We would be near George and Mindy, who are moving to DC in
a few weeks for George's latest assignment at the Pentagon. We'd
be near my aunt in New Jersey, and Barrett's brothers in Alexan-
dria. And yet I feel a lead weight in my gut. I don't want to leave
my friends and family in Berkeley. What will the people be like
in Carlisle? Can I ever feel comfortable? I don't want to live on
an army base. But what's the alternative? If we stay here I know
how things will be. Barrett will have more to do than is humanly
possible. He'll have the police job and the army and then the correspondence course on top of everything. As opposed to: *Gentlemen's
course, time with family, time to renew.*

By 6:00 a.m. the next morning, Barrett has e-mailed his com-
pleted form 1058, "Application for Active Duty for Training, Active Duty for Special Work, Temporary Tour of Active Duty, and
Annual Training for Soldiers of the Army National Guard and U.S.
Army Reserve." At 8:39 a.m., he receives his "Resident Student
Welcome" e-mail, which urges him to fill out a number of forms
and return them the same day:

biographical sketch, housing and social name tag applications, Carlisle schools pre-registration, family medical screening and Academic Pre-Assessment Survey, security clearance verification and photograph (Head & Shoulder, no flags in background) for you and your spouse (spouse photo is optional). Suspense for completion of the above actions is 17 May 2004.

At 11:36 a.m., Barrett receives an e-mail flagged as "urgent": *Your Housing Application has not been received!* By 7:00 p.m. that night—after consultation with me—he has submitted our request for a four-bedroom. Under "Family Information," Barrett types, "Sophia Raday, Niko McAllister, and New Baby."

I lie in my bed, suitcases and boxes strewn around me. Outside my door, in the kitchen, I hear Niko's high voice. "I want Mommy! I want my mommy!"

Barrett's voice murmurs a mantra: *Mommy doesn't feel well. Mommy is sad. Mommy needs to rest. Mommy loves you.*

We won't be needing a four-bedroom house on post in Carlisle. A few days ago, I went to a doctor's appointment and he couldn't find the baby's heartbeat. So yesterday, Friday, I went back to his office to have a D & C. Afterward, in that fake cheerful medical professional voice, he suggested, "Why don't we try to get up?"

I was pinned to the stretcher by how much I hated the doctor. I hated the way he said that about half of pregnancies end in miscarriage. I hated the way he swept aside my experience, all the dreams I had for this baby, as if you could fit that into a statistic. Today is the Saturday of Memorial Day weekend. I've almost never thought about what Memorial Day really is, how it is a day to remember the dead. Up until now, it's always just been an extra day off to me, a day to have a barbeque. But now it has come home to me that Memorial Day is a solemn day, set aside to honor loss.

When I got my legs on the floor, the walls spun and I put my hands on the white paper coverlet to steady myself. I lowered my head toward the crimson Rorschach prints where I'd lain, the red so bright and fierce. I rested, half lying on the table. Then I slowly stood up, still dizzy, and leaned against Barrett.

The doctor was washing his hands and drying them. The very same doctor who touched me, who just finalized my miscarriage, then turned on his heel at the door and said cheerfully, "Have a great three-day weekend!"

It was all finished for him, he was a million miles away, already playing golf or whipping up a smoothie or playing with his cats, whatever he is doing this weekend, this three-day Memorial Day weekend. But it was just beginning for me. How did I make sense of this hurt? This loss? We had been on our way. We wanted two children and now we were having the second and everything was going to be fine. It was even okay that we were moving to the War College because I had a job, a role: I was going to be pregnant, take care of myself and Niko and the baby. That made sense to me. But now nothing makes sense. I don't know how to tell myself a story about the future that makes it okay. Right now I just feel how all kinds of possibilities have been amputated. No long afternoons of swimming at the local indoor pool. No Christmas infant. No contemplation of names. No warm family gatherings after the baby's arrival.

Listlessly I roll over and pick up my journal. I see a few entries from our trip to see George and Mindy, then lean on an elbow and scrawl on the page, "I *hate* Dr. Rosenberg." My mind plods along, each thought a monotone of gray. A little while later I write, "Will the hurt go away if I can get pregnant again? Or will all this pain be in vain?" And I remember back to something George said: "No one can say Jeff Benton died in vain."

I wrap the comforter tight around me, watch the dust dance in the slanted morning sunlight. I remember the way George's armor dropped briefly. I wonder what I could have done differently so that maybe I wouldn't have lost the baby. And something obvious hits me. George questions himself for that young man's death. How could he not? I didn't read the signals right. And of course he was trying to hide it. But a big part of the reason I didn't understand what was happening right in front of me was because I was too busy having a *political* discussion. The whole time I was speaking in those distancing, theoretical tones about something that wasn't theoretical at all to George. It was *personal*. He was trying to tell me that Jeff Benton got killed. *Jeff Benton died.* He was trying to share the weight of that, of seeing the gun with the helmet hanging on it, someone he *knew*, someone under his command. He was trying to make sense of it. And I did the same thing my doctor did. Instead of accompanying George as he tried to give meaning to his experience, I talked about "stovepiping" and "phase IV operations" and "intelligence failures."

An elfin face appears by my bed. "Are you still sad, Mommy?"

I put down my journal to help Niko scramble up. "I love you, my sweetest," I say, "but yes, I'm still a little sad."

And then for quite a long time, my son, the perpetual-motion machine, lies quietly next to me and strokes my hair.

ELEVEN

Culture Wars

Do not linger in dangerously isolated positions.
—Sun Tzu, *The Art of War*

S EMINAR 12 SOCIAL AT THE BOWLING Pavilion," the invitation reads, noting that spouses and children are invited, sandwiches will be served, and casual dress with nametags is suggested.
The War College sends weekly updates of all activities via e-mail
and I am amused to see that they always include a dress code for
the students (and sometimes for the spouses). "Class A" is indicated
for formal occasions, or when a bigwig is coming to speak; "Class
B/business dress" is the most common designation and what is required for daily classes; and lastly the War College equivalent of
"casual days": "BDUs (basic daily uniform)/business casual."

A major goal of the Army War College is to encourage the army's future leaders to think strategically, to innovate, to transform
the army into a learning organization. I remark to Barrett that it
might be hard for officers to become innovative thinkers when the
army still tells them what to wear.

I pin on the silver nametag that reads "Sophia Raday" with the
AWC crest next to it, issued to us by the War College. Silver for students and their spouses, gold for faculty members and their spouses.
The nametag is de rigueur at the War College for all social events.
At the recent opening ceremonies at the parade grounds, I quickly
perused the list of students and their mates and noted that I was the
only woman among the three hundred or so wives and twenty or
so female students who did not use her husband's name. The posts
of the nametag are thick and I have to press hard to get it through
the silk fabric of my blouse.

Each War College class is broken up into "seminars" of about twenty students. Barrett has been named chairman of his seminar because his date of promotion to colonel is the earliest. I, consequently, have been assigned to be leader of the spouses. It will be my responsibility to organize monthly get-togethers and other social activities. I will also have to attend a monthly meeting of seminar spouse leaders in which information for families will be disseminated. In an odd twist of fate, I have become part of the army chain of command.

"C'mon!" Barrett yells from the foot of the stairs. "Time to move out!"

I hold Niko's hand as we walk down the steep stairs of our quarters to the basement and garage. Our quarters are half of a stately brick duplex, built on a gentle knoll with a green lawn in front and a narrow alley behind. Barrett heaves up the creaky garage door, then stands in the middle of the narrow road, hands outstretched like a crossing guard. "Clear!" he yells.

Brad, our gangly twelve-year-old neighbor, is shooting hoops. As we emerge, he says, "Hello, Colonel. Hello, Mrs. McAllister." Brad's dad, Colonel Underwood, is active duty, hoping to finish up his twenty-year career here in Carlisle so his kids can go through high school in one place. Brad's mom, dressed in gingham shorts, with Brad's nine-year-old sister Alycia at her side, presented us with a ground beef casserole on our first night in the house. Now Brad indicates the best way to walk to the bowling alley where we are headed for the social.

We cross the street and make our way to the creek path that leads to the bowling alley. The Army War College is housed on Carlisle Barracks, a picturesque post full of green lawns and leafy maples. The buildings are red brick or white clapboard, and LeTort Creek runs along the western edge. We pass a homemade swing, a square of wood knotted at the bottom of a stout rope, gently swaying below a broad tree branch.

Just before we left Berkeley, the Army War College had been in the news. President Bush had made a speech here after the Abu Ghraib photos broke. But that didn't stop my friends from staring when I told them where we were going. It didn't stop them from saying, "You're going *where*? The Army *War* College? As in W. A. R.? As in *what is it good for?*"

And yet, contrary to its name, this is a remarkably peaceful place. The landscape is bucolic; there are no fences allowed around the quarters and the wide green expanses are soothing to the eye. Perhaps this will be a good year for our family after all. Perhaps I can regroup here, recover from the miscarriage. Maybe Barrett will also be able to relax a bit and spend more time with us.

Just then, behind us, the basketball thumps off the backboard. I remember the conversation I had yesterday with Colonel Underwood while he and Brad were playing "H-O-R-S-E" at the portable hoop set up between our two garage doors. Barrett and I were on our way to the playground with Niko. Colonel Underwood had started telling Barrett about some war book he had recently bought, then followed up with, "Yes, I'm something of a bibliophile."

I looked up from chasing the India rubber ball that had bounced off Niko's open arms. "Really? So am I. What kind of books do you like?"

He stopped dribbling the basketball a moment and looked up at me, sort of surprised. "All kinds. I collect them. Lately I've been reading poetry."

"I love poetry!" I exclaimed, a little burst of excitement exploding in my chest.

"You do? Hunh. Who do you like?"

I doubted he would know Ann Carson, my favorite poet. Czeslaw Milosz? Maybe better to think of an American poet. Then it hit me, the perfect poet to mention. "I really enjoy Walt Whitman," I said.

Colonel Underwood was a pale man in his forties, more professorial than warrior-like. Now his eyebrows drew together above his eyeglasses. He resumed dribbling, saying, "That guy? Naw, that guy's whacked!"

"Really?" I paused, not sure what to say next. "I think his stuff is beautiful."

No answer. Just a shot at the hoop, a rebound, and a toss to the son.

I squinted at him. "Why do you think Whitman is whacked?"

"Just is."

My new neighbor seemed to be avoiding any further eye contact with me. On a hunch I offered, "I suppose there's a lot of homoeroticism in his work."

"You got it," Colonel Underwood said. "Like I say, whacked." I shake my head at this memory as Barrett glances at his watch. "Range walk," he pronounces, the command for an extremely rapid stride that—although my legs are longer than Barrett's—I have never quite mastered. As Niko and I jog alongside, Barrett explains we'll meet the twenty other students, including two international students (from Taiwan and Canada) and the faculty members who are assigned to be part of our group, with their spouses and families. (There is one female War College student in the seminar.)

"After Colonel Johnson introduces me, I'll make a brief welcome speech," Barrett tells me. "Then I'll introduce you."

Right. I start composing my own remarks. *I am looking forward to a stimulating year of exchange and learning.* Nah. Too pretentious. *Hi—I am excited to spend the year together learning together.* Jesus, too kindergarten. *Hi, everyone. It's a pleasure to be here and I look forward to spending the year together.* Good. Simple and straightforward. I repeat this to myself and try to breathe deeply.

The event is outside the bowling alley in a little covered picnic area on a concrete pad. I step gingerly across the muddy perimeter and place one foot up onto the concrete, then swing Niko across. Barrett is shaking hands with various strangers. While murmuring my welcome remarks to myself, I smile in a general way, grab a plate and a turkey sandwich, and find a place for us to sit.

Colonel Johnson begins. He is proud to welcome this year's group of War College students. He reminds us of some of the great men who have graduated from the Army War College: Omar Bradley, George Patton, Dwight D. Eisenhower, Norman Schwarzkopf, Tommy Franks. He refers to the War College students as "the next leaders of our country." I lose the thread briefly as I peel some cheese away from mayonnaise-soaked bread for Niko, open a milk carton, place the straw in it, and hold it for Niko to drink. Then Barrett is speaking. It is an honor for him to lead the group. I take a deep breath and make sure Niko can manage his milk carton if I stand up. Barrett will do his best to make this a productive year for all. He would like to introduce his family, "My wife Sophia and my son Niko." I struggle to extract myself from the picnic bench, noting he skirted the last-name issue. I am beginning to raise my buttocks from the bench. Barrett looks at me, and I take in the eyes widening, the tension in his jaw, the way he crunches his teeth together, and

I register these as alarm. I am doing something wrong. Raising my hand, I sit back on the bench and smile mutely at the group.

Everyone claps.

Clutching a white plastic laundry basket full of Barrett's dirty black wool socks and Niko's pee-soaked pajamas, I pass Barrett sitting at the dining room table, reading Strobe Talbott. I read Talbott's book *Endgame,* about the SALT II arms control talks between the United States and the Soviet Union, when I was at Stanford. When I come in later from the commissary with a load of groceries, he's still there, reading George Kennan. At Stanford I read various Kennan articles, most notably his famous "long telegram" entitled *The Sources of Soviet Conduct,* which outlined the basis tenets of containment theory and influenced American foreign policy from Kennedy until Reagan. When Niko and I tramp up the stairs after riding our bikes home from the childcare center, there's Barrett, reading Graham Allison. Yes, I read him too, over fifteen years ago.

After dinner Barrett hastily loads the dishwasher then walks down to the library in Root Hall to do some more reading. All day long a familiar thought has been tripping through my brain. How come he's reading and I'm doing the laundry? *I'm the intellectual.* Barrett, on the other hand, has long preferred TV to reading. In political arguments I chide him for his penchant for oversimplification, for his lack of nuance. And now *he's* being *paid* to read! For the tenth time today, I remind myself I am not being fair. Barrett has earned this opportunity through years of hard work in the military, much harder work than I have ever done. I wanted a family, I remind myself. I wanted to stay home while my children were young. *My children. Scratch that. My child.* "Just the one?" everyone asks as we introduce ourselves. Yes, just the one.

I glance at the unread copies of the *New Yorker* piling up on our pine dining table. On top of the pile is the May 10 issue, which features an article by Seymour Hersh about Abu Ghraib. This morning, after I delivered Niko to school, unloaded the groceries, and started the laundry, I spent about fifteen minutes reading it. Now I put a video on for Niko and quickly straighten up his toys. Then I steal back to finish the article.

After Niko's video is over, I give him his bath, put on his pajamas, and read him *The Little Engine That Could*. Then I lie next to him resisting my next task. When Niko's breathing has become easy and regular, I have no more excuses, so I push myself out of his low bed, grab some supplies, and head down to the basement bathroom. My mom is coming out for a week's visit to coincide with my upcoming fortieth birthday, and George and Mindy and the kids are coming for a small party. The prior tenants and the movers left the basement toilet filthy. It has to be cleaned and there's no one else to do it but me. The shit lies in dry streaks in the toilet bowl, above the water line. I flush a few times to loosen it up and get the toilet cleaner to stick. I put on the clammy yellow latex gloves that come up to my mid-forearm. I eschew the typical toilet scrubber, that horseshoe-shaped brush on a stick. My weapon of choice is a good old yellow sponge with the scrubby green side. I think back to Abu Ghraib. I feel a similar disgust, a similar desire to close down my senses.

How did it happen? Why did it take an enlisted guy to blow the whistle? Where was the chain of command?

I turn off the water to the toilet and flush it so the water level is lowered. Then I lean over the toilet with my elbow almost in the water, hold my breath, and give it an aggressive scrub. I feel my mouth screw up into a little compressed raisin.

Even I am familiar with the seven army values: loyalty, duty, respect, selfless service, honor, integrity, and personal courage. Barrett, like many soldiers, has a small laminated card listing the values hanging with his dog tags around his neck. The ethos embodied in the army values makes Carlisle Barracks a quite nice place to live. Several times when I've parked outside our quarters with groceries, uniformed soldiers have stopped their bicycles and inquired, "Can I help you with that, ma'am?" This is the first place I've ever let Niko play outside alone for more than a few minutes. It's not just that the speed limit is fifteen miles per hour and people really respect it. It's that if they see a little kid wandering off, they will stop and help him. I am confident of that. *Even the teenagers* are nice, with their "Hello, Mrs. McAllister." Ten-year-olds have paper routes, sixteen-year-olds come around with flyers about their Eagle Scout projects. They are gathering old soccer cleats for kids in Iraq, or identifying and cataloguing the trees on post, or repainting all the fire hydrants bright red. Barrett leaves the house unlocked. *At night.*

I can't reconcile the politeness and rectitude of the troops here with people abusing prisoners, taking pictures, and then passing them around for entertainment.

The toilet requires more cleanser. I dip the sponge back in the water, extract one hand from a yellow glove and vigorously shake the green container of Comet. When I'd heard about President Bush making a speech at the War College, I'd been worried. What if he came to speak while we lived here? Could I listen respectfully? Or would I embarrass my husband by being carried out for heckling? We were in contact with a student here who unwittingly settled these concerns for me. He said that on the day the president flew in for the speech, "the wives and kids really got a kick out of watching the helicopter land!"

Got it. Spouses weren't invited to the speech.

I turn the water back on, flush a few times, peel my latex gloves so that one envelops the yellow sponge, and throw the whole lot in the garbage. I swallow and wipe the back of my hand across my eyes, as if to wipe away a painful thought. *Nobody wants to hear* my thoughts or confusions about Abu Ghraib. Recently a neighbor stopped by, another War College student, to say hello to Barrett. He nodded briefly to me after surveying the emerging living room, boxes piled in every corner. "It's really starting to come together in here, Sophia," he said.

Nobody wants to hear my theory that American foreign policy is characterized by codependence, that we focus on the external enemy in order to avoid looking at our own social ills. I am the toilet-cleaning colonel's wife, mother of just the one.

On a beautiful Sunday afternoon in late August, Niko and I head across the street to the neighbors'. Barrett is in his study carrel at the library. Niko and I now spend many afternoons outside with Jane and Tracy, each of whom has a girl and a boy. Jane is a boyish competitive marathon runner who gets up every morning at four-thirty to run for several hours, and Tracy is a bubbly brunette who sings in an award-winning local choir.

Today, like many other days, I sit at the patio table in Tracy's green backyard and fold laundry. The kids raid the toys stored in Tracy's and Jane's open garages, skipping over Wiffle ball, jump ropes, finger paint, and scooters to settle on sidewalk chalk. Jane marks out big hopscotch grids for them to jump on. Tracy brings out a pitcher of iced tea. Tracy's husband Jack is in Civilian Affairs, six months back from a year tour in Iraq. She's shown me the camel saddles and the jewelry he brought back. But as to what his experience was like, what she thinks about the war, what she thinks about Abu Ghraib: nothing.

Don't Jane and Tracy think Rumsfeld should be fired? I've gleaned from George and Barrett that many soldiers don't particularly care for the secretary of defense. They don't agree with his vision that technology will make ground warfare obsolete and his consequent disdain for the army's infantry and armor. They don't like the way he publicly humiliated former Army Chief of Staff General Eric Shinseki after Shinseki told Congress that an invasion of Iraq would require "several hundred thousand troops." And they don't like his repudiation of the Powell doctrine (force, when used, should be overwhelming) in favor of small, light, and fast military operations emphasizing air power and Special Forces.

But as Barrett has explained to me, there are certain unwritten rules. The military serves at the pleasure of the president. The officer corps is loyal to the chain of command, so for the most part they keep doing their job and they don't complain, at least publicly. I wonder if Tracy and Jane, like me, see Abu Ghraib as a symptom of loyalty gone overboard. I'd like to introduce the topic, but something stops me. It's not simply the pressure I feel to conform, the pressure that propelled me to use Barrett's last name on my new magnetic social nametag. It's the way my body feels when I contemplate beginning the conversation, the way my skin tingles with adrenaline about to be released, the way I start to tremble. I am afraid.

The screen door of Jane's house swings open with a slap, and Jane's husband Dan appears on the stoop, exclaiming, "Wow, it's so calm. Mind if I fire up the leaf blower?"

I look around at the couple dozen leaves spread out over the big backyard and laugh ruefully. The people here are devoted to their lawns. I have never done anything to my crabgrass lawn in California except mow it and occasionally water it. Even Barrett mows our lawn here every two weeks with a lawn mower I pick up from the post's "U-Do-It" shop, a sort of tool lending library. Returning the lawn mower to the U-Do-It my first time, I discover that the blades on all the mowers they lend out are soldered to the same height. "For uniformity," the U-Do-It lady says in explanation. I don't point out the logical flaw in this reasoning—that this only makes sense if everyone mows his lawn at the same time. I just nod and say, "Of course, I understand." And then I watch as each weekend, like clockwork, out come the men and boys to mow the lawns. I want there to be music, for the lawn mowing to be choreographed, like water ballet.

There will be no discussion of Abu Ghraib amid the whine and whir of the leaf blower. I don't ask if Jack or Dan has ever run across Antonio Taguba, the two-star general who was asked to investigate abuse at Abu Ghraib back in February of this year. His secret report, recently leaked to the press—in which he called the "Gitmo-izing" of Abu Ghraib contrary to doctrine—has embarrassed the Department of Defense. Military sources say it will cost him his career.

"What is Niko going to be for Halloween?" Tracy asks when Dan finishes.

"He's not sure yet," I say. "He's still deliberating between Scooby-Doo and the Cat in the Hat. How 'bout Rick and Taylor?"

"I got a beautiful Snow White costume for Taylor, and get this, Ricky is going to be Nemo! You should see these costumes. I'm really happy with their quality."

"You already have 'em?"

"Of course!"

I look over at Jane. "How 'bout you?"

"Oh, yeah, both Casey and Jasper are going to be M&M's. Makes it easy. I've had the suits for a couple of weeks. I always order before Labor Day."

If only Janis Karpinski, the general in charge of Abu Ghraib, had run that prison like these women run their households. In one of the *New Yorker* articles I've read, she describes the many nonuniformed people running around the prison whom she didn't know, who would smile and wave at her. I want to ask Jane and Tracy, "Don't you think she should have said to those people, 'Who the hell are you and what are you doing here?'"

Tracy raises a well-manicured finger and taps it in the air toward me. "Oh, hey," she says. "I've been meaning to tell you—I saw these new frozen Crock-Pot dinners at the commissary. You might want to check them out." Once I mentioned that every day at 1700 hours when the cannon goes off, I panic because I haven't given any thought to dinner. The very next day Tracy introduced me to the Crock-Pot, flipping through her recipe binder and clipping out specific recipes for me to photocopy.

I conceal a sigh. I want to tell them what I think: that Rumsfeld has deftly used the loyalty of the army leadership against it, that he manipulated military planners into promulgating only the most optimistic scenarios, that he has railroaded the most competent military leaders and set up yes-men in the highest positions at the Pentagon. That the military leadership has, to some extent, been *played*. But I'm not going to. I didn't yesterday and I'm not going to today. I'm afraid my ideas will make me a traitor.

Despite all the trappings of relaxation (mild sunny day, lawn chairs, iced tea) our conversation does not feel free and easy. With each step I am careful not to step on the mines that have been laid across our country since 9-11: What does it mean to be a patriot? How does one support the troops? When is loyalty the right thing and when is dissent the right thing? Instead I survey possible safe places to step next, something involving kids, domestic challenges, or the eccentricities of husbands. "Oh, wow!" I finally offer. "Hey, thanks for the tip. Did I tell you I got a rice cooker?"

A week or so later, Barrett takes me out to a birthday dinner at the nicest restaurant in Carlisle. We eat outside in the warm evening amid trees strung with garlands of white lights. After we order, I try to tell Barrett what forty means to me, how many roads now have "Closed" signs across them, when Barrett interjects, "Well, I'm not a very successful person, but I try to—"

I feel a spark ignite in my chest, and suddenly I am interrupting, "What do you mean *you're not successful*? The guy who's being paid to *read*? The guy with all the awards? And what about the Medal of Merit? What about 'SWAT team member of the year?'"

Barrett glances around him nervously, which tells me that I am getting loud. All I can do is constrain my fury in a low hiss. "Jesus, if *you* are not successful, what the hell are we doing? We've moved the whole family out here, so that *you could have more opportunities.* God knows we didn't come here *for me.* We didn't come to the Army *War* College because it is important to my ideals, *did we?"*

Barrett says very softly, "I'm not doing this to be successful, I'm doing this...I mean...I thought...I thought I was doing this— *for us."*

I look at Barrett's face. He is surprised, confused, and—I see from a shadow across his eyes—wounded. Barrett, who always takes my side in conflicts with my friends or family. So much so that he sometimes can't forgive the other person, long after the original issue has been resolved. Jesus, I've mixed him up with the enemy.

I mumble, "I'm sorry, Barrett, I'm sorry I am so angry. I just feel so excluded. Did you hear Georgie talk about Rumsfeld this weekend? He called him the 'Sec-Def.' He said that in meetings at the Pentagon, the 'Sec-Def' still refuses to grasp the kind of war we are dealing with in Iraq, that 'Rapid Deployment Operations' didn't work." I am moving my water glass in small circles as I speak. "Think about it. Georgie rubs shoulders with the goddamn Sec-Def and I rub shoulders with—with—with shitty toilets! Tell me—why is that?" I put the water glass to my lips and take a sip, and when I put it back on the table, it lands with an unexpected thud. "Yes, I wanted children," I say. "I wanted to have more than one. I know it's romanticized, but I had this idea of a family living in harmony, in a community where I could be both a mother and...and *a thinker.* Barrett, I'm forty years old and where am I? It doesn't seem fair to me that wanting to be a mother should erase everything else that I am!"

Barrett strokes my forearm, "Maw Deuce, you didn't like working in politics, remember? You would really hate working with the Sec-Def, I assure you." He laughs. "How is your writing going, anyway?"

I manage a little smile at the pet name. Barrett dubbed me Maw Deuce shortly after Niko's birth, around the time Bush refused to sign the Kyoto Protocol. Maw Deuce refers to the army's fifty-caliber machine gun, designed during World War I by John Browning. Barrett said I reminded him of it because I am constantly spitting out opinions, *rat-a-tat-tat rat-a-tat-tat.*

"What writing? I don't have time to write." I explain that there are still boxes to unpack, cabinets to organize, food shopping, laundry, cooking. I organize spouse outings. I go to spouse leader meetings. I forward e-mails to my group about the Carlisle Barracks Spouse Club luncheon, the tour of homes, the chili cook-off, the holiday gift wrap fund-raiser, and my personal favorite, the shooting of the colonial cannon. Using a mock-deep voice, I cite this latter one to Barrett: "The colonial cannon will *not be fired* on Thursday, October 14 at 1700. *The date has been changed to Wednesday, October 20 at 1700.* All are invited to watch the event. Please use extreme caution when standing in the vicinity of the cannon."

Barrett laughs. I tell him I just manage to do my bimonthly column at the Web site my writing group launched a year ago, but that's all. I don't see how I can go any farther with the writing. Whenever there's a little space in the day, it gets used up editing other people's work for the site.

"Well, why are you doing the editor thing, anyway?" Barrett asks.

That's a good question. As the Web site has grown, new people have come in, people with more writing experience than I. And they want things run their way. It's a typical start-up scenario, where founders become obsolete because of the enterprise's success. I explain that I am nervous about letting the position go: even though it's not paid, it gives me a tiny toehold in the literary world. It gives me something to write at the bottom of my e-mails: "Sophia Raday, Memoir Editor."

"I don't know," says Barrett the ever loyal. "They sound like a bunch of fucksticks! Put Niko in full-time childcare if you need to. But I recommend you lose the editor thing. Because you want to be a *writer,* not a *fuckstick integrator!*"

Barrett is not being fair to the people at the Web site. But he is right about one thing: I *do* really want to be a writer. And the only thing keeping me from trying is fear. Even Maw Deuce can't argue with that logic.

• • •

When Tracy invites me to be a "sub" at a Bunco game, I'm both nervous and excited. Bunco leagues are the big social events for military wives. I just need one person, one kindred spirit—then she and I can laugh together about this place. Maybe I'll find her tonight. The evening's hostess, Kathy, is an athletic fiftyish woman with short silver hair cut in a mod wedge. Her husband is a retired colonel. Kathy is a photographer and her work—stark black-and-white landscapes, and hand-painted black and whites of children—adorns the dark-toned walls of her warm house. After we shake off coats and exchange introductions, Kathy points out the mulled wine simmering in the Crock-Pot and the spinach and artichoke hors d'oeuvres just out of the oven.

As we wait for a sixth person to arrive, there is nothing to do but chat. We sit at an oval table and eat puff pastries. I realize how much I was counting on the game to protect me, give me cover. I imagine what the ladies would think if they knew me, my past, my beliefs. What if they knew that after being arrested at Stanford, I did my community service at the Center for Nonviolence in Palo Alto? That I've smoked pot, don't go to church, am passionate about keeping abortion legal?

I squirm a little in my chair, feel a now-familiar trill of fear. Yet why should I be so scared? I want to be accepted as I am. I am not such a horrible person. I am kind. I care about people. I am tired of being on guard, of watching what I say. I am tired of listening to the War College speeches: about how we are all so proud to be supporting freedom and democracy abroad. We spouses are so proud to make family sacrifices because we believe so much in the mission. I'm tired of the smug certainty that I agree with the rhetoric and the war and the lockstep role of quiet housewife. If only they weren't all such Stepford wives, maybe they could tolerate someone among them who is a little bit different.

When Kathy asks me what I think of Carlisle I describe how odd I find the social life at the War College. That although everyone is warm, jovial, the men and women break off into separate conversational klatches, where the men talk about their schoolwork or the softball team they are required to field, while the women talk about recipes or their kids. I recount trying to break into a conversation about world affairs with some of the men, how I couldn't get a word in edgewise. I tell them that when my uncle attended the War College twenty-five years ago, my aunt dubbed the place "Ego Mountain," and I'm beginning to understand why. I say that there are four or five members of Barrett's class who once they start, can't stop talking. They don't engage in dialogue, they pontificate. I describe a recent conversation:

> COLONEL: "I just picked up an interesting book, called *What Should I Do with My Life?*"
> ME: "Oh! I know that book."
> COLONEL: "It was a collection of stories about people who had made drastic changes in their lives."
> ME: "It's by Po Bronson, right? He was my same year at Stanford. He also wrote some great stuff on Silicon Valley start-ups."
> COLONEL: "My *favorite* part was…"

We are sitting at Kathy's dining room table, each cupping a warm glass of mulled wine. We have given up on the sixth person. There will be no Bunco tonight. Tracy is laughing at my story and so is the one other Carlisle Barracks resident in the group. It is so nice to be listened to, finally. Why not continue? I tell the group that in desperation I play the Condi card. At a strategic moment in conversation, I drop the simple phrase "Actually, Condi Rice was my professor at Stanford." It's virtually magic. It's like that *tink, tink, tink* on a wineglass. Condi has the power to stop the monologues. I playact how I press my advantage with Colonel Steamroller, adding, "She was a Democrat at the time, actually. Brent Scowcroft noticed her at a panel discussion at Dinkelspiel Auditorium." I imitate myself bending my head toward my new army colonel friend. I pantomime a conspiratorial whisper, like I'm letting him in on something.

In the warm glow of the mulled wine I convince myself that the performance has gone over well. Ignoring the slight pressing together of Kathy's lips, I focus on the nervous titter of the rest of the gathering. I yield to the loosening and lightening in my stomach. Kathy says, "So, what do you all think about the debates?"

My body registers dread before my mind does. No one answers.

Kathy presses forward, "What I don't understand is why they keep saying that so many people are undecided. *I don't see how anyone can be undecided.*"

The sudden rush of saliva in my mouth tells me that something bad is coming.

"Well, Sophia, with your policy background, I'd be interested to hear what you think of the debates. Did you see the last one?" Kathy asks.

Deep in my sacrum I feel a twist of terror. I won't lie about what I believe. But now I will certainly be reviled for my views. And doesn't that suck? Doesn't it suck that I am around such provincial people? People who are so closed-minded? "You *really* want to know?" I say, glaring at Kathy for putting me in this position.

Kathy's "Of course" comes out in a huffy laugh. She stands up a little taller and pulls her shoulders back like we are two boys squaring off in the playground. She's just a bully, isn't she? She is just angling for a fight. I feel a sudden gut-kick of adrenaline. Fine. If she wants a fight, I'll give her a fight.

"Actually, I don't watch the debates; I have to turn off the TV anytime Bush appears." I shake my head, and half stand in my chair. "I just can't look at his face; I can't bear to hear his voice." I sense a drawing back of everyone at the table, a shock, and that releases an electricity of anger that spurs me on. I say he took us to war under false pretenses. There were no WMD. Did he or didn't he know that all along? I assert it is equally criminal either way. "I suppose it could have been sheer *stupidity*," I say. "*Maybe he's not a liar.*"

After I stop talking, I hear the ticking of Kathy's grandfather clock, the space between the ticks a whole lifetime. Little fingers of embarrassment inch up my face. Everyone looks at her lap or the tablecloth except Kathy, who squints at me open-mouthed. I myself begin a studious examination of the needlework in the white cloth. My breath still comes in quiet gasps, which I try to control. I glance up and see Tracy hunched beside me. She catches my eye for a second, then abruptly looks away, baffled, betrayed. She was my entrée into the group, and this is how I thank her?

As Tracy turns away from me, all my past interactions here in Carlisle become puzzle pieces, and in my mind, they flutter up and rearrange themselves into a different whole, a different picture. The new picture has dimensions and meanings I couldn't make out before. Tracy. What has she ever done but be nice to me? She helps me with cooking ideas. She watches Niko while I run to change the laundry. She invites me to Bunco. And Kathy. What was her crime? She asked me what I thought. Isn't that what I've been longing for? So why did I rain hell on her? I don't like the way the puzzle pieces are fitting together now; I don't like the story they are telling. I try to defend myself: they don't see who I am, they don't see that I have something to say, they assume I am only interested in recipes.

I remember myself chiding Barrett earlier this evening as he hurried to get Niko to bed so he could work. I told him that before we came to Carlisle, he'd always explained that his tense moods came from the anxiety of being on patrol, or the pressure of the workload at the army. But now, when he's on a safe army post where the workload is reasonable, he can't stop. He's still tense. He's still anxious. He can't stop overworking. He thinks his feelings are caused by his external landscape when really they are caused by *his internal landscape.*

I feel a hot crumpling shame. If Barrett's perspective on the world is shaped by some internal conflict, what about *me?* Kathy said she didn't see how anyone could be on the fence. I felt provoked. But *I was the one who used the angry tone of voice. I was the one who was argumentative.* I had wanted so badly for someone to ask me what I thought. And yet when they did, I attacked. I assumed they were going to hate me, so I'd already started hating them. I'd put all these women into a two-dimensional box. I'd demonized them because of my own fears of rejection. Yes, I am different. Yes, I have strong opinions. But perhaps I could express them without so much anger, without so much fear. Fear that comes from the odd climate in our country to some extent, perhaps, but also fear that comes from my own self-loathing, fear that comes from struggling with my own self-worth after losing a baby. My struggle with my lack of accomplishments as I turn forty, with having only one child. My own feeling of powerlessness. *My* internal landscape. I have been girding myself for battle, and the War College provided such a perfect enemy.

Just then, a voice quavers from the other side of the table,

"Well," says the spectacled mother of four whom I have met once at the Carlisle Barracks pool, "I'm—I'm actually, well—*I'm* on the fence."

It's Election Day, 2004, and I am in line at the security gate to get back on post. This morning, as a volunteer for Get Out the Vote, I teamed up with a disabled man. In his van, we cruised around the poorest parts of Harrisburg taking elderly people to the polls for the Kerry campaign. As my car nears the guard shack, I carefully peel off the Kerry/Edwards sticker on my T-shirt, along with the cheery "Hi—I'm Sophia" nametag below it. It's easier if the guards at the barracks gate don't see it, or the childcare center staff, or my neighbors. To my great relief, despite the Bunco debacle, Tracy is still friendly to me. I've decided to quietly go about my own pursuits. I have been canvassing for Kerry for the last few weeks. I have quit my editorship and signed Niko up for childcare every morning. I have sent query letters out to two magazines and have gotten one favorable response.

I tuck the Kerry/Edwards buttons into my glove box and throw Barrett's poncho liner over the yard signs in the back seat. While the rule at the War College is that all conversations that occur within Root Hall (the main lecture hall) are for "nonattribution," Barrett has told me that the members of his seminar—or at least the loudest of them—are considerably more conservative than he is. He also told me that the seminar recently discussed a survey by Richard H. Kohn and Peter D. Feaver that revealed that the officer corps of the military has become increasingly politicized and increasingly Republican. Later I find a *New York Times* article on the same study. It says that while in the seventies, 12 percent of the officer corps identified as Democrat and 33 percent as Republican (with the other officers claiming they were independent or apolitical), now 8 percent identify as Democrat and 64 percent as Republican.

Recently General John Abizaid, CENTCOM commander, came to speak at the War College. Only the students could go; spouses were invited instead to hear Mrs. Abizaid speak. I have watched Abizaid's career with interest because he was Barrett's company commander when Barrett was in the Ranger battalion. Barrett has had great respect for him ever since they parachuted into Grenada together in 1983. As usual, Barrett couldn't tell me any of the specifics of the speech, just broadly that General Abizaid encouraged the students to go out and speak to community groups to counter the media image that the war was not going well.

Once I've picked up Niko from the childcare center and brought him home, I cut up some apples and check the election returns. No winner yet; it is still very close. I wonder how Barrett voted. Because I don't talk politics with anyone on post, Barrett has become my swing state. I have been pulling out all the stops to convince him to vote for Kerry. But it's a surprisingly tough sell. While he is highly critical of Bush, he also doesn't like Kerry, feels he will not make a good commander in chief.

"Why not? He's a *frickin'* war hero, for God's sake!" I'd said recently.

Barrett hemmed and hawed, then mentioned Kerry's involvement in protests against the Vietnam War.

"What are you talking about?" I went on to ask him why he assumed that just because a citizen objects to a certain foreign policy or military adventure, that citizen must not be patriotic, must not "support the troops"? I explained to Barrett that those of us who protest wars and those of us ready to serve in wars are really not all that different. I reminded Barrett that when he describes his sense of duty, of service, he describes it as wanting to "be a part of history." I felt the same way as a young activist.

"Mmm...maybe," Barrett said.

I told him I considered joining Peace Brigades International, an organization that sent Americans into poor areas of El Salvador to serve as human shields against further bombing of the peasant countryside. I explained that the motivation of a protestor and of a brave soldier are actually very similar. Both roles require the moral courage to act on strongly felt beliefs, and to put yourself on the line. It's easier both as a soldier and a citizen not to "stick your neck out," but some people are compelled to because of their convictions and their mettle. Was it so crazy to think both should be acknowledged as playing an important role in the political arena?

"I dunno," Barrett said.

It is a citizen's *duty*, I went on, as strong as the duty of a soldier to follow orders, to speak out against government wrongdoing. If the government is making a mistake—and even the most superficial reading of history demonstrates that the U.S. government has made quite a few—speaking out and preventing the misuse of military troops protects them!

Barrett nodded, then said, "All I know is Reagan brought pride back to the military in the eighties. It seems like the Democrats—ever since Vietnam—just haven't valued the contribution of the military. But whatever you say about Bush—he sees us as heroes." He added that Clinton was completely uninterested in the military. Had I heard that rumor that Clinton supposedly wanted to delegate oversight of the military to someone else?

I had not.

"As if he could delegate being the commander in chief!" Barrett snorted.

Barrett and I have always had a little more conflict during election years, but this year has been much more intense. Partly it's because the choice between Bush and Kerry feels more stark and more important than in prior election years. But it's more than that. I know Barrett doesn't approve of a lot of what Bush has done. And yet he can't seem to make that final step toward change, toward compassion, toward *me,* that it would take to actually vote for Kerry. In my mind the election isn't just about the two candidates but also about Carlisle and Sophia: Whose opinion does Barrett value more? Whom does he respect more? Whom does he trust more?

Last night I found myself making a little speech before bed. "This isn't a threat," I began, "but I feel it's only fair that you should know."

He put down *Nuclear Terrorism* by Graham Allison. "Yes?"

"Well, I just want you to know—if you vote for Bush, I'm not sure I could ever have sex with you again." I added hastily, "It wouldn't be a punishment. It just might gross me out too much."

He just smiled.

Niko looks up from his plate and notices Tracy and Jane and the kids out the window. They are walking through our yard to the playground by the creek. I yell out the back door that we'll be right down. I grab my fleece jacket and tie it around my waist for later, when the warmth of the afternoon sun wanes.

The kids play on the teeter-totter and the monkey bars and run around and chase each other. I give Niko his special "over and under" push on the swings, and the other kids clamor for a turn. "One per person," I say, and make my way through Ricky and Taylor and Casey and Jasper and Alycia from next door. Then I go back to stand with Jane and Tracy. A few minutes later, as my body cools, I untie my jacket to put on against the impending chill.

"*Eeewwww! Gggrrrooosss!*" shrieks Alycia, pointing at me. She presses her nonpointing hand, clawlike, toward her chest, and sits on air to punctuate her outbursts. "Eeww, eeww, eeeewwww! Oh, my *God!* Oh! My! God! *Gross! Gro—oss!*"

I look down at myself, heat rising to my face. What is she making such a fuss about?

"You have a *Kerry sticker* on!"

Oh, Christ. But I took those off! Shit, those were on my T-shirt. I forgot to remove the campaign stickers I'd placed on my jacket early this morning. I put my hand to the edge of the sticker and gently pull. The blue fuzz of my jacket adheres to the back of the sticker. I try to be nonchalant. "Oops..."

I am drowned out by Alycia's keening, "*You have a Kerry sticker on. Gross! Gross!*"

Jane's daughter Casey starts in. "*No way! No way!*"

For a moment the moms are all paralyzed while Alycia and Casey start a sort of improv spoken-word session: "*Oh, my God, oh, my God, ewww, ewwww,*" continues Alycia, while Casey brings in the percussion, "Bush! Bush! Bush is right! Bush is good! Bush is right! Kerry is evil!" Then she segues into a cheerleading session. "Give me a B!"

"B!" says Alycia.

"Give me a U!"

"U!"

I feel a sick ripple in my gut. No one is going to hurt me here, and yet I am inexplicably afraid.

Jane begins shushing, "Now girls, we don't all think the same way..." and Casey falters briefly, but Mrs. Underwood, Alycia's mom, is not here, and Alycia cannot contain herself. She finishes the cheer herself, doing both parts of the call and response, "Give me an S! S! Give me an H! H! Bush! Bush! *Yay!*"

Then she looks at me, still yelling *"You like* Kerry?! *You voted* for Kerry?!*"*

An intellectual part of me views this from afar and could laugh, but my body is right there in the playground, under attack, adrenaline flooding through me. My teeth are grinding with the effort of not moving, of not striding up to Alycia and grabbing her by the throat. You wanna piece of me? Bring it on.

It's the plaintive note under the accusation that stops me, the hint of hurt or betrayal in her intonation. I can see the confusion in her face. She's thinking, *Miss Sophia?* The one who gives her over-under swings, which she loves? One evening after dinner a few weeks ago Tracy's husband Jack mixed margaritas. Barrett was home unusually early and the parents all had a drink or two and sat around in lawn chairs laughing and talking in the warm Indian summer evening. For once there was no bickering among the kids, just dancing in the sprinklers. I was considering expounding on the magic in the air when Jack snuck up and dumped a kids' bucket full of water over my head. Water dripping down my nose, I caught Tracy's eye and she winked. Then she chatted with Jack at the grill and signaled to me when he was within firing range. Just as the fireflies came out, I nailed Jack with the garden hose. A general water fight ensued. No one—parent or kid—wanted it to end. Alycia is always asking me if we can have another night like that. She can't understand how *that Miss Sophia,* who lives next door, whose husband is in the military, *whom she likes*—how can that Miss Sophia be one of those Kerry supporters?

To be fair, someone wearing a Bush sticker on his or her jacket would probably meet an equally hostile response walking into Totland, a favorite kids' park in Berkeley. When we are at home I can't ask Barrett to pick up some milk on his way home from the Army Reserve. He doesn't want to be seen in Berkeley in an army uniform. He is afraid of the reaction he might get in the land where "Kill your television" bumper stickers are outnumbered only by those that say "Question authority." Tie-dyed canvassers stop by our house regularly asking for our support to "tear down the military-industrial complex." Recruiters are banned from many college campuses. The library puts labels on children's videos about helicopters or airplanes or submarines: "warning: depicts helicop-

ters/planes/submarines in *military* settings." In a few years, after
we have moved home, the Berkeley City Council will make national
news by passing a resolution that the Marine Corps is not welcome
to recruit within city limits.

If we were at home, I would have to defend Barrett. Friends
would sidle up to me at the playground, at the supermarket, or at
parties, and say sotto voce, "So, what about Barrett? I mean, he's—"
(glancing back and forth to be sure no one nearby might hear)
"—not a *Republican*, is he?"

I'd be giving my little speech about him being a Republican like
the Republicans used to be: a pro–civil liberties, small government,
pro-defense Republican, as opposed to a pro-life, antigay, teach cre-
ationism in schools Republican. Or perhaps I'd be talking about how
interesting it is to have a Republican partner who sees the world so
differently from me, how it has helped us maintain our individual
identities. Either way would be going over like the teacher in the old
Peanuts cartoons: *wonh wonh wonh wonh Republican.*

Eventually my head narrowly wins the war with my body.
I decide to take a schoolteacher approach. Standing as tall above
Alycia as I can, I hiss, "I don't appreciate your tone. I can vote for
whomever I want. *Get it?*" Except my voice doesn't sound much
like a schoolteacher. There is an edge to it. In fact I am pretty
much shouting. *"That's* what this country is about. And *yes,* if you
must know, I voted for *John Kerry!"*

Alycia stares at me. I stare back at her. She looks at her shoes. I
look at my shoes. I feel the other moms behind me, probably looking at their shoes. We all stand there, frozen with awkwardness.

The truth is that—other than Barrett and my cousins George
and Michael—no one from "my world" is in the military. No one
I know from college, no friends from my hometown outside Phila-
delphia or friends in the Bay Area, where I have lived for the past
twenty-five years, have chosen that path. My world, pre-Barrett,
was essentially a world in which being a soldier was considered a
bummer, that is, if it was considered at all. In fact, before 9-11, soldiers were about as visible to my peer group as toilet cleaners. To
the extent we considered military service, we thought in horror of
the reinstatement of the draft and how we might spirit our children
away to Mexico or New Zealand as necessary. In college a friend

gave me a T-shirt I thought was really funny. It said, "Join the military, go to interesting places, meet interesting people . . . and kill them." Recent demographic studies of the military back up my personal experience. The military has long drawn disproportionately from rural, southern, and western areas of the country. Graduates of elite colleges are underrepresented, and, surprisingly, so are low-income people.

So *this* is what it feels like to be demonized, dismissed as wrong and evil? Once again I feel a hot wash of shame remembering myself that night at Bunco, remembering how I hated the women for maybe hating me, the way I called them Stepford wives in my mind. Isn't that the root of violence, the denial of the other's humanity? Isn't *that* what led to Abu Ghraib? My instincts tell me to fight back, but that just continues the spiral of misunderstanding and anger. But how do we talk about this? When has anyone ever changed his or her mind in the middle of a shouting match? The shouting and the slurs, they just harden us in our respective sides. I have to try to express my differences more gently.

I want to tell Alycia it is okay to be curious about my views. I begin, "Listen, sweetie, it's okay to talk about this. It's okay to be curious. You can just ask—"

But suddenly there is a shriek from across the playground, a wail from the sandbox. "Stop it! It is *not!*" Tracy's little boy Rick sobs, "Mom-*mee!* Casey called my truck a *Kerry* truck!"

TWELVE

Drive On, Soldier, Drive On

Surrender is not a Ranger word.
—U.S. Army Airborne Ranger Creed

BARRETT IS UP AND OFF TO the library early, per usual, a vague kiss in the gray dawn while the speakers broadcast reveille. There is no change in our routine for the day after the election. It's over. Bush won.

Niko doesn't want to eat his breakfast, doesn't want to sit in the high chair, doesn't want to go up the stairs to retrieve his shoes. "Niko," I say, "let's get your shoes on. No. No Legos now. Put that down and let's go to your room. *Now.* Niko, come with me now. It's time to put on your shoes. Niko! Get over here this minute!" I rush toward my son, who is lifting the yellow plastic bin up off the floor and looking at me with a defiant grin. "I am counting to three, Niko. One...Two..." My voice takes on a guttural quality. "*Three!*"

Keeping his eyes on me, Niko upends the bin and the multicolored tiles tumble out of the bin with a resounding crash. The sound fills me with seething energy, and I prepare to do battle. I am almost eager to have a conflict with Niko, for here's something I can prevail in, something I can control. "You are going to put your shoes on right *now!*" I put him sideways under my arm like an overgrown football and start marching up the steps.

"Mommy, stop! Mommeee!"

Some part of me is watching myself and saying this is not good. This is not me. This screeching woman should stop and calm down, but the feeling of shame that washes over me only makes me more angry, only propels me forward. Breathing hard, I toss Niko on his

159

bed, sit beside him and pin him down with my leg over his torso. He struggles but I don't let him up. He starts crying. Between gritted teeth I say, "You. Need. To. Put. Your. Shoes. On." I take his socks and yank them onto one foot one at a time. He thrashes his arms so I take my leg off of him and lean over him, holding his shoulders down. "Stop it, Niko! *Stop it!*" I bellow. Then I pull him up by the arms, turn myself and him until we are sitting on the side of the bed. I cram and twist one of his sneakers on. He kicks at me with his other foot, catching me right in the mouth.

"Goddamn it, Niko!"

The pain breaks the spell. I slide off the side of the bed to the floor and put my hands to my face. I start to cry, sitting on the floor, letting Niko do whatever he wants, which it turns out is to lie on the bed and kick for a while, cry a little, then crawl down onto the floor next to me, slide his head into my lap and pull at my hands so I can look at his worried little three-year-old face. I pull him into my lap and tell him Mommy is a little upset today, and it's not his fault that Mommy is crying. He sticks his unshod foot out and wriggles his toes. I remind him that he can't go see Miss Annie, his favorite teacher, until he puts his shoes on. He smiles at me. I walk down the upstairs hall to the office I share with Barrett. Retrieving my coat from a chair, I glance at my e-mail.

There is a new message, with a subject line that says, "Upset about the election? The Buddha says Breathe," a bit of wisdom from Tibetan Buddhist Lama Surya Das:

> To loosen my own attachment to opinions, I remind myself that if I really knew everything there was to know—past, present, and future—about any particular person, subject, or situation, my opinions and feelings about them would be quite different. Since I don't know that much, I have gradually learned to not to be so judgmental and invested in my own views, although I certainly do have them.

I stare over at the bronze bust of Theodore Roosevelt that sits next to Barrett's monitor. Barrett bought the bust for a presentation on leadership, along with a replica of the original Teddy Roosevelt–inspired Teddy Bear, which leans against the bust.

Could I let go of the fierce certainty that all the people who were flashing thumbs-up signs last night at the bowling alley are well meaning but clueless? Or if I couldn't get *there*, what about releasing my conviction that it is up to me, personally, to convince them of the error of their thinking? A friend once pointed out to me that conflict is like a rope with a giant knot in it. You can't even begin to untie the knot if you are still pulling, pulling the knot tighter. Is the answer so simple? Could I simply release my side of the rope?

I unearth Niko's remaining shoe from among the toys at his bedside. To let go would mean, in effect, to acknowledge my own limitations. Walking downstairs, I grab my warm hat and Niko's jacket from the pegs by the front door. I call out to Niko that it's time to go, that Miss Annie is waiting for him at school, that he is missing story time, that I have a surprise for him. He comes bounding down the stairs. I hoist him up and carry him out to his car seat and then, when he is buckled in, I hand him his surprise (a bag of leftover grapes) and gently slide the shoe on.

The next time I see Tracy at the playground, she chucks me affectionately on the shoulder and says, "Ya know, Sophia, I've voted Democrat in the past."

In the weeks following the election, Barrett starts reading articles about the Israeli-Palestinian conflict in both the *Economist* and *Al Jazeera* online. He discovers Thomas Friedman and begins leaving the columns out on the breakfast table for me. I almost spit out my breakfast cereal when one Saturday morning he wonders aloud if his next vehicle will have to be something more fuel efficient than his Chevy two-ton.

On the Sunday after Thanksgiving, we are speeding along the New Jersey Turnpike in the Chevy two-ton. Leaving the family gathering in Princeton, we are taking a feverish Niko to the Children's Hospital Emergency Room in New Brunswick for some stronger antibiotics. When they usher us into a tiny white and silver room that smells of ammonia, I sit down in a white plastic chair. Niko slumps against me, while Barrett stands against the wall, his arms crossed over his chest. The doctor, a woman with short brown hair, gently presses her fingers along the swollen side of Niko's neck.

"Yes, we've seen a couple cases of this," she says, and rolls across the room to pick up a phone. She speaks in doctor-speak, but I pick up "retropharyngeal abscesses," "pediatric ward," and "CAT scan." She explains that Niko has a massive infection in the spaces of his neck. If the tissues swell too much they can close down his windpipe. Niko needs IV antibiotics, a CAT scan to evaluate how much his windpipe is compromised, and possibly, in a few days, a surgical procedure in which they will insert a large needle in the back of his neck to drain the abscesses.

I can't take it all in. "You mean we have to stay here?"

She says, "Oh, yes, probably for two weeks."

I suck in a breath. Barrett walks over to Niko and me, kneeling down and grabbing both sides of the chair so that we are encircled in his arms. "Okay, it's going to be all right," he says. "We will get through this." He turns to the doctor. "I assume we can stay with him." While his voice is polite, there is a commanding tone to it. It really says, *We're staying with him and there's nothing you can do about it.* It reminds me of a running joke with my mom. Whatever story I tell about our joint adventures, no matter how much I emphasize my own impressive actions, she always reacts the same way. "Oh! Thank God *Barrett* was there!" Right now that's exactly what I feel. Thank God Barrett is here.

The doctor rearranges the stethoscope around her neck and makes a note on her clipboard, telling us that there are foldout cots in each of the rooms for one parent. She tells us that they need to get Niko's IV going right away and then take him over to radiology for the CAT scan. She glances at her watch. "Let me know when you are ready."

Niko is still sitting on my lap with his shirt off, his head cradled against my breasts, my arms around him. A slender kid since birth, his ribs now stick out—he hasn't eaten for the last few days. He looks like a fragile little bird, out of place in this big mechanical hospital with all its sharp edges, cold surfaces, and weird beeps.

The nurse arrives to put in an IV. She picks up Niko's arm at the wrist and flips it over to evaluate his veins. She starts tapping the needle. "Hang on just a sec," I mumble. She shakes her hair back off her face in a gesture of impatience. The hospital doesn't wait for us, we wait for it. Scowling, the nurse says, "He's dehydrated. It's going to make it harder to find a vein."

They decide to check his fluid level. Can he pee in a bag? They want to measure his urine. Gently I take off his pants and they put a sort of plastic bag around his penis. I hug him to me and tell him it's okay to let it go. Try to pee. He does and half of it ends up in my lap. So much for measuring it.

Again the nurse taps Niko's inner wrist. At three and a half, he won't understand why we are letting these people hurt him. I feel panic spinning inside me, but I can't let Niko see it. I try to explain what's happening to him. "Baby," I tell him, "you need special medicine and they have to put something in your arm. You'll feel a little prick but it won't be long."

"No!" Niko says and immediately starts to cry, "No, Mommy, don't let them!"

Barrett picks Niko out of my lap and lays him on the examining table. Barrett's tenor voice is strong. "Niko, I'm going to be right here with you."

I stand behind Barrett, stroking Niko's legs. As the nurse brandishes the needle, I begin to feel lightheaded. Barrett says, "Just look at me Niko, look at Papa." When Niko cries I turn my head away and close my eyes and steady myself against the table. Barrett grunts and I realize that they haven't gotten it in, and when they stick Niko the second time, he screams. Barrett says, "Almost there now, baby boy, almost there." Barrett looks at the nurse and she nods. Niko's crying trails off as Barrett rocks him in his arms.

Taking Niko from Barrett, I sit back down with him on my plastic chair. I tell Niko what a good boy he is, what a strong boy. Barrett turns his face to the wall and puts his knuckles to his eyebrows for a minute, then quickly wipes a thumb under each eye. The nurse says one of us can go in the room while he has the CAT scan, which requires him to lie still on a rolling platform that will slide inside a dark tube. One of us can be touching his leg and talking to him, helping him stay calm. The other will have to wait outside.

I sigh. I am the obvious person to go with Niko. I am still the person who dresses him, feeds him breakfast, makes his lunch, takes him to preschool, picks him up, spends the afternoon with him, takes him to the doctor when he needs it, gives him his bath, brushes his teeth, and puts him to bed. Even though the War College was supposed to be a midcareer break for army officers, an opportunity to spend time with their families, we still don't see Barrett that often. He has trouble believing he is doing enough work, believing that the work he is doing is good enough. And though he already has an outline of his strategic research paper while many other students are still hunting for topics, he is not sure he will be able to finish on time. When he is not reading or writing, he walks around the house nervously fidgeting.

Occasionally I can convince Niko to ride his bike down the path along the creek with Barrett. But that's about as far as it goes. Whenever Niko gets hurt, it's always Mommy he goes to for comfort. If I try to suggest maybe Daddy do the bath one night, or Daddy put him to bed, Niko cries and protests.

Nothing undoes Barrett more than his son's indifference. He just doesn't understand it. What little boy doesn't dream of having a dad who's a soldier *and* a policeman? I try to coach Barrett on how to play with Niko, how to sit down on the carpet and play Legos or trains instead of taking him along to Wal-Mart or to get the oil changed. I encourage Barrett to follow Niko's lead, to try to be more in the moment with him. Barrett will try for ten minutes or so, but then he'll start looking at his watch or glancing at his computer on the dining-room table. Eventually he will say something like, "Well, that was good; I think we really bonded. Mind if I hit the library?"

Niko is sitting with his legs across mine, his face in my shirt, as I rock him gently and stroke his hair. His voice, muffled against my sweatshirt, is weak and reedy. "What did you say, baby?" I ask.

"Daddy," he says. "I want Daddy."

I sit on a bench outside the CAT scan room, my pants still damp and clammy. I stand and shake them away from my skin. There is a stretcher with a patient lying on it a little way down the green hall. I listen for what is happening behind the thick door marked X-ray. The technician's voice is a low murmur, but I can hear Barrett telling Niko not to be scared of the machine, that Daddy is right next to him making sure he is safe. Just so he knows Daddy is right here with him, Daddy will sing to him. I catch snippets of Barrett singing the ABCs. Then "Row, Row, Row Your Boat." "Mary Had a Little Lamb." The ABCs again. Then there is a pause. I lean my ear against the door to hear Barrett's next song:

Peas, peas, peas, peas,
Eatin' goober peas,
Goodness, how delicious,
Eatin' goober peas!

It must be five minutes by now. If Niko were crying would I hear him? When are they going to be done? For a while the singing stops, but then, just before they emerge, I recognize the refrain of the army fight song:

Then it's hi! hi! hey!
The army's on its way.
Count off the cadence loud and strong, two, three;
For where'er we go,
You will always know
That the army goes rolling along!

Once Niko is settled in his room, I call Tracy's husband Jack and ask him to go find our army insurance card. When he hears Niko is in the hospital, something in his voice shifts, signaling that he is snapping to attention. He follows my instructions on how to jimmy open the window next to our back door, how to wrap his arm through to the door and unlock it. I talk him up the stairs to my desk, direct him to the third drawer on the right. He leafs through a stack of papers he finds there, reading me what he finds, and I tell him to keep going. Fleetingly it occurs to me that he will see things we normally keep private: drafts of my writing, our investment statements. But I dismiss this thought almost before it registers. In situations like this, military people shine. We can count on Jack. He will help us. The solidness of that is something I let myself rest into. He unearths the card and reads me the numbers. Anything we need, he says, just call him back.

When I rejoin Barrett in Niko's room, we sit down on the small banquette next to the bed, where Niko is hooked up to an IV drip that will simultaneously rehydrate him and deliver strong doses of antibiotics. He is deeply asleep, worn out by the late hour, the infection, and the day's proceedings. Our little area is enclosed by green fabric on a wire to give us privacy from the other patient across the room, a little boy who hacks and wheezes with pneumonia.

Many doctors have already been through to see us: the resident, various students, the internist. Finally the three of us are alone. My pants have dried. I haven't stopped for a moment since early this morning. I haven't eaten anything. I don't have a toothbrush or any other clothes. The vinyl sofa is a colorful pattern of green, blue, and yellow swirls. I let myself sink into it. Barrett takes one of my hands and clears his throat. "Babe, I was thinking..." he says and looks at his watch. "It's only 9:30. If I took off now I could still get back to Carlisle by midnight."

There are no windows in our area because we are in an interior corner. TV blares *Blue's Clues* from the other little boy's room. At first the vinyl of the sofa felt cool but now I feel a rush of heat, of sticky discomfort.

"You want to go back to Carlisle?"

"It's not that I want to. But that way I could make it to class tomorrow."

I don't get it. He could stay one more day. He could stay close by us for at least one more day, be here to talk to the specialists, wait and see if the antibiotics are lowering Niko's temperature. Surely no one would fault him for that. It's not that class is so important to him; I know there are times when he feels like it's sort of pointless. It isn't a matter of life and death that he sit in the classroom tomorrow. So why?

"This is a big deal," I say, and my voice comes out small. "We haven't even seen the specialists yet."

"I know, but I'm not on leave. I have to report."

"So? You call your adviser and tell him what happened. End of story."

"Well...I don't know if I feel right about that. You're here to take care of Niko, right? Do we really need both of us? And if you need anything you can call me. I'll be here in two hours."

Around the house, Barrett loves to sing his own praises. Sometimes he assumes a sportscaster voice, talking about himself: "It's *amazing* the way he completely *dominates* the kitchen battlefield. Garbage taken out! Dishes put away!" On Sunday mornings, he'll cry, "Time me!" and dash around the kitchen, making bacon and eggs. After sliding the eggs onto our plates, he'll stand in his bathrobe with hands on his hips, puff out his chest, and proclaim,

"Your husband is a national treasure. Your husband is an American hero."

Yet in terms of the army, Barrett can never do enough. West Point instilled an ideal in Barrett, the romantic notion of an officer and a gentleman. This ideal—which goes back to General Mac-Arthur's famous "Duty, Honor, Country" speech—is so lofty that Barrett can never quite reach it. Barrett has often imitated Mac-Arthur giving the famous speech, deepening his voice and pausing dramatically between words: Those. Three. Hallowed. Words. Reverently. Dictate.

> *What. You. Ought. To. Be.*
> *What. You. Can. Be.*
> *What. You. Will. Be.*

Years later I will listen to the whole speech and be transfixed by its emotion and poetry:

> I listen vainly, but with thirsty ears, for the witching melody of faint bugles blowing reveille, of far drums beating the long roll. In my dreams I hear again the crash of guns, the rattle of musketry, the strange, mournful mutter of the battlefield.
>
> But in the evening of my memory, always I come back to West Point.
>
> Always there echoes and re-echoes: Duty, Honor, Country.
>
> Today marks my final roll call with you, but I want you to know that when I cross the river my last conscious thoughts will be of The Corps, and The Corps, and The Corps.

Then, blinking away my tears, I will think, really? Your last conscious thought is going to be of the military? C'mon, don't you have a wife? Or children?

I press my cheek against the blue hospital wall. I am falling, swirling down. The vertigo of a heavy snowstorm, when you can't tell if your skis are stopped or still sliding. I can't say exactly what lies ahead, in what situations I will need to tap Barrett's strength. But I know that we will have to advocate for Niko, make sure he is not left in the hall on a stretcher, ensure that the many different medical opinions are integrated appropriately. I sense I will have to be ever on guard here. And I am right. After Barrett leaves I will begin my solitary sentry duty: jumping up at the nurse's approach at midnight and 4:00 a.m., convincing her she doesn't have to wake him up in the middle of the night to take his temperature, or pinch his toe with the blood pressure monitor. In the morning after fitful sleep beside Niko in his single bed, I will continue my watch. I reason with the different nurses as the shifts change. I simper. I cajole. Anything to get them to flush the IV slowly so he doesn't cry out in pain.

I don't argue with Barrett. I know what he will say. C'mon, this is nothing, we have to be strong. Barrett's classmate Matt has just found out he will be pulled out of the War College to be sent to Afghanistan right after Christmas. Now *that's* hard. On short notice, to let your husband leave for a year. This is nothing to complain about. This month, November 2004, will match last April for the month with the highest number of U.S. service members killed in Iraq since the invasion began. It could be so much worse. There are soldiers dying. Families whose Daddy isn't coming back. Ever. This is no big deal, compared to that. He'll just be two hours away.

I don't know how to say, "Please, I know all that, but I'm tired of being strong. I need to feel you at my side." I can't ask him because I'm afraid he'll say no. And that would mean something I can't face up to right now. It would mean he has let me down.

When we were first dating, Barrett and I used to playfully argue about his desire to open the door for me, or pull out my chair, or build the fire. When I told him that I was perfectly capable of doing those things myself, he'd answered, "I know that. It's just that I want to do the hard things for you." And I had stopped for a moment, cocking my head as I thought about his reply. There was something so sweet and noble about his desire; it made my protestations seem churlish. Somewhere around that same time, Barrett dubbed me "Scrumpshkin," and then, to show the depths of his feelings for me, he recast MacArthur's rallying points into a more intimate code of "Duty, Honor, Scrumpshkin."

"No, no," I laughingly corrected him. "I prefer 'Scrumpshkin, Duty, Honor.'"

Now I say nothing, and stare over at Niko asleep in the hospital bed, attached to myriad tubes. Some part of me realizes that there is a little hard sharp-edged thing—a sliver—wedging its way into a tender place in my heart. But I don't know how to get it out.

.

On a cold March morning, tired of my house, tired of the cold, tired of being tired, I strap on my CamelBak and head for the frozen trails of the post's golf course. I trudge through the gray landscape, longing for spring. Niko got out of the hospital after nine long days, a remarkable recovery. Returning to Carlisle with that saggy feeling of relief that comes after an adrenaline rush dissipates, I realized that Christmas marked the halfway point of our year at the War College. Barrett and I started making plans for life after we move back home. We decided that if he gets command of a brigade after the War College, then he will minimize his hours at the police so we can have more time together: time to fix up our house, to work on adopting a child, to just relax and be together.

In January, Barrett's colleague Matt left for Afghanistan and I began pursuing adoption. Barrett and I decided to focus on Guatemala because I speak Spanish and feel somewhat familiar with Central American culture. Then, in February, a few days after our social worker's first visit for the home study, I stood in our bathroom with the peeling linoleum and the dirty grout, staring at a home pregnancy test. After I saw the second pink line, I was oddly depressed. I missed imagining our blond son holding hands with his adopted Hispanic sister. Seeing them laughing, sharing childhood secrets. And I was ashamed of my grief. I should be grateful, elated to have a baby of my own.

Hoot-hoot-hoot interrupts my reverie. *Hoot—hoot—hooaw.* I look up and see a barred owl, maybe twenty feet from me, on a branch of a near tree. We stare at each other for a long time. When I walk on, I feel lucky, like I have been chosen. I walk a little faster. Rolling from heel to toe, I spring into the next step. Vitality flows through my body, my arms swinging back and forth, carrying me forward. But suddenly I stop, spooked. Wait a minute. I'm not struggling against a pulling tide. I don't weigh three hundred pounds. I feel better. Feeling better is bad. The sicker I feel the better the chance of carrying the baby to term. Oh, God. Oh, shit.

I'm going to lose the baby.

• • •

Barrett and I, along with other seminar members, take care of Matt's wife Sylvie and their children while he is gone. We stop by to mow the lawn. In the mornings when it has snowed, we call to lend a hand with shoveling the walk. I gather up donations from the spouses in our seminar to get Sylvie a gift certificate for a massage, and I stop by from time to time for tea and a chat. With Sylvie I discover it doesn't matter that we have not known each other long or that we have different worldviews. Her husband is in a war zone and she needs support. I learn what it means to be bonded by shared adversity and shared mission. This is something I have never really experienced, never having belonged to a big family, or a church, or any other large social organization. This is the first time I've felt this sense of connection that transcends value systems, and it's at the *Army War College*, of all places.

It turns out Sylvie is also checking up on me. One day, on the way back from lunch, as she maneuvers her tidy minivan expertly through the roadblocks and up to the security gate, I tell her that my human growth hormone count didn't go up at all, when it should have doubled. "It looks bad," I say.

"Don't give up yet. You don't know for sure."

"I think I do."

Sylvie drops a hand from the wheel to touch mine. "Have faith. Leave it up to God," she says gently.

A few weeks later I miscarry. Soon after Sylvie invites me out antique shopping and I buy a beautiful wrought-iron garden chair to grow vines through. Sylvie asks if I would mind if she started attending the meetings of the spouse leaders, something that is my duty as the seminar chair's wife. She broaches the subject cautiously, looking at me intently, and I realize she wants to make sure she is not usurping my status in any way. The truth is I have forgotten to attend the last several meetings and her offer is a relief.

My thoughts are not on spouse meetings. The first miscarriage was a searing pain; this one is more a dull ache. Akin to the war in Iraq, which drags on like the northeast winter: hopeless, neverending. Proud Iraqis with blue voting smudges on their thumbs are false harbingers of spring. While even Barrett is now very critical of Bush, he still admires his "resolve." My cousin Georgie goes even further, saying, "We know he won't abandon us. We know he's morally in the fight."

For many nights I talk to Barrett about the empty feeling in my body. My sense of physical void. Many nights he holds my hand and listens. But there is distraction in his manner, a growing impatience. Then one night, as our time in Carlisle draws to a close and the packers and movers are on their way again, he is silent for a long time. It is June, just after General Abizaid publicly concedes that the insurgency is as strong as it was six months prior. Barrett says softly, "C'mon now, hon, isn't it time to move on? It's getting too hard for me to watch. I know it's sad, I am sad too, but I just drive on. That way I don't feel it as much. Please. I don't want to feel it so much. Can't we just drive on?"

Wearing a knit cap and a fleece sweatshirt along with my shorts and sneakers, I make my way to an aerobics class at the YMCA a couple blocks from our house. We are back in California; finally, we are home. No more of the stifling noonday heat of central Pennsylvania in summer. No soft green late-afternoon light. California is brighter and brasher, the ocean colder, the mountains bigger, and the sky bluer.

My hometown is made up of unpretentious little houses, homes built for the workers at the Richmond Shipyards during the Second World War. It's ironic that my neighborhood, adjacent to Berkeley, an area where people like to pretend that war doesn't exist, was born out of the struggle to win the Second World War. Of course, that was such a different war: everyone was impacted by it, not just a minority of soldiers and their families.

Shortly after we got home, Barrett took command of a Reserve brigade. At the change-of-command ceremony, the commanding general began with an elaborate explanation of how we really didn't lose the Vietnam War. In retrospect, he boomed, we can see that Vietnam was the beginning of the end of Communism. Our soldiers did not die in vain there, he cried. They were really victorious; we just couldn't see it at the time. I wondered if that would make people who lost a loved one feel any better. And then I wondered about the implication that it is only through victory that the troops earn our appreciation. The general went on to call Barrett an outstanding warrior, the first person he'd want by his side in battle. We must show resolve in the conflict in Iraq, he said, we must persevere. Gamely trying to capture a British accent despite his pronounced southern twang, he imitated Winston Churchill: "Nevah give up!" he cried. "Nevah! Nevah! Nevah!"

Unlike the smooth rolling lawns of the East, here each house is cramped up next to its neighbor, the small house and yard—a tiny canvas—framed with a fence. They are painted an array of colors: terracotta, olive, pale yellow, burgundy, misty green, sea blue, usually with two or three contrasting accents on the windows and doors. And they are small, mostly two bedrooms and one bath. Many are somewhat dilapidated, but others are obviously well loved. The latter might have a rain chain of copper fish or flowers that guide the rainwater downward or a front-stoop bench sculpted out of old metal. Many have gaily colored Tibetan prayer flags streaming, or pots overflowing with succulents. They have signs of active lives—kids' bikes tossed over in small front yards, piles of shoes visible on front porches—all amid California poppies, climbing roses, and ornamental grasses.

On a recent walk together, Barrett asked about the adoption progress. "What about the INS approval? How is that coming?"

I told him I needed to get yet another set of fingerprints because of my college protest arrests. It will delay us another four weeks at least. That my medical form certifying I was "free of communicable diseases" was delayed because I once had genital warts.

Barrett said, "So we'll wait four weeks."

I began to shake. Wrapping my jacket's lapels tightly across my chest, I tried to joke. "Yeah, I guess it takes a little longer when you're promiscuous and a criminal."

Barrett reached for my hand. "We will have another child, babe, I promise you."

"Am I a bad person?" I mumbled, my vision clouding, I have long held the barely conscious belief that if something bad happens to me, I must have caused it somewhere along the way, by my own behavior. It can be helpful when you are looking forward, hoping to change a person or the world, but at that moment I was caught in a backhanded twist of this logic. I was responsible somehow for this latest obstacle. "Do I not deserve another child?"

Barrett took a deep breath. "Honey, we just have to keep marching. We just won't stop until we reach the objective. Do I need to recite the Ranger creed? 'Readily will I display the intestinal fortitude required to fight on to the Ranger objective and complete the mission, though I be the lone survivor'?"

Now I pass the elementary school where Niko will start kindergarten in another year. After walking north half a block, I round the corner and turn down the main street of our town. Colorful banners hang from faux-antique streetlights, advertising our yearly street fair. Since I have owned my house for thirteen years now—ever since my father died—this is a walk I could do in my sleep. Everything is pretty much the same as when we left a year ago. When we got back home, one of the first things we did was stand Niko against the spot on his wall where we mark his height, to see how much he'd grown. Almost two inches this past year. And what about me? What have I to show for my year? Have I made progress, gained any territory on the map of my dreams?

Before Carlisle and after Carlisle, everything here is the same. And yet I see it differently. I note the "Code Pink" T-shirt my neighbor wears ("pink-slip Bush!") or the "Bring the troops home now!" bumper sticker of a passing hybrid car, and I'm surprised to find there is something other than pure relief in my gut. I do feel relief, but I also feel little pricks of resentment. You don't know what it's like, I think. It's so easy for you to say, you there in the sunshine sipping your latte. I bet you don't know a single person who is serving in the military. Or you, making reservations on your cell phone for dinner at the latest trendy place. You have no idea what it's like to take care of your family while your spouse is in harm's way. Your opinion's all air. It's got no weight.

I've arrived at my old gym. Same equipment, same smell of sweat and mold. I hand my membership card over. Same card, same receptionist. Here at home I often find myself thinking of Sylvie, remembering the farewell luncheon at which I presented Sylvie with an Army War College ornament in front of our group of spouses. I started to cry, realizing she had seen my despair; I didn't think anyone had noticed. But she had, and she quietly tried to ease my burden.

In the gym, I pull my hair into a ponytail. I am a little bit early.

While stretching and waiting for class to begin, I remember sitting with Barrett in a tapas bar last night. I was excited to be drinking a mojito. You can't get a mojito in Carlisle. Nor are there tapas bars, or any restaurant for that matter, with burgundy walls and a black ceiling, where sparkly pendant lights spill off the black clothes and goatees of the patrons. I was enjoying myself, taking in the tattoos, when Barrett said that the new police chief wanted Barrett to be his chief of staff.

"And you told him no, right?" I said, my mouth full of Chioggia beets and goat cheese. I reminded Barrett that we've agreed on a plan in which he lies low at the police. Remember the plan?

He said he was afraid to pass this up. It was an opportunity to do something with his War College education, to be a leader at the police department, to do something for the rank and file.

I swallowed hard, not tasting my food. "But what about more time with me and Niko? What about getting the house ready for another child?"

Barrett said, "I'll just have to limit what I do at work. I'll just have to be really efficient."

The aerobics instructor, dressed in flowing sparkling pants and a short halter top, announces that this is a new class called Nia. Something tells me this class would never be given at the Army War College, as loud whooshy music swirls, and the teacher encourages us to touch earth then sky. We are weightless in the sky, we are flying, she says, can we feel it? Our feet are like hands massaging, connecting with the earth, can we feel it? She tells us to shepherd our intuition. She extols the joy of movement. She exaggerates her exhalations into the microphone: *HeeAAAH, HeeAAAH.*

I remember how at the tapas bar, I wanted to scream at Barrett, "No!" There were words in my mouth, waiting to be spoken. I could hear them in my head. "I love you, Barrett, but you are breaking me. I love you but I don't want this." I could feel my lips touching each other, forming the sounds. But something stopped me. Old patterns, old fears that if I ask for what I want I will be abandoned. Fear I will lose him. If I ask him to turn down the job, won't he always resent me for it? Bitterness in my throat. Why did he put me in a position like this? Why did I have to always advocate for the family? Why didn't he want to put us first?

I crossed my arms over my chest, stared at the mint in my mojito. Barrett reached a hand out. "Do you think we could try it? Just
see how it goes? I love you guys, you know that. It's just...it's an
opportunity to make a difference, you know, for the troops."

"Six months," I heard myself say. "Tell the chief you'll try it
for six months."

In class, we are waves, swooping, then breaking. We are cats,
growling, *Raer, raer, raer.* We receive, jutting our hands forward
and scooping into our bellies an imaginary bounty. The music grows
louder and some class members begin to whoop. The instructor is
telling us we must balance strength and flexibility, fortitude and
surrender. We can't be all fortitude, she says, marching around the
room energetically, punching her arms in front of her. We can't
always go go go with no rest. Nor, she says, can we be all surrender.
Here she dangles her arms and her head forward like she is collaps-
ing. If we're all surrender, we'll just become a puddle. We need
both, in balance.

As I swing my hands over my head, graceful and flexible like sea
grass, then swoop my arms down like scythes, I think that my instructor's attitude sure wouldn't go over very well on Capitol Hill.
In just a few months will come the time in the United States Congress where Jack Murtha—a hawkish Democrat, retired Marine,
and decorated Vietnam vet—will call for our withdrawal from Iraq
in a tearful press conference. And Republican congresswoman Jean
Schmidt will respond by parlaying the recent funeral of a young
Marine from her district into an imperative to continue the war,
adding, "Cowards cut and run; Marines never do."

Now send the energy out, the instructor cries. We are punching
now: side, side, front. *I want to hear your voice, HUNH! HUNH! I want
to hear you say No!"*

I feel ridiculous but I allow myself a tentative "hunh." It feels
damn good, and soon I am hammering with my fists and bellowing,
"Hunh! Hunh!" During the final crescendo of sound, the teacher
tells us, *Follow your own bodies, just let it all go, no one is watching, no one is watching, just let it go.* I writhe and whirl while being
careful to avoid the lady near me, who is curled up on the floor in
fetal position.

Let it all go, no one is watching. I close my eyes and let my body follow an internal current. I feel something silver pulsing through my muscles, the glint of sunlight on water. Colors flashing up from the deep and spreading out around my body, through my shoulders and elbows and down my legs to my toes. I hear Sylvie saying leave it up to God. I don't conceive of God the way she does, but she's right about one thing. I can't make sense of it all. I can't make all the painful memories, or even the joyful ones, line up into some perfect story.

Finally I let all the pieces of the past, pieces of me, who I used to be, who I wanted to be, who I am right now, pieces that I have been struggling to corral into line, fall where they may. And the answer I have been waiting for finally arrives, so simple after all these months. The answer is to acknowledge what's been lost. Two times now, the dreams of a little girl or boy who looks like me or has my father's nose or Barrett's mom's voice. All the times that I have been alone, the nights in the hospital with Niko, all the times with Niko that Barrett has missed. Every fleeting smile, every slip and fall, every milestone, so many moments unshared. Lost time with me, his wife, his lover. I don't believe in ignoring that loss. It is real. I can't deny it anymore.

Any more than I can deny the country's loss. The mothers, fathers, sisters, brothers, sons, daughters when the twin towers fell, at the Pentagon, in Pennsylvania. Gone. The opportunity we had after 9-11 to, as Pete Seeger painted on his banjo, "surround hate with love and force it to surrender." Gone. The opportunity after the invasion of Iraq to gain the trust of the Iraqi people. Gone. All the soldiers who have died in Afghanistan and Iraq. The spouses who have lost their partners, the children missing a parent. The untold number of Iraqi civilians who have lost their lives. The Iraqi children. Gone. It's hard to accept, it's easier not to think about it. Or to explain it away as part of some grand plan. Some people would say that to stop and tally the loss, let it register, is some form of defeat.

But it doesn't feel wrong, it doesn't strike me as cowardly to feel it. I don't even know that a hurricane is forming over the Atlantic that will reach land in just a few days and cause shocking devastation. That the help that will come will be too little, too late. That warning signs were ignored, and basic maintenance neglected.

That the most vulnerable people—the hospitalized, the elderly, the young—will be most likely to die. Katrina will feel like a terrible sign of what can happen when we focus on an ill-conceived foreign adventure, and in our desire to justify past losses, forget to take care of things at home. It feels right to cry—in the middle of the gym with basketball hoops that fold up to the ceiling so we can dance. Cry for all that we've lost.

And so I do.

THIRTEEN

Quagmire

Tell me how this ends.

—General David Petraeus, as quoted in
In the Company of Soldiers, by Rick Atkinson

A FEW MONTHS AFTER KATRINA, on Christmas Eve, I put our son to bed and go in search of Barrett. The rain pounds against the roof, and I cringe whenever I think of the excavated area underneath my feet, our half-built basement addition, filling up with brown water. We are waiting for the contractor's workers to come back from Christmas vacation, and for the incessant rain to stop, so they can pour the new basement slab and put in the steel beams to replace the jacks that currently hold our living space up. I've prepared a shot of scotch for Santa, and I look forward to wrapping and arranging the presents with Barrett, then sipping our drinks and nibbling cookies in front of the tree. We've put the Christmas tree in the kitchen this year. That way we don't have to stare at the plywood nailed up where our fireplace used to be, which collapsed when the old foundation was removed. To placate Niko, I wrote a sign, zipped it into a plastic bag, and taped it up securely to the exterior of the plywood patch. "Santa, please use the front door."

Barrett is not in the living room or in his office. Padding back to our bedroom, I find him in the bed asleep, the *Combat Lifesaver Training Guide* open next to him. He is lying on his back, and I gently shake his shoulder, whispering, "C'mon, help me do the presents." He grunts. Barrett has been asked to prepare a task force to train foreign security forces. Up until just yesterday, he was at Fort Hunter-Liggett working with his brigade, trying to whip four hundred Reserve soldiers—dentists, administrators, lawyers, teachers, most of whom can't pitch an army tent, let alone fire their M-16—into shape for a possible deployment. "Some of 'em don't even know how to march! And they're supposed to train the Iraqis?" Barrett exclaimed to me. Last night, I woke up to the sound of Barrett shouting into the darkness, "No, Sergeant Major, these troops! S3, S3, where is the FRAGO? Lower the muzzle. Sergeant Major.... troops...troops...aren't ready...Soldier, lower the muzzle...tourniquet...IV bags...can't find...where.... IV bags!"

When Barrett took over this brigade a few months ago, I drove down to Fort Hunter-Liggett for the change-of-command ceremony. Barrett moved out of the barracks to stay with me in Motel 6–style officers' quarters for the night. I sat on the bed while he unwrapped the plastic from two disposable cups then opened a bottle of wine with his Swiss army knife. After splashing the wine into the cups and handing me mine, he sighed. Then grabbing my hand, he said, "Let's make a run for it, tonight. You and me. Let's drink this and run."

"Yeah, right. You? Go AWOL?"

"What the hell. We could be four hundred miles away by morning." Then he'd laughed. But his eyes were tired.

The last few years have loosened the skin of his face near his ears, brought creases below his eyes where tears might fall if he let them. I feel a familiar struggle between tenderness and resentment. I am proud of Barrett, proud of what a competent and honorable leader he is. But much stronger than my grown-up pride in him is a child inside me who stamps her foot and says, "It's not fair!" Duty is pulling him away from us. With each passing day, he is slowly leaving.

"Babe, wake up," I say halfheartedly. "Time to be Santa with me!"

He rolls on his side and tugs the covers up around his chest.

We get the dregs. If his pager went off or his Blackberry vibrated, he would get up, drag himself out of bed. The army and the police department keep giving him more and more difficult tasks. Why wouldn't they? Because whatever he's asked, he does, and he does everything they ask so well. They use up all his energy, and because I love him and know he needs to rest, I ask him for less and less. And where does that leave me? A few weeks ago, two suicide bombers hit the Baghdad Police Academy, killing thirty-six people and wounding many more. So many people tell me Barrett is just what they need over there. I respond by repeating what Barrett tells me: Barrett is infantry, not military police; the army is too bureaucratic to realize Barrett's civilian job skills. But I feel in the ache of my shoulders, in the dead weight of my limbs, a dull certainty. He is going. That's where this is all leading. It is inevitable. I could cry about it, but I'm getting tired of crying. Like the catharsis in Nia class a few months back, I've learned that acknowledging loss helps me make peace with the past, but it doesn't tell me how to move forward.

Mechanically, I wrap the last presents alone. To set the scene for the morning, I pour half the scotch down the drain and bite a cookie, dry in my mouth.

On the fourth day of rain after Christmas, our foreman calls. His voice cracking, he tells me that our contractor has taken his own life. It turns out that months ago a big customer stopped paying, and for weeks our contractor was using money from the paying jobs like ours to try to cover his supply bills. But he couldn't keep it up.

For a few days I am numb. Then I can't think of anything else. I know this man's tragedy is far greater than mine, and yet my sympathy for him is quickly overwhelmed by the desperateness of my own situation. I try to pinpoint the exact point where our renovation went wrong, where one of my actions might have contributed to the disaster. I picked the wrong contractor, clearly, but was there any way of knowing? I read back over the references he gave. They were glowing. I go over my decisions in detail trying to find my misstep. I hired an engineer who was recommended. He did a preliminary drawing and recommended several other contractors. I met with them. I got bids from all of them. I got references.

It wasn't anything I did wrong. Except maybe...I feel a tender thought lingering in the back of my consciousness. What is it? I review my thoughts, palpating for the bruise. And I find this thought: it's because I was so alone. It's because I had to do it all by myself. It's not that I made the wrong decision anywhere, it's just that I didn't know how to read the warning signs. I didn't have the broader base of knowledge, another person's take—that Barrett's involvement would have allowed. I remember again the numerous times the various engineers and contractors and city officials asked if my husband would be part of a meeting or decision. "No," I'd said over and over, my brain slipping down a familiar groove, "he's too busy. I'll handle it."

As winter turns to spring, I trudge forward. A friend who works in construction comes and adds additional jacks under the house, attaches firefighter-style hoses to large temporary pumps to carry the water from under our house out to the street. The only way to keep despair from pulling me under is to shut everything out. I see only my list of things to do: find a new architect, revise structural engineering, resubmit for permits, hire a concrete guy, hire a plumber. . . . I put one foot in front of the other, mechanically responding to each new crisis as it comes. I know that if I stop, I will go under.

Meanwhile congressional reports show that despite spending billions on rebuilding Iraq's basic infrastructure—drinking water, electricity, sewage service, all the most basic elements of civilized life—we cannot bring the country up to prewar levels. Insurgents regularly bomb what we have just rebuilt. And it doesn't help that corruption is rampant. "Bricks"—shrink-wrapped packages of hundred-dollar bills—have been found stuffed in footlockers and file cabinets around Iraq.

There is no dramatic moment when it becomes certain that Barrett will be deployed, no tearful conversations, apologies, pep talks. It all happens incrementally and inexorably. But in April 2006—a month when the morgue in Baghdad tallies 1,091 bodies—it surprises no one that Barrett is named commander of the task force going to Iraq. He will leave in January 2007, train in Fort Riley, Kansas, for three months, then go for a year to Baghdad in April 2007. He will leave us for fifteen months.

As I sink under the weight of the construction project, I watch Barrett gear up. He is marshaling resources, planning, training, getting ready to go away. One of his responsibilities is dealing with Reserve soldiers who don't want to go: the father reluctant to leave his troubled teenage son, the mother with young children, the husband with the depressed wife. I tell Barrett he is too hard on these people. They just love their families. They are just putting them first. Can't he understand that? In response Barrett's voice gets hard with contempt. "That's a reason to shirk their duty?" And I wonder if we are really talking about other soldiers, or talking about us.

One typical Bay Area June evening, cold and foggy, I ask Barrett to watch Niko while I head out back, avoiding the muck by treading along a makeshift path of pavers. I round the back of the house to get to the lean-to that is my temporary laundry room, so I can switch the laundry. Returning with a basket of clean clothes, I hear Niko crying. I run up the back steps and into the house, dropping the laundry aside. The wails are getting sharper. Niko is in the bathroom, curled into a ball, holding his knee. Grabbing him under the armpits, I sit on the toilet and pull him into my arms. "Baby, what happened? Let it out now, try to breathe, where does it hurt?" He is wailing and can't explain. I can only surmise he fell against the hard ceramic of the tub. When he has quieted, I take his hand and walk into Barrett's office.

I stand in the doorway holding my son's hand, Niko and I on one side of the threshold, Barrett on the other. I think to myself that Barrett is halfway out the door already. We're second string. Second fiddle. Second in his heart. Second, second, second. "Barrett," I say. Without inflection, without a question mark, just a statement of fact: "Barrett."

He is sitting on our blue couch with the Bluetooth piece at his ear. He looks up at me, puts a finger to the earpiece, and says without pausing, "Okay, gotta go. Over and out here. Maw, I'm sorry. I'm sorry, but something big is going on. I had to—"

"Niko was hurt. Didn't you hear him?"

"I know, but—it's just that, someone at the brigade, one of my guys—"

"Your son was crying. Your son was hurt."

"One of my guys has *cancer.* He just found out. I had to—"

"Your son!" I shout. "*Your son!* You didn't even get up to look!"

"I know, but—"

"I don't care, Barrett! Stop. Just stop. Can we be part of the brigade, Barrett? *Then* would you pay attention *to us?* All you think about is the brigade. I don't want to hear it anymore. Because I don't...I don't fucking care."

I turn on my heel and walk out of the room, still holding Niko's hand. I close the French doors behind us. This is not the way marriage is supposed to be. This is not why I married Barrett, someone I could depend on, someone who would not let me down.

I stare ahead of me, at the plywood nailed up where our fireplace used to be. I can feel the cold air seeping through the cracks. We have no heat; the furnace is sitting outside in the rain, strips of insulation hanging off of it. *The military keeps taking more and more. Eventually there is going to be nothing left.* I remember the night the fireplace collapsed, the pouring rain outside. At first we thought it was an earthquake, the whole house shuddering as the bricks tumbled into the driveway. I ran to the living room, then stopped, stared. I couldn't understand why my neighbor's bushes were visible from my living room. Then I realized the hole was above the hearth, where the fireplace used to be. I stepped toward the vacant space, hoping to do something, fix something. But the more I approached, the more the plaster around the hole split open, tributaries cracking, spreading in all directions.

FOURTEEN

Hearts and Minds

*[O]nce the realization is accepted that even between the
closest people infinite distances exist, a marvelous living
side-by-side can grow up for them, if they succeed in loving
the expanse between them, which gives them the possibility
of always seeing each other as a whole and before an
immense sky.*

—Rainer Maria Rilke, from *Letters,* in
Into the Garden, by Robert Hass and Stephen Mitchell

BARRETT AND I TRACE THE ROUTE on a map to a bleak part
of Oakland. Over the past few weeks, since our argument over
the brigade, we have reached a détente. I am wary, as I imagine a
wife might act after her husband has had an affair, watchful for
signs of his greater love for the military. I look at him and wonder,
what is he thinking about now—them or us? He tries to placate.
When he has unexpected military duties, he tries to sandwich the
unwelcome news between announcements of family activities he
can attend. Like today, he'd said, "I can pick up Niko from school,
then I have to go visit the family of that injured soldier, but I'll be
home in time for dinner."

"I'll go with you," I'd said suddenly, surprising myself.

"You don't have to," Barrett said.

"I'll go. Maybe I can help with my Spanish."

He'd nodded and I'd put on my coat. Wordlessly, he'd handed
me my umbrella. Once we were in his truck and on the freeway,
I stared out the window and said, "But please, Barrett. You know
I can't say that bullshit about how their sacrifice has furthered the
cause of freedom."

"Don't worry," he said grimly, "that's my job."

Our destination is a drab two-story concrete apartment building surrounded by a concrete parking lot. Where the downspouts spill out, puddles darken the corners of the building. There is no vegetation, not even a potted plant. A door is open to a lower-level unit, and we approach it and peer in. About ten members of what I assume is the extended family are gathered in a virtually unfurnished living room, a few folding chairs on a tan wall-to-wall carpet. We stand awkwardly in the doorway. A stout gray-haired man finally notices us and steers a young woman dressed in gray sweatpants and sweatshirt around to look at us. She is just starting to show her pregnancy. "This is Mariela. His wife," he offers in a heavy Mexican accent.

The other people don't introduce themselves or approach us. I smile and say, "Hola, mucho gusto" to Mariela, then turn to another young woman—who appears to be Mariela's sister—and present the Starbucks coffeecake we have brought. She motions us toward two folding chairs, then serves the cake to us—and no one else.

Our job is not to bring information. The family already knows Daniel was hit by an IED and lost both legs two days ago. At least we don't have to notify them of that. Although Barrett would do it. He wouldn't hesitate; he would do whatever he had to. And I guess I would go along, but not with the same resolve, not with the same strength. But they already know that Daniel is in a hospital in Ramstein, Germany, and that he will likely be brought to Walter Reed when his condition stabilizes.

With no place to put his napkin and cake, Barrett finally sets them on the floor. He clears his throat and asks if there is a family member who could translate to the young Spanish-speaking wife. The sister who served us the cake steps forward. Barrett stands up and takes off his beret and places it on the chair behind him. He says, "I want you to know I thank you for your husband's service. When the country called, he answered."

I close my eyes for a moment, trying to summon up some image to help me through this moment. When I open my eyes, there is Barrett, looking the young wife right in her eyes as he speaks, even though he knows she doesn't really understand him. I realize this moment is critical to whether this family will feel understood and acknowledged, or swept aside and forgotten. Or is that inevitable?

Barrett never met the injured soldier; he was "cross-leveled" (lent to another unit) from the brigade before Barrett took over. Barrett pauses to nod briefly to the sister for the translation, but immediately returns his full attention to Mariela. Somebody's cell phone sounds. Barrett doesn't flinch. He doesn't look away. He looks right at her, unwavering.

Mariela looks at the floor.

Barrett says, "Daniel put his life on the line for his country, for all of us. I want you to know I, for one, will never forget him."

I'm sure many commanders would tell the family that there was a reason for their son's permanent injury, that it was "worth" it because it protected our country and brought freedom to the Iraqi people. I'm glad Barrett doesn't say that. I realize for some families that idea is a source of great comfort, but I think it is a double-edged sword. I think if it rings false, it will engender deep feelings of betrayal.

"On behalf of myself," Barrett finishes, "the United States Army, and the American people, I thank you for your service and for your sacrifice."

Watching Barrett, I feel a wave of simultaneous grief for this family and pride in his courage, and I have to push down tears. He is doing everything right. And yet, I wonder how Barrett and I look to this family, the white colonel from the other side of the tracks and his tall wife. What do we know of their grief? Daniel is twenty-three years old, his wife barely twenty-one. She got pregnant while he was on leave a few months ago. They are so young, still waiting for their lives together to begin. And now this. Now their whole world has changed. Although underneath the shock and sadness, I also feel in the room an undercurrent of relief. At least he is alive.

What Barrett is here to do, while it can't reverse the loss this family has sustained, while it is intangible, is not insignificant. We offer what we can: acknowledgment. And embedded within our acknowledgment is the undeniable fact that this trauma could happen to my family, too. Like Mariela, I am expecting a baby, mine an adopted little girl. Barrett and I were recently "matched" with our daughter, which means the legal proceeding began in Guatemala while she lives with a foster family. We have a photo of her, looking serenely up at the camera. I know something may happen to Barrett in Iraq; and our daughter may never know him as our son does.

But for Daniel's family and the other families—who've lost their loved ones, or have had to contend with their physical and psychological injuries—what does a mere acknowledgement provide? It is natural to seek a deeper, higher meaning to explain the harm done. God, let there be a reason, a very important reason, for this to have happened.

Many Americans tell the story this way: the death of and injury to soldiers in Iraq is the high price of freedom. Our soldiers are to be lauded because they are willing to put their lives on the line for our country, and when they make the ultimate sacrifice, the family can take comfort in the fact that their family member is an American hero. But many others, people who sympathize with Cindy Sheehan and Gold Star Families for Peace, are moved by the death of American soldiers into decrying the war. They don't feel comforted by the hero label; in fact, they find it manipulative. They believe the soldiers didn't die for a good reason, and that we must stop this pointless war. Each of these two sides finds the other story a betrayal. They feel the other side diminishes or dishonors the enormity of their grief. And so as a nation, we are locked in a bitter battle over how to make meaning of our loss.

I translate for Daniel's mom what Barrett said to her daughter-in-law. I promise to help round up some winter coats for the family's imminent trip to Walter Reed. She tells me that on the phone this morning, Daniel told her *que soñó con ella*, she was in his dream last night. In Spanish they say I dreamt "with" you, instead of I dreamt "of" you. She tells me with a slight smile that Daniel said to hurry up and come meet him at Walter Reed, that he wanted her to bring some of his favorite tamales.

I picture Niko when he is older, and imagine hearing that he has lost his legs. I think I would surely start a crusade of my own, to somehow make meaning of the loss. Months later, when Barrett has already left, I will go to a retreat with returning soldiers and their families, and I will see parents walking on either side, steadying their sons who are struggling with traumatic brain injuries. I'll see a female colonel break down when she confides that she has seen her husband through two tours to Iraq, but now the Marines want her nineteen-year-old son, a brand-new lieutenant, to go. She will say quietly, her cheeks glimmering with tears, "I'm just not sure anymore. . . . I'm just not sure."

When I meet Daniel's mom, something falls into place for me, and I realize why Barrett feels he has to go. It's because he can't look at Daniel's mom and all the moms like her and say, "I'm sorry, Sophia and Niko and Gabriela need me at home," when her son, *her child*, is going into harm's way.

When we say good-bye to Daniel's relatives, it is hard to catch people's eyes. I write down our e-mail addresses and our cell phone numbers. "Let us know if you need anything." Outside, I pause under the overhang to open my umbrella, the metal security door against my back. Barrett doesn't stop; it is against regulations for army officers to carry umbrellas while in uniform. With a click and a swish mine unfurls, a temporary shelter against the rain. Then I look up and see Barrett out in the parking lot. He is holding open the passenger door to the truck, staring blankly ahead, the rain pelting his beret and shoulders.

It's 9:30. I am perched on the side of the hotel room bed, beginning to sweat. The baby won't be used to air-conditioning so we are trying not to use ours. Barrett, Niko, and I are at the Guatemala City Marriott, a hotel that caters to business travelers, but even more, to adoptive parents. They rent out strollers at the concierge. They have set up a special "parents' lounge," equipped with a rocking chair and toys and a bottle warmer. I stand up, walk to the mirror, rearrange my necklace, sit back down. Looking through my backpack, I finger my U.S. passport. Barrett keeps his own passport as well as Niko's and the baby's new Guatemalan one. Everything in order. I rearrange the brightly wrapped packages, gifts for the foster family. Picking up the multicolored toy horse for the baby, I press its saddle, listen to its cheerful neigh.

In the elevator, we let Niko press all the buttons. The lobby is large and cool and dim, with many different seating areas. In the few days we have been here, we have seen several other Americans seated in the lobby with foster families. Most of the couples or single moms are just coming to visit the children, and everyone's eyes widen with excitement when we tell them we will be taking our daughter home. I feel odd currents of emotion that start in my chest and ripple out toward my arms and legs, leaving me shaky. Bubbly excitement combines with a jagged fear that makes my breath come in little sips. When the elevator door opens, Niko sprints out and around a large potted plant. Barrett squeezes my hand, then gives chase. "Niko, come back here!"

I scan the various knots of people, trying to make out our agency liaison, a tall red-haired Guatemalan lady who has guided us through our various embassy appointments to get Gabriela's final visa. Having corralled Niko, Barrett waits for me at the foot of a grand stairway leading to the banquet rooms. As I pass them, I pull at Barrett's shirtsleeve, crying, "There they are!" I start to jog and then slow down, suddenly shy as I approach. "Oh, my God, there she is!" I recognize our baby from the photos. She has dark eyes, so dark you can't tell if they are a deep brown or black. A perfect pert little nose. Her short black hair is like a cap, emphasizing her round cheeks, as does the stretchy pink ribbon, like a garter belt, that she wears around her head. She is calm, nonchalant, and sits up high in her foster mom's arms, playing with her hair. The intimacy of this gesture knifes through me. She has no idea her life is about to change irrevocably, as is mine.

I smile quickly at Yolanda, the foster mom, whom I recognize from photos, then turn my gaze to the baby. "Nenita," I say softly. "Hola, bebe." I stroke the baby's arm. Then I smile again at Yolanda, who comes barely to my chin, and introduce myself in Spanish. Baby Gabriela is alert, curious, yet shy. I start to reach my arms out to her, then remember the advice of the bonding experts. I ask Yolanda in Spanish, "Could you please hand her to me?"

The baby doesn't cry when Yolanda gives her to me. Niko is bouncing up and down at my side. "Let me hold her! Let me hold her!" and suddenly everyone is talking; the men are shaking hands. Yolanda and I are hugging and laughing and crying at the same time. The baby sees the colorful beads of my necklace and reaches toward them. I hold her close, breathing in her scent, sunshine on wood. Then I remember the gifts we have for the foster family: chocolates and a necklace to match mine for Yolanda. Awkwardly, while still holding the baby, I reach into my backpack and take them out for her. I show Gabriela the toy horse, giddyup it along her leg, as Yolanda opens the gift and puts the necklace on. I tell her I gave her one like mine because we are sisters now, and she wipes her eyes.

We sit and chat for about ten minutes. I feel desperate to know everything about the baby and focus mostly on Yolanda and of course Gabriela, who is now pulling quite intently at my necklace. Niko asks every few minutes if he can hold the baby, and when I tell him no, he leans in and kisses her, or tickles her and laughs. Yolanda tells me the baby's eating and sleeping and bathing routine, and gives me back the disposable camera I sent her along with some baby clothes. Then, as the conversation falters, we sit with smiles lingering on our faces, even Niko surprisingly still in Barrett's lap. The midmorning light streams in through a window. Suddenly I feel very tired.

The liaison lady gives a cheerful smile, pats her thighs, and stands up, signaling that it is time to say good-bye. When I hug Yolanda, I murmur gracias over and over. Barrett snaps a photo: I have my arm around Yolanda, and she has her arm around both me and Gabriela. We are wearing our matching necklaces and crying. Afterward, Yolanda whispers, "Portate bien" (Be good) to Gabriela, then puts her handkerchief to her eyes. She leans against her husband as they walk toward the door. Just as the automatic doors open, the mom turns and calls out to me in Spanish, "She loves music!" We watch as the doors close behind them and they get into a beat-up blue Toyota truck. And then they are gone.

Later, back in our suite, I can't get the baby to sleep. She doesn't cry, but she is alert, watchful. She has had her bottle. She didn't eat much of the rice cereal we brought, but she loves the apricot baby food. She watches as Niko cavorts around the room, putting his swimsuit on, looking for his goggles. She surveys the scene as if she is trying to figure out what to make of it. She doesn't seem scared, really, but neither is she relaxed.

I can get her to settle in my arms, and even drift off, but she wakes immediately whenever I try to transfer her to the crib. I sigh. Barrett says, "You want me to try?"

I laugh at the notion that he will do any better, but am glad to take a break. Passing Gabriela to Barrett, I start to get my swim stuff together to go to the pool with Niko.

When we come back an hour later, Barrett is sprawled out on the bed, reading *Terror in Breslan*. "You were able to do it?" I ask. "You got her to go down in the crib?"

Barrett yawns. "Yeah, I just went real, real slow and she was fine. Been sleeping nearly forty-five minutes now."

The next thing I notice happens that afternoon. It is the first time we hear Gabriela laugh, her eyes widening and her little nose crinkling up: Barrett is making animal sounds while showing her a book. "Oink, oink," he says, and a dimple reveals itself across her upper left cheek. As our first days together pass, she slowly relaxes, slowly lets go of her guarded, watchful quality. But she seems most comfortable, most at home, when she is with Barrett.

On our last night in Guatemala, Barrett holds up one of Gabriela's hands in his own. "Look at her fingers," he says. "Aren't they amazing? Look at how long they are." He has the baby in his lap and is starting to rock her to sleep. Niko is sitting on the big bed watching a video while I pack our things. We leave tomorrow for home. Home, where construction should finally restart soon, after eight months of turmoil.

I look over at the baby's hands and it's true. Her fingers are remarkably slender and lean. "They are lovely," I say. "Maybe she'll become a pianist."

"Or maybe," he says with an impish grin, "maybe she'll be the first female I've ever met who can handle a .45."

In the background a disc with Latin American folk songs is playing softly, to soothe Gabriela. "Maw Deuce, we did it. Look at us," Barrett whispers. "Look at our beautiful family."

A selection called "Naranja Dulce" is playing. It is a nursery rhyme in Spanish, set to the beat of a march. Barrett doesn't understand Spanish, but I do:

> *Sweet orange, a slice of lemon*
> *Give me the hug I ask of you*
> *If they were false, my promises to you*
> *In other times, we'll all forget*

> *The march is playing*
> *My breast is weeping*
> *Good-bye, my lady,*
> *It's time I go.*

• • •

Two months later, Barrett and I sit with our kids on a log outside our cabin at Stanford Family Camp, "camp" thankfully being a euphemism at Stanford. The cabins, wedged onto the edge of Fallen Leaf Lake, have plumbing, electricity, and views of the lake and Angora Peak. Barrett is clad in a T-shirt, shorts, black socks, and army boots, his black combat pack in the dust next to the log. He and I just got back from a hike, a scramble, really, straight up the mountain trail behind the camp. We lost track of time and on our way back, half ran, half slid through the scree to get to the children's program in time. As Barrett pulled ahead of me, I called, "It'll be okay, they'll wait for us," but he kept going. By the time I stumbled, panting, into camp, he had Gabriela in her stroller and Niko beside him.

I bounce Gabriela in my lap while Niko looks for pinecones. The sun is warm on our backs, and in the stillness, we can hear the Jeffrey pines creaking in the breeze. Even though I am grateful that construction has finally begun again on our house, it is a pleasure to forget about it for a week. Away from all-day meetings, away from e-mail and the cell phone, the clipped-word, tense-lipped commander is sliding off Barrett, and underneath I can see the goofy, boyish man I married.

Next year he will not be here at camp. He will be in Iraq. And the year after that? Will he be back? Barrett chides me for constantly thinking about it, says I am driving myself crazy. He says of course he's scared, too, scared of dying a gruesome death, scared of dishonoring himself somehow. But he learned back in Ranger school that when you have to jump out of an airplane, you don't think about it every second for all the hours preceding it. You put it out of your mind until right before. Then you just jump.

They say this war in Iraq is particularly psychologically damaging to soldiers because the front is everywhere. There is no safe place. They can never be sure who is the enemy. I can relate. Because I fight a war in my mind 24/7. I fight to keep calm, to tell myself I can do this. I fight not to think about it. Courage for me is pretending I'm not falling apart.

In the afternoon, with the kids busy with their counselors, we lie on the bed in our cabin, the lake lapping outside. Barrett's thighs are still sore from the downhill run so we've opted for relaxation this afternoon. The grabby nylon of the comforter catches on the ridges of dry skin on my fingers. This is so unusual, we are almost awkward: alone together in a quiet place with nothing urgent to do. We lie next to each other, flipping through our respective books. I have been waiting for a moment like this, but now that it has come I am afraid to start.

"Barrett," I finally begin, "I want to talk about how it's going to be—" I stumble, stop before I say the word "if," "—how it's going to be *when* you get back."

"What do you mean?"

I tell him my fears. For fifteen months I won't be at his side, to insist on the breaks from time to time, the outings to the beach, the dinners together, the picnics. I won't be there to make sure we weave our lives together. I'll be left in Berkeley surrounded by people who know nothing of the military experience. Meanwhile he's going to go fully into the mode of army, army, army, all the time. I'm afraid we will spin out into separate worlds.

After I have spoken I am surprised to find I feel stronger. There is a trill of fear, too, as I wait to hear his response, but overall it makes me feel both more solid and more free to declare my fears. I used to think speaking them aloud would force us to a breaking point. But now I realize it doesn't work that way. It's okay to say what you fear and what you want without guarantee of results. It is powerful, somehow, just to put your hopes and worries calmly into words. It's definitely better than not saying it, holding it in, and being angry at your partner for not understanding.

I lean on my elbow to look at him. I tell him the predeployment family trainings emphasize one thing: your partner will come home changed. And the spouse at home will change, too. They can't say exactly how, but we will both be different. So will there be an *us* after all the months apart? I point out that I've been in a tug-of-war with the military over Barrett McAllister. "I'm afraid the military will win. I mean…completely…" I trail off.

Barrett laughs reflexively: short, mirthless grunts.

"It's not what I want," I say. "I want us to be a family. It's just what I'm afraid of."

Then we are both quiet for a long time. Finally Barrett says softly, "I don't know why it's so hard for me. I do love you guys. You are the reason for everything I do. I love you more than anything, but I guess it's true that family isn't as...well...quite as exciting as work. It started at West Point. I got this feeling there of urgency and accomplishment, of being part of something big, bigger than me. With my father and my brothers, the way we lived after my mom died—geez, I just couldn't wait to get out of there. I know how to be a good soldier, but being a family man—I really don't know *how*."

I take a deep breath and my body fills with cool mountain air and a blend of hope and sadness. I am amazed at how gentle, open communication transforms the differences between Barrett and me. It is not that honestly talking makes us agree or see the world the same way, but somehow it changes the distance between us from something vast, hard, and impenetrable into something softer, something approachable—from a shadowy threat to something tractable. This is the first time he's ever admitted it. The first time he's conceded that he has trouble giving the same kind of intensity to his family as he does to his work.

I tell him my hopes for the future: that he will work less, that he will help the kids with homework, take them biking or fishing or to music classes, teach them to throw a baseball. That he will spend more time with *me*.

He reaches over and strokes my hair. "I want that, too. I really, really do. This is the last big thing," he says firmly. "When I get back, I'm going to find a way to spend more time with you and the kids. You know...you know I'm always loyal to you, don't you?"

On one of the last nights of camp, we arrange with one of the counselors—all friendly Stanford students—to babysit Niko and Gabriela so Barrett and I can go on an Astrocruise on the lake. At dusk, we join other parents on *Boatster*, the camp's well-used pontoon boat with eighteen plastic seats bolted to the deck. Our guides hand out hot chocolate, red wine, and yoga blankets as needed. The mood is festive, like kids let out of school for summer. I wrap myself in a blanket (Barrett declines) and we all chug quietly out to the center of the lake. One of the two guides, a long-haired engineering student, produces a powerful laser pointer to aid with the presentation. The other guide, who sports the fashionable patch of beard Barrett refers to as "chin music," announces he is minoring in classics and will tell us some of the stories behind the constellations. Chin Music points out Vega, the bright star above us, which is part of Lyra the Harp. Angling southward with the laser pointer, he points out Altair, Aquila, and Deneb, the three points of the summer triangle. We see Cygnus the Swan, the Big Dipper, Polaris, the Little Dipper, Draco the Dragon. Around the time we start looking for Cassiopeia, the laser pointer dies. I am getting a little sleepy by the time we get to Arcturus and Alphecca and Corona Borealis (the Northern Crown). The riffles of the water against the side of the boat are rhythmic and I am holding Barrett's hand inside the pocket of his jacket. He has pulled on his black watch cap and allowed me to put our blanket around his shoulders. Chin Music is saying that the Corona Borealis represents a crown given to Ariadne by Theseus on their wedding day. Ariadne fell in love with Theseus because she saw in him the heart of a hero, and she gave him a sword with which to kill the Minotaur and a silken thread to guide him out of the Labyrinth. After his deed is done, Theseus and Ariadne start sailing back to Athens and stop on the island of Naxos where, although the stories vary as to why, all agree Theseus leaves Ariadne behind.

I am not sleepy anymore. My seat is too hard. Ariadne. Abandoned. A thought sneaks up on me, unwelcome: am I a modern-day Ariadne? I think back to a few weeks ago when Barrett and I went back to see our couples' therapist, my fear at his leaving spilling into all our interactions. The situation in Iraq is as bad as it has ever been, sectarian violence reaching gruesome levels, the government itself said to be infiltrated by militia members. Sitting on a floral sofa in the little therapy office, I addressed the air between Barrett and the therapist, told it that when I'd kissed Niko good night the other night, he'd grabbed my arm and pulled me back. He was afraid his Daddy was going to "get dead" over there. Was Daddy going to be okay? he'd asked. I didn't know how to answer. I couldn't look at Barrett and the therapist as I told this story. I just stared in front of me, saying my son wanted to know if his daddy was ever coming back. Please, tell me, I asked: what was I supposed to say?

Barrett and the therapist answered in unison. "You say yes."

A fish flops. The lights across the lake bleed yellow across the water. I look up at the black bowl above me, dotted with points of light. We have been waiting for the moon to drop behind the ridge-line so we can see the stars more clearly. I recently read somewhere that we are losing our relationship to the stars. There is too much light pollution; we don't see them. I wonder where I got the idea that if life frightens me, I must have made some wrong decision along the way, that fear and heartache must be some reflection of my own missteps. Perhaps I came to this notion because I liked believing I could be in control: if I could conduct myself perfectly, life would always be pleasant. If I chose wisely, marriage would be effortless. When I found someone I truly loved, he would never leave me.

Thich Nhat Hanh says that if you look deeply into a flower, you will see garbage. Within the purity of a rose, there exists the rottenness of garbage. And, most remarkably, he says, "The rose and the garbage are *equal.*" They need each other. Things inter-are. Perhaps we need to confront our fears in order to find our strength. Perhaps we need the darkness to help us see the stars.

Some geese fly over the boat, so close to us I can hear the thwack-thwack of their wings. Barrett has taught me that I can love someone who is very different from me. I have learned that differences allow the space for a dance. Maybe the important thing is *how* differences are expressed: gently, with curiosity about the other, without the fear and judgment and self-doubt that make curiosity impossible. Maybe true love is not having the same beliefs or even having the same goals, but supporting your mate in striving for his or her best self.

The moon is gone, and now we can make out the Milky Way. When *Boatster* gets back to the dock, Barrett steps onto the dock first, then turns and extends his hand to me. I grab hold and jump over.

In the months to come so many people will say to me, "I don't know how you do it." Or: "You must be so strong; I would never be able to survive!" I usually just shrug and point out that I don't have all that much choice. But I should say more about how you do it, or at least how I did it. You tell yourself a story, a story that goes something like this: Everything will be okay. Everything will be fine. One day at a time. We'll get through this. I am strong. I can do this.

You write your husband long missives, telling him of the baby's new words, of your son learning to ride a bike, of loose teeth, and boo-boos, and how the construction is finishing up. You tell him how your writing is going. At night after the kids are down you curl up in bed and pull out your husband's latest letter—an actual old-fashioned handwritten letter—and read it over and over. Because he is eleven hours ahead, you whisper good morning to him as you drift off to sleep, and when you wake up you send him a good night kiss.

You avoid the news. You start out desperately lonely, a military wife in Berkeley. Although you don't know even one other person in your situation, you learn to stay away from gatherings of soldiers and their families. That way you don't risk seeing men with multiple scars across their scalps, where bullets entered and exited. You avoid military officers who will ask logistical questions. "Does your husband have his key volunteers in place? Because he's going to need them when the casualties start rolling in!"

Sometimes things happen that are not in your story. Your car breaks down in Tahoe during a snowstorm and you and your two children and your new au pair get stuck at a ski resort because your car battery is dead. When you get the battery jumped, the car alarm goes off, and you can't turn it off because your keyless remote battery died long ago and you haven't had the time to replace it. When you hitch a ride with a Triple A guy down the mountain to get the battery, and they close the road back, you remember your husband's offhand comment, "If you ever have to sway a male cop, just start to cry. They can't handle it." So you let the tears fall, tears you'd normally hide, and you tell the highway patrolman that your husband is in Iraq, that your children are up the mountain, that you have to get back to your children.

I promise you: he will let your taxi through.

You spend a lot of time trying to do too much. After a few instances of getting overtired and yelling at your kids, and then hating yourself and crying on the floor of your bedroom, you start asking for help. You learn that while some friends turn away from intense situations like yours, others turn toward you; and these become your second family. You find there are a lot of kind people in your neighborhood who want to help, but they are not military people and don't know how. You will ask one to mow the lawn occasionally and another to pick you up an extra quart of milk on her Saturday shopping trip. Your writing group will start not only giving you critique but trading off bringing you dinner. Your au pair will turn out to be amazing and when she takes care of the kids, you buy groceries and do laundry and manage the bills and the investments and the house maintenance and the children's activities, and you write. And you leave some time at the end of most days to take a walk with the dog. You get back into swimming.

About twelve months into the fifteen-month separation, on a neighborhood walk, you will stop short as you come to a surprising realization. While you are still anxious about your husband's safety, still miss his laugh, his smell, his strength, you nevertheless *like your life.* You smile at the irony in the fact that it took your being alone, took your husband "abandoning" you, for you to learn that completeness is not bestowed upon you by a perfect partner. It does not come from your lover figuring you out and taking perfect care of you. It comes, instead, from *deep inside you,* from seeing your own limits and gently challenging yourself to move past them. It comes from facing adversity, and through it, discovering your own inner strength and wisdom.

But still, I am forgetting to tell you something, something important. And that is how to find the courage to let him go, how to say good-bye. I will tell you one way, my way. When it is time to say good-bye, you drive down to Camp Parks where your husband has been staying for the last couple days getting the troops assembled to go to Fort Riley. You give him a shy grin as he drives you to the "Team-Building" area, isolated on the northwest edge of the post. You walk with him around the various "rooms" of the Ropes Course, not paying much attention to the ropes, boards, nets, barrels, things to jump over and through, but looking more at the ground and whether it is soft and whether there is enough space and whether you are facing the road or not.

You guide him to a bay that is covered with chopped-up bits of old tires and away from the road, and lie down and draw him to you. With your hands you try to warm his thighs that are getting goose-pimply from the wind blowing off the dun-turning-to-green hills. As you make love you invoke Ariadne, not as the woman who was abandoned by her lover, but as the woman who gave her lover the silken yarn. You rock with him while your heart whispers to his: Here is the filament of my love, my warrior. I will be here holding my end while you go, with your hero's heart, into battle. Don't let go. Hold on tight. When you are lost, follow the thread. Follow it out of the Labyrinth.

Follow it back to me.

Acknowledgments

Two realizations gave me the courage to pursue this book: first, that persistence, not raw talent, was the key to success; and second, that I didn't have to do it alone. There are many, many people who helped make this book possible.

Caroline Paul encouraged my writing, let me be her date to Grotto events, introduced me to my agent, gave me vital critique, cajoled me when I was down, listened when I despaired, and got lost with me on Angel Island when I was searching. Caroline, your friendship is one of the great blessings of my life.

Thank you to the members of the Motherlode Writers, soul sisters all: Marian Berges, Ursula Ferreira, Caroline Grant, Rebecca Kaminsky, Sarah Kilts, and Sybil Lockhart. Every aspiring writer should have a circle of support, insight, and encouragement like you.

I could not have survived the deployment without the support of Mike Beaver and his family. Whether it was bringing jacks and sump pumps, making sure all our holidays were special, stepping up when I needed someone to take my son bowling, putting up towel racks, or coming over to investigate the mysterious locked bathroom door in my cottage, Mike and family were always there for us (sometimes in SWAT uniform!).

Many others helped as well. Nick and Joni Tooliatos assisted with everything from contract disputes to lawn work to hunting-trophy repair. Rima Kittner read the article in the *SF Chron* and saw we needed help: she became Luna's fairy godmother and a dear family friend. Dick Dickerson came over during visits from Tennessee and asked me to put him to work, without saying a word teaching me some of the meaning of Semper Fi. Chris Dickerson, who, like me, is intrigued by the in-between places, kept me and the kids company. Tamara Friedman and Dirk Husselman kept an eye on us from next door, regularly had us over for dinner, and took care of many of my technology challenges. Glenn Alexander, Missey and John Dore, Phil Donnelly, Floyd and Betty Garrett, Rebecca Hawley, Rob Teigen, Julie and Francesca, Dr. Robert Brod, Lauren Breeze, Susan Widmer, Renee Hassna, Paul and Natalie Figueroa, Josefina Guerrero and family, Sandra Lewis, Lily Brum, Joe Bobrow, and Eric Hoffmann all helped us in some specific way, emotional and/or logistical, before, during, and after the fifteen months of family separation.

Thank you to my mom, Maria Geczy, who, like oxygen, is vital to everything I do, yet too often unheralded. To my aunt, Liz Zuckerman, the closest thing I have to a big sister, thank you for coming when I needed help, and for working so hard holding down the fort at my house after B.'s midtour leave. I thank my brother Tom Raday, who has always believed in me, and my late father, Tamas Raday, who taught me to love adventure and who recognized my strength.

Manuela Chesney, Katja Pinkston, Tonna and Jim, Kelly and Dave, David and Wiebke Jablonsky, Anne Allen, Judy Devlin, Kaye Rovegno, and all the students and family members of the Dirty Dozen: thank you for your friendship at the War College.

Thank you, Misfits, for finding me a real man, a quintessential sheepdog; for teaching me about military culture; and for your unwavering love and support. Additional thanks are due to you both and also to Jessica Grant for your grace in being part of this story.

To my editor, Amy Caldwell, thank you for being such a wonderful guide. You told me gently when something wasn't working, soothed me when I was anxious, and were generally insightful, inspiring, and encouraging.

Thank you to my agent, Michelle Tessler, who saw the potential in this story early on and didn't give up on it.

Thanks are also due to: Mary Stanley Dore and Deborah Davis

for critique; Kira Sturney Keane for assistance with PR and so much more; Anna Goldstein and Joe Lamb for help with promotion; Steve Ostrover, Margo Perin, Joanne Hartman, Jennifer Eyre White, Rachel Sarah, Jon Kaplan, and Ellen Manerud for encouraging me to write; and the San Francisco Writers Grotto, especially Po Bronson and Stephanie Losee, for generous advice and encouragement. To our au pair, Ilknur Erduran: thank you for making it possible for me to concentrate, and for the light and laughter you bring to our family. Most importantly, thank you to B., my muse, for your generosity in being the subject of my work, and for all the things you have taught me, including that once the good idea cutoff point has passed, it's time to take action. And to my children, for your patience with me during this project, for giving my life its anchor and purpose, and for loving me so well.